Anarchism and Ecological Economics

Anarchism and Ecological Economics: A Transformative Approach to a Sustainable Future explores the idea that anarchism – aimed at creating a society where there is as much freedom in solidarity as possible – may provide an ideal political basis for the goals of ecological economics. It seems clear that it is going to be impossible to solve the problems connected to environmental degradation, climate change, economic crashes and increasing inequality, within the existing paradigm. The anarchist aims of reducing the disparities of rank and income in society and obtaining a high standard of living within environmentally sound ecosystems chime well with the ecological economists' goal of living within our environmental limits for the betterment of the planet and society.

The book refers to the UN's sustainability development goals, and the goals expressed in the Earth Charter, viewing them through an anarchist's lens. It argues that in order to establish ecological economics as a radical new economy right for the 21st century, neoliberal economics needs to be replaced. By connecting ecological economics to a solid philosophical tradition such as anarchism, it will be easier for ecological economics to become a far more potent alternative to "green" economic thinking, which is based on, and supports, the dominant political regime.

Innovative and challenging, this book will appeal to students and scholars interested in economics and the politics surrounding it.

Ove Daniel Jakobsen is a professor of Ecological Economics in the Business School at Nord University, Norway. He has more than 30 years of experience in transdisciplinary work: including philosophy, economics, business administration and systems theory.

Routledge Studies in Ecological Economics

For more information about this series, please visit www.routledge.com/series/RSEE

Anarchism and Ecological Economics

A Transformative Approach to a
Sustainable Future

Ove Daniel Jakobsen

LONDON AND NEW YORK

First published 2019
by Routledge

2 Park Square, Milton Park, Abingdon, Oxfordshire OX14 4RN
52 Vanderbilt Avenue, New York, NY 10017

Routledge is an imprint of the Taylor & Francis Group, an informa business

First issued in paperback 2020

British Library Cataloguing-in-Publication Data
A catalogue record for this book is available from the British Library

Library of Congress Cataloging-in-Publication Data
A catalog record has been requested for this book

ISBN: 978-1-138-59758-7 (hbk)
ISBN: 978-0-367-66445-9 (pbk)

Typeset in Sabon
by Integra Software Services Pvt. Ltd.

To Vivi

Contents

Illustrations

Figures

Tables

Boxes

Preface

If one of philosophy's goals is to enlarge our ideas of what is possible, then "a philosophical exploration of anarchism is surely a valuable exercise" (Suissa 2010, p. vii). My intention is to discuss the extent to which philosophical anarchism is relevant as a political platform for ecological economics. The ambition is not to come up with a ready-made recipe but to provide a contribution to the process of rethinking the political ideas embedded in ecological economics. Or, more precisely, to reflect on anarchism´s relevance and capability to facilitate the system conditions that make it possible for ecological economics to succeed in handling the challenges it is supposed to handle. To make this goal as clear as possible I refer to the UN's sustainability development goals and the goals expressed in the Earth Charter. Even though most people still harbor intensely negative feelings about anarchism I find it both stimulating and relevant to put this aside and dig further into what is largely unexplored material.

Anarchist thinking has an inspiring variety and richness and I became aware of a wide range of ideas that anarchism and ecological economics held in common. Most importantly, they share a structural homology in their approach to nature, society and economics. Since ecological economics has no explicit political platform it is difficult to counteract the ideas of mainstream economics, which are based on neoliberal capitalism. If history shows us anything, it is that once a particular view of reality becomes dominant then social and economic processes adapt and become consistent with that worldview.

To establish ecological economics as a radical new economy right for the 21st century, we need to reject and replace neoliberal economics as the political platform for ecological economics. Anarchism offers an interesting and relevant context for ecological economics, a context which is necessary if we are to meet the many challenges which arise at the intersection of environment, society and economics. By connecting ecological economics to a solid philosophical tradition such as anarchism, it will be easier for ecological economics to become a far more potent alternative to "green" economic thinking, which is, of course, based on and supports the dominant political regime.

Any attempt to solve the environmental crisis within the bourgeois framework must be, according to Murray Bookchin, "dismissed as chimerical" (Bookchin 2004, p. viii). Eliseé Reclus argued that a fundamental shift is required, away from a system of economic inequality and exploitation such as that robustly embodied in capitalism. The domination of nature and society will continue "as long as humanity remains under the sway of a vast system of social domination" (Clark and Martin 2013, p. 29) that has caused a rupture in the harmony of both the eco-system and the social system. It is from within this serious state of affairs that a clear alternative arises – to merge ecological economics with the radical political platform of anarchism – and this presents an area of great interest and influence for the future.

Since it has appeared almost impossible to solve the problems connected with environmental degradation, climate change, financial breakdown, and the increasing gap between rich and poor, a reconsideration of the ideas behind the dominating economic and political ideology is long overdue. According to Bookchin, "the destruction of the natural world (…) follows inexorably from the very logic of capitalist production" (Bookchin 2004, p. ix). Competition and accumulation of wealth are the very laws of capitalism. In a society with such principles at its heart, nature necessarily becomes nothing more than a mere resource to be exploited and abused for profit. Though we run the risk of being characterized as unrealistic and fictional utopians, the search for change at a deeper systemic level is vital. Bookchin maintains that "Dropping out, becomes a mode of dropping in – into the tentative, experimental, and as yet highly ambiguous, social relations of utopia" (Bookchin 2004, p. viii). In describing utopia as anarchism, he refers to a stateless, classless and decentralized society. Anarchism also draws attention to spontaneity, a conception of praxis as an inner process, not an external, manipulated process. "Every revolutionary epoch is a period of convergence when many different and apparently separate processes collect to form a socially explosive crisis" (Bookchin 2004, p. xii). Clark and Martin exemplify Reclus's well-known image from 1905, "Humanity is nature becoming self-conscious", by maintaining:

> That (humanity) can only fulfill its weighty responsibility by acting with an awareness that we are an integral part of nature, rather than continuing under the illusion that we are a power over and above the natural world.
>
> (Clark and Martin 2013, p. vii)

Reclus's analysis parallels the division of the natural world (the first nature) and the social world (the second nature) made by Bookchin. For Reclus, "humanity is emerging within nature rather than out of it" (Clark and Martin 2013, p. 21). We are creating a radically new nature that acts as a counterweight to the first nature from which we are emerging. Ecology deals with the crossing of the first and second natures. From this perspective ecology becomes a means of changing the world rather than objectively observing it. In addition ecology provides the compass for assigning humanity's place in the first nature.

To throw light on and interpret anarchism as a political platform for ecological economics, it is of vital importance to anchor the approach in history. Even if anarchy, in all its details, is not necessarily the significant answer, it is fascinating to consider the relevance of its critique of both capitalism and communism and the solutions it puts forward. To overcome the challenges we face today, we cannot struggle back to an earlier stage in history; rather we have to master the problems as they are, without minimizing them, and we have to go through with it. "But we shall only get through it if we know where we want to go" (Buber 1996, p. 132). Capitalism has been more than happy to let the dust settle on anarchism, but I think the time has come to brush that dust off and look again at some of anarchism's basic ideas in terms of our current knowledge and state of affairs. Mannheim (1936) argued that thinking transcending reality was of the greatest importance both to understanding and shaping history.

The Norwegian anarchist Jens Bjørneboe, who once warned against misusing the concept of anarchism, refers to Kropotkin as one of the most interesting and clear-thinking representatives of anarchism. Bjørneboe maintained that anarchism is misinterpreted and has been connected with such negative feelings that anarchism was characterized by our society as an area of "dangerous thought". In reality it is quite the opposite, as "anarchism has survived the persecution, and without being a great prophet I predict that it will reappear in the coming decades, probably as the most vital political impulse from now on" (translated from Norwegian) (Bjørneboe 1972).

According to Bjørneboe (1972), anarchism is not a question of either-or, but rather it is a question of degree. The degree of anarchy varies; anarchy can occupy a higher or lower degree, i.e., society may be more or less anarchic. Anarchy at the higher level is characterized by a high standard of living within an environmentally sound milieu. Disparities in rank and income in the society are generally minimized. Bjørneboe's idea is that the more characteristics of anarchism a society has, the healthier it is, while complete anarchy, which means removing all forms of authority, is neither possible nor desirable.

I illuminate and discuss the extent to which anarchist philosophy gives a relevant political platform for ecological economics in the light of how a great number of distinguished scholars over the last few decades have seen ecological economics as a transdisciplinary field of science. One main point emerges: it is not enough merely to reduce the negative symptoms of the current capitalist economy; the entire economic system has to be addressed. One interesting question on which to reflect is the extent of the chances of success in implementing ecological economics, something which is of crucial importance if we are to solve the challenges we face, correlated with the amount of anarchist tendencies in the society. Today we are, on the one hand, heading very quickly in the wrong direction and the chances of success are decreasing rapidly; but, on the other hand, we also see interesting moves towards a breakthrough of new ideas in many branches of society. To describe the challenges and to explain the connection between them, I refer to the UN's Millennium Development Goals (MDGs), the UN's Sustainable Development Goals (SDGs) and the Earth Charter.

In the following chapters I have a double undertaking: to understand the urgency of the challenges facing humanity, and, secondly, to evaluate if ecological economics, anchored to an anarchist political platform, represent a realistic gateway to meaningful change.

Acknowledgements

This book is the result of many years of reflection on the connection between economic practice and its philosophical and political contexts. My supervisor, and source of great inspiration, Professor Leif Holbæk-Hanssen (1917–1991), introduced Kropotkin to me in the late '80s. After that the idea emerged of a possible connection between anarchism and ecological economics.

Issues related to anarchist philosophy have been the subject of many conversations with good friends such as Elling Willassen and Stein Sneve over the decades. Issues arising from the problematic link between ecological economics and neoliberalism have been the subject of regular discussion among good colleagues at the Centre for Ecological Economics and Ethics at Nord University: Stig Ingebrigtsen, Are Ingulfsvann, Øystein Nystad, Amsale Temesgen, Kaja von Kwetzinsky-Stetzenkow and Vivi Storsletten. Vivi Storsletten has also been an important energizer in the task of linking anarchism and ecological economics.

For many years my dialogues with Anders Lindseth, Fritjof Capra, Laszlo Zsolnai, Knut Ims, Gunnar Skirbekk, Torsten Graap, Peter Garrett, Emil Mohr, Dag Andersen, Jostein Hertwig, Johann Galtung, Christian Egge, and many more have been most revealing and encouraging.

Julie and Rasmus (my children) are vital sources of inspiration in my work for a sustainable future.

My good friend David Beake, in addition to improving the language, has provided important input to the content. The two reviewers of the proposal and the people in Routledge deserve great honour for giving inspiring comments during the whole process. Thanks to all of them.

This book, in the true spirit of anarchism, is the result of the interaction between my free thinking and the free thinking of others.

1 Introduction

In the following chapters I examine some of the central philosophical assumptions and principles in anarchist theory in order to find out if anarchism represents a relevant political platform for ecological economics. Economics is a constructed lens that "support either a struggle for fairness, equality and justice, or a legitimation of greed and ´free enterprise'" (Westoby and Dowling 2013, p. 108) and cannot be separated from politics. I focus on those ideas, which are of special interest in organizing the economy in the context of anarchist political philosophy. "The challenges of our time require us to rebel against the disabling faith in the idea that oppression, hierarchy, and captivity are somehow the natural consequences of human evolution. Our revolt is our emancipation" (White, Springer and de Souza 2016, p. 1). Our revolt is to practice freedom; to practice freedom is to perform anarchism.

Anarchism is a political philosophical position which aims to create a society where there is as much freedom as possible and a minimum of pressure on individuals from authorities. Innovative social change depends on the ability to choose to "adopt different attitudes towards the other, attitudes of openness towards the other which are opposed to domination" (Westoby and Dowling 2013, p. 30). No one is morally entitled to rule over others. All forms of authority harm human beings. Anarchists want a free society based on cooperation between a diversity of equal parties. "Diversity and not unity (...) creates the kind of society in which you and I can most comfortably live" (Ward 2004, p. 82). Basic principles are cooperation, mutual aid, sympathy, solidarity, initiative and spontaneity. The living community is an open universality "in that it is the terrain on which the dialectic between universality and particularity endlessly works itself out" (Clark 2013, p. 6). The members can never simply identify with the community as a complete being in itself.

Anarchists are often referred to as people who believe that all good comes from the people and all bad comes from the authorities. This is obviously not true and the anarchists know it, but still they argue that the State, as the highest form of hierarchy, represents a threat to liberty, equality and fraternity. Anarchism claims that the State is unnecessary and requests to remove or, to a large extent, reduce all forms of its power structures. For anarchism, the term

"State" is not only a state power, i.e., a national superstructure (government), but rather a way of organizing society hierarchically. In other words, it is not the State as such that is the problem; it is the hierarchical power structures which disqualify and emasculate the people. Consequently, anarchism is primarily a movement against hierarchical organizational structures which include authorities. This explains why giant globalized companies could be a bigger problem than national authorities based on social liberal or reformist political principles.

The problem in many Western countries has been the rise in inequality when free-market liberalism takes over the social processes. A consequence of this is that community development has lost its capacity for solidarity and empathy with poor and marginalized people. Here it is of great importance to notice that the notion of freedom in anarchism is very different from the notion of freedom in an egocentric competitive market. Freedom in anarchism is connected to cooperation and solidarity. Bakunin puts it more strongly: "liberty without solidarity is privilege and injustice, while solidarity without liberty is slavery and despotism" (Clark 2013, p. 1). The anarchists argue that instead of centralization, in which the world is divided into a powerful, wealthy, and hegemonic core and a weak, poor, and dominated periphery, we have to develop a world that has its centers everywhere and its periphery nowhere. In other words, society is organized as nested networks.

The anarchists consider society to be a self-regulating organism that develops best when subject to least interference. Despite this strong communitarian dimension it is "the human person, the primary element in society, which is the source of the creative will that constructs and reconstructs the world" (Clark and Martin 2013, p. 6). According to Kropotkin, anarchism represents "the creative, constructive power of the people themselves, which aimed at developing institutions of common law (...) which would insure a free evolution of society" (Kropotkin 1909, p. 6). Anarchism was an attempt to apply the natural-scientific inductive method to the study of social sciences, politics and economics, and an attempt to "foresee the future steps of mankind on the road to liberty, equity, and fraternity, with a view to realizing the greatest sum of happiness for every unit of human society" (Kropotkin 2002, p. 192). Kropotkin's ambition was to form a scientific concept of the universe embracing the whole of nature, including man. Based on an organic worldview Kropotkin maintained that anarchism could have a great influence on the development of human institutions and, at a more general level, on practical life. More defending anarchist philosophy, my goal is to explore these ideas in order to spell out their relevance and application to ecological economics. The question is to find out the extent to which the ideals and principles of anarchism are relevant for ecological economics. To put it another way, is it possible to discover a "hidden" connection between anarchism and ecological economics?

Ward concludes his book on anarchism with the following statement: "Anarchism is the only political ideology capable of addressing the challenges posed by our new green consciousness" (Ward 2004, p. 98). Hence, there are strong indications that anarchism, as an alternative to both capitalism and socialism, has the potential to be a relevant political platform for ecological economics. Owing to the complexity of the global crisis, the merging of anarchism and ecological economics, as an alternative to the dominant system, will become more and more relevant in the 21st century. The goal of anarchist political philosophy is to inspire the development of a free, ecological society in which humans actualize self-realization through participation in a non-dominating community, and further "planetary self-realization by playing a cooperative, non-dominating role within the larger ecological community" (Clark 2013, p. 250). Clark maintains that such solutions depend on acceptance of the need for diverse, multidimensional experiments in democratic processes, and recognizing that ideals such as liberty, ecology, and solidarity remain the guiding inspiration for anarchist theory and practice.

The chapters are organized in the following way. Chapter 1, "Introduction", gives an overview of the ideas described, illuminated and discussed in the book. Chapter 2, "Structure of the discussion", gives a synopsis of the philosophy of science's perspectives and the methodological approaches relevant for understanding the discussions in the following chapters. Chapter 3, "Challenges facing today's society", focuses on some of the main problems of our time, such as the degradation of soil, water and air, the overexploitation of natural resources, the increasing gap between rich and poor (within and between countries), food safety, climate change and decreasing quality of life. The discussion is anchored in the UN's 8 MDGs and 17 SDG's, and the 16 principles of the Earth Charter. The UN's description of different goals gives an interesting overview of the most demanding challenges today. The Earth Charter speaks on behalf of all species and eco-systems on earth. The declarations agree that all problems are connected to how we organize the interplay between economy, nature and society. Chapter 4, "Liberalism and Marxism as political platforms", gives a political philosophical context of interpretation, relevant for understanding the ideas advanced in anarchism. Different blends of liberalism and Marxism represent the basis for the political platform characterizing the dominating economic systems worldwide today.

Chapter 5, "History of anarchist philosophy", gives a historical overview of the development of anarchism, with a focus on the great 18th-century anarchist contributors such as Godwin, Proudhon, Bakunin, Kropotkin, Reclus and Tolstoy. They all argued that the good life in a good society should be anchored in freedom from authorities of all kinds. They had a positive image of humans, meaning that people would find the best solutions if the society had a decentralized structure. The classical anarchists thought that order based on individual empathy was much better than structures implemented by authoritative use of power. In Chapter 6, "Outline of anarchist philosophy", I put forward some of the main principles of anarchism as a political philosophy relevant for ecological economics, such as scientific anarchism, Darwinism, human nature, freedom, pedagogy and education and pacifism. Chapter 7, "Anarchism and the good society", launches a critical discussion of how anarchism could be practiced in society through associations, communes and the economy. I focus on the relevance of anarchist political philosophy as a practice, looking at both its positive and negative traits.

Chapter 8, "Principles in ecological economics", gives an introduction to some of the main sources of inspiration behind the establishment of ecological economics. Ecological economics is defined, on the one hand, as an integrated part of the eco-systems, and on the other hand ecological economics learns from nature instead of dominating her. The core principles of ecological economics are synthesized. "Utopia inspired by ecological economics" is spelled out in Chapter 9. "Anarchism as a political platform for ecological economics" is examined in Chapter 10. I argue that without a certain level of anarchism in a society, ecological economics are suppressed to become little more than "green" economy. Green economy is interpreted as an economy focused on environmental (and social) challenges within the dominating system. In Chapter 11, "Concluding reflections", my focus is on how anarchism could be developed to have greater relevance in ecological economics in the future. Amongst other topics I question the Socratic idea that knowledge leads to good action. In other words it may be naive to accept Rousseau's idea that the individual becomes good as soon as he frees himself from any form of authority and that goodwill or good motives necessarily lead to good action. Hence it is more an ethical precondition that freedom presupposes responsibility – and vice versa – than it is a demonstrable empirical fact.

Anarchism has conceived an ideal that leads to its own methods of action which differ from other political philosophies such as liberalism and socialism. Kropotkin argued that criticism of the existing system is impossible unless the critics have a picture of a better alternative. "Consciously or unconsciously, the ideal of something better is forming in the mind of every one who criticizes social institutions" (Kropotkin 1908, p. 62). All change begins with the people.

2 Structure of the discussion

Introduction

As a context for the reflections concerning the connection between anarchism and ecological economics, I will be giving an overview of some relevant topics in the philosophy of science. Imre Lakatos and Alan Musgrave (1982) argued that science only makes fundamental changes when problems in the current society cannot be solved within the established scientific research program. Karl Mannheim (1936) claims that it is necessary to develop utopian solutions outside the established ideology if we are to solve the most challenging problems. As examples I discuss the differences between green economy and ecological economics and argue that, respectively, they represent ideology and utopia.

We stand at a critical moment in history: humankind has to decide if its future lies down a track anchored in economic models based on the exploitation of nature – a track which is driving humankind towards ever more serious environmental, social and economic problems – or a track towards a future characterized by the protection and valuing of the vitality, diversity and beauty of the Earth's eco-systems. The future direction required simply cannot be under a capitalist growth economy. "The growth economy is leading to an inevitable series of ongoing crises, creating harm, death and destruction" (Spash 2017, p. 14). According to the Earth Charter, fundamental changes are needed in our values, institutions, and ways of living. "We must realize that when basic needs have been met, human development is primarily about being more, not having more" (The Earth Charter). The change process has consequences for how we think, for our philosophy of science, and for our moral and political philosophy.

In the following paragraphs I explore more deeply some dimensions that are relevant in understanding the nature of the change process. Firstly, a distinction between what is possible and impossible, actually and ideologically, is discussed. The idea is that ideology can encourage or hinder the implementation of change, even if that change is possible and necessary in the actual world. Secondly, I introduce paradigms and research programs to explain different levels of change. Thirdly, I look at the tension between ideology and utopia to explain how energy and direction in the change processes can be created. And fourthly, the clear distinction between green economy and ecological economics is introduced to throw light on two opposing directions into the future. The chapter concludes by stating that ecological economics goes to the very heart of the challenges and that green economy merely reduces the negative symptoms within the dominating economic system; ecological economics changes the system. Implementation of ecological economics is actually possible but impossible within the existing ideology.

Actual and ideological possibilities

John P. Clark (2013) distinguishes between different interpretations of possibility – what is actually possible given the concrete situation, and what is ideologically possible according to the actual political and economic system. Referring to these two categories, four alternatives are probable: actually possible – ideological possible (possible possibilities), actually impossible – ideological possible (impossible possibilities), actually possible – ideological impossible (possible impossibilities), and actually impossible – ideologically impossible (impossible impossibilities). The point is to indicate that what is possible in practice could be impossible to implement because of the characteristics of the existing ideology. It is also sound to argue the other way around and say that ideology defines the opportunities and that, for example, technological developments can change what is possible in practice.

In Cell 1, we find actual politics, doing what is possible within the existing economic and political system – in other words, actuality. Green economy illustrates this well: politicians and businesses want a green shift using the tools that exist within the dominating ideology. In Cell 2, politicians and economists argue that it is possible to solve today's environmental and social problems with solutions that are ideologically possible but practically impossible – in other words, false promises. One such example is to say that we can have exponential growth in the use of natural resources on a globe which is finite. A society built on and dependent upon the depletion of natural resources will sooner or later collapse. The basic logic is that the planet's natural resources are limited and human societies are dependent on the Earth's capacity to

		Actual	
		Possible	Impossible
Ideology	Possible	1. Actuality	2. False promises
	Impossible	3. Potentiality	4. Fantasy

Figure 2.1 Possible impossibilities

regenerate resources. Cell 3 illustrates what is actually possible and ideologically impossible. To implement the suggested solutions, we have to shift to another ideology. In other words changes in ideology will actualize the potentials. Guérin argued that equality, liberty and fraternity are impossible within the current system and that "poverty and proletariat are the inevitable consequence of property as presently constituted" (Guérin 2005, p. 74). Today ecological economics is an example of a possible impossibility. To implement ecological economics, a shift in ideology (systems level) is necessary. Cell 4 represents what is both actually and ideologically impossible – in other words, pure fantasy. An example of such wishful thinking is the advice of the late Stephen Hawking: "The human race must move to a planet beyond our Solar System to protect the future of the species" (BBC News 2018).

In the following chapters I will be elaborating on possible impossibilities – namely, that implementing ecological economics is impossible within the existing ideology but entirely realistic within an anarchist political platform. Karl Mannheim (1936) explained the connection between actuality and potentiality as the tension between ideology and utopia. The question is to decide what kind of theory and practice is needed in order to actualize the potential of a society. Martin Buber (1996) argued that the greatest challenge today is the gigantic centralization of economic power covering the whole planet and devouring all free communities. "People have increasingly given up their sense of personal responsibility, lost faith in their traditional communities, and abandoned their fate to mass society" (Clark 2013, p. 158).

In response to the complex and serious challenges currently faced by society, the increasing conflicts between economy and nature, between people, and within individual human beings, much has been written telling of the end, or certainly the decline, of Western civilization. It has become more or less impossible to inquire and seek out explanations on a deeper philosophic and systemic level. Basic beliefs are untouchable and whatever fails to fit into the established theories is viewed as either something quite horrifying or, more frequently, "it is simply declared to be non-existent" (Feyerabend 1975, p. 7). This is close to what Lakatos (1982) named the hard core of a research program. However, due to global crises, there is a new and demanding thirst for economic, social and political alternatives to the dominating system.

Paradigms

In the next paragraphs I will describe and explain the philosophy of science frame of reference for the discussion in the succeeding chapters. To do this it is important to introduce and deliberate on Thomas Kuhn's concepts of paradigm and of revolutionary paradigm shifts. Kuhn (1962) rejected the idea that scientific knowledge can be regarded as a cumulatively growing system of statements and theories. He argued that knowledge is not the knowledge acquired through the research process; instead knowledge is the research process in itself. According to Kuhn, the evolution of science is characterized by the fact that normal scientific periods are replaced by irregular revolutionary leaps where all the scientific understanding of the foundation is replaced by a new one. When the frame of reference changes, the previous knowledge has to be re-interpreted. The paradigm consists of reality perception, and norms for scientific activities: exemplary problem areas, methods and theories. Not all issues are accepted within a paradigm. Kuhn drew a distinction between local and global definitions of the concept paradigm.

Local definition of paradigm

• Universally recognized scientific achievements that provide model problems and solutions to a community of practitioners

Global definition of paradigm

• The entire constellation of beliefs, values and techniques shared by members of a scientific community (because they were all trained on the same paradigm examples of good practice)
• Revolution is a transformation of vision; crises are terminated by a gestalt switch
• After a revolution, the data themselves change and the scientists work in a different world
• Progress is not simply a line leading to the truth
• Progress is more a movement away from less adequate conceptions of the world

The process by which a new paradigm substitutes the old paradigm cannot be done step by step; it happens all at once like a Gestalt switch. The transfer of commitment from one paradigm to another paradigm is a conversion experience. According to Kuhn, since changing people is difficult, new paradigms are normally introduced by researchers from other disciplines or younger researchers who feel no loyalty to either the traditions or the authorities of the discipline. Max Planck explains changes in science in a similar way: "A new scientific truth does not triumph by convincing its opponents and making them see the light, but rather because its opponents eventually die, and a new generation grows up that is familiar with it" (Planck 1968). Scientists representing different paradigms are characterized by disagreeing about these issues:

• What are the problems?
• What counts as a solution?
• What data actually are?

Because of these discrepancies they will talk over each other in debating their respective paradigms. Kuhn argued that different paradigms were incommensurable, meaning that communication between them is impossible; they speak different languages.

Hard core and protective belt

Imre Lakatos criticized Kuhn's understanding of scientific development and introduced a theory of research programs. Research programs provide a framework that is shared by those involved. A research program consists of a hard core and a protective belt. When the hard core is threatened, theories in the protective belt are modified in order to save it. Thus, research can go on without being disturbed by dramatic breaks in the basic assumptions. Lakatos, inspired by Popper's critical rationalism, puts down the foundation for an evolutionary understanding of scientific development. When it comes to changes in the hard core, caused by disturbances in the environmental conditions, Lakatos is close to what Kuhn called a paradigm shift. Seen this way, Lakatos could be described as a mediator between Popper and Kuhn.

Because of the introduction of the protective belt, Lakatos assessed and challenged Kuhn's assertion that science is always based on a limited and comprehensive set of rules and ideals. Rather, he claimed, there are extensive theory complexes that form the primary tools for understanding and appraising scientific progress. He was critical of Popper and argued that scientific knowledge cannot be regarded as a cumulatively growing system of statements and theories. The evolution of scientific knowledge is characterized by long periods in which the hard-core ideas are protected by a belt of theories that are continually adapting to environmental changes. When the challenges become too dramatic, critical questions are asked of the hard core, and an evolutionary period is replaced by irregular revolutionary leaps in which the very foundations of scientific understanding are challenged and replaced by new ones.

Theories associated with larger superstructures are, according to Lakatos, a scientific research program. On the one hand, the hard core of theory is central to the scientific research program, as hard-core theoretical assumptions cannot be rejected or altered without falsifying the whole research program. The researcher will therefore be anxious to protect it, and, on the other hand, this is done by changing the auxiliary theories and hypotheses in the protective belt in order to adjust to the changing environmental conditions. Lakatos divided the procedures within a research program into negative and positive heuristics. Negative heuristics point at methods and approaches to avoid changes in the hard core, and positive heuristics refer to methods and approaches to make changes in the protective belt.

While the negative heuristic protects the hard core, the positive heuristic makes it possible to change the protective belt. The negative heuristic tells us not to reject the hard core even when counter-evidence arises; instead "we should use our ingenuity to develop other explanations which protect the hard core, re-examining the evidence, or rejecting or modifying one of the less important hypotheses" (Darwin 2010, p. 42). The positive heuristic is derived primarily from the hard core and "tells us what paths to pursue so that we can develop and enrich our research program" (Darwin 2010, p. 42), and it consists of articulate rules about how the theories in the protective belt can be improved. The positive heuristic "defines problems, outlines the construction of a protective belt of auxiliary hypotheses, foresees anomalies and turns them victoriously into examples, all according to a preconceived plan" (Lakatos cited in Darwin 2010, p. 43). Lakatos defines the main concepts in his theory in the following way:

> the negative heuristic specifies 'the hard core' of the program which is 'irrefutable' by the methodological decision of its protagonists, the positive heuristic consists of a partially articulated set of suggestions or hints on how to change, develop the 'refutable variants' of the research program, on how to modify, sophisticate the 'refutable' protective belt.
> (Lakatos and Musgrave 1982, p. 135)

Even though the hard core is rigid and slightly changeable, continuous development is achieved by improving the surrounding theories, leading to increased complexity. Lakatos defines a research program as theoretically progressive if it provides the basis for new and unexpected explanations and predictions. A research program is empirically progressive when any explanation or prediction is verified. Over time a research program will often change from being progressive to becoming degenerative. A degenerative research program is often saved by its followers by launching ad hoc explanations as opposed to empirical evidence.

Research program – hard core

- Theories are part of broader structures
- Within such a program theories develop in a dynamic way
- A theory that is shown to be inadequate is replaced by a better one but typically one which belongs to the same family
- We have a sequence of theories – T(1), T(2), T(3) and so on – each of which explains more than its predecessor and thus supersedes it
- A sequence of interrelated theories is a scientific research program

Research program – protective belt

- The part of the research program containing the auxiliary hypotheses is thus called the protective belt or positive heuristic.
- It indicates what needs to be done in order to increase the explanatory and predictive power of the program.

- A research program R1 is falsified when there is an alternative research program R2 that can explain and predict as much as research program R1 does.

According to Illich, critical reconsideration becomes more difficult when an assumption has been left "unquestioned long enough to be taken for a certainty and to even congeal into perception" (Illich 2015, p. 15). The adherents of the research program consider changes in the protective belt expendable. Theories in the protective belt may be altered or abandoned when empirical anomalies require some adaptations in order to protect the hard core.

Based on the research program's hard core, study can be conducted on the basis of some fundamental principles that are not discussed. Hard-core assumptions are protected by the set of auxiliary hypotheses that aim at increasing the predictive power of the program and in this way "protect" the hard core. In this regard, the hard core is similar to Kuhn's conception of a paradigm.

There are limitations to modification and changes in the protective belt. As an example, Lakatos claimed that not all changes in the protective belt of a research program are equally productive or acceptable. He argued that changes in the protective belt should be evaluated not just in terms of their ability to defend the hard core by explaining anomalies, but also by their ability to come up with new explanations and understanding. He defined adjustments as degenerative if they did not accomplish anything more than the maintenance of the hard core.

Lakatos' model provides for the possibility of a research program to be progressive even if it contains troublesome anomalies. He argued that it is essentially necessary to continue with a research program even if it has problems as long as there are no better alternatives. In order to falsify a research program, there must be a better alternative available.

Anything goes

In *Against Method* Paul Feyerabend claimed that Lakatos' philosophy of research programs appears liberal only because it is "anarchism in disguise" (Feyerabend 1984, p. 181). Feyerabend playfully dedicated *Against Method* to "Imre Lakatos: Friend, and fellow-anarchist." Feyerabend described science as being essentially anarchistic and he argued that the hallmark of anarchism is its opposition to the established order of things. Insofar as methodology of research is "rational", it does not differ from anarchism. Insofar as it differs from anarchism, it is not "rational" (Feyerabend 1975, p. 198). He represents an anarchist position in philosophy of science that recommends us to ask questions which fall outside the ideas dominating the current society. To reach any new understanding we have to use hypotheses that challenge and contradict well-established theories and even those which have been scientifically confirmed. Given any rule, however fundamental and necessary for science, "there are always circumstances when it is advisable not only to ignore the rule but adopt its opposite" (Feyerabend 1975, p. 23).

The consistency condition – the condition that demands that new hypotheses are consistent with accepted theories – merely serves to keep the older theories in place. Only those hypotheses that contradict well-confirmed theories are capable of improving our knowledge. We should therefore be quite happy to "invent and elaborate theories which are inconsistent with the accepted point of view, even if the latter should be highly confirmed and generally accepted" (Feyerabend cited in Darwin 2010, p. 40). Feyerabend rejects the view that the dominant science would under any circumstances be prepared to make pluralism the foundation of research. In other words only fresh and critical thinking will develop a science that is able to break out of the dominating paradigm.

Feyerabend argued that there are no absolute rules in science and, furthermore, he claimed that any such rules would restrict academic freedom and prevent scientific progress. In his view science would benefit by not imposing rigid rules on scientists and accepting a kind of theoretical anarchism. Feyerabend's philosophy of science is radical in comparison to that of Kuhn and Lakatos because he claims that philosophy of science can neither succeed in defining a demarcation line between science and non-science, nor in defining absolute criteria for research methodology. He also maintained that scientific progress depends on scientists breaking the rules.

Backing his position, Feyerabend gave support to research questions that were inconsistent with well-established paradigms or research programs. Furthermore, scientific pluralism improves the critical power of science, and a pluralistic methodology would improve the articulation of each theory. He concluded that science might proceed best not by induction, but rather by counter-induction.

Starting from the assumption that an historical universal scientific method does not exist, Feyerabend argued that science does not deserve its privileged status in Western society. In his opinion, science has become a repressive ideology, even though, arguably, it started as a liberating movement. Feyerabend thought that a pluralistic society should be protected from being too influenced by science, just as it is protected from other ideologies.

Since scientific points of view do not arise from using a universal method which guarantees high-quality conclusions, Feyerabend thought that there was no justification for valuing scientific claims over claims by other ideologies such as religions. Scientific success has traditionally involved non-scientific elements, such as inspiration from mythical or religious sources.

Based on these arguments, Feyerabend defended the idea that science should be separated from the state in the same way that religion and state are separated in a modern secular society. He envisioned a "free society" in which "all traditions have equal rights and equal access to the centers of power." For example, parents should be able to determine the ideological context of their children's education instead of having limited options because of scientific standards.

Feyerabend's key points

- All methods have their limitations.
- Therefore, the most reasonable position is that of methodological pluralism.
- The importance of creativity in science: anything goes
- Science has no universal, unchanging method: any rule that one would wish to lay down (and has been laid down) will have to be broken (or has been broken) to make progress, in light of any rationalist account: epistemological anarchism.
- The enforcement of epistemological "law and order" is a limit on human creativity and freedom (and crucial opportunism).
- Nothing distinguishes science from non-science

Method

- Sometimes use induction.
- Sometimes use counter-induction.
- Sometimes be guided by the observable facts.
- Sometimes challenge the observable facts.
- Sometimes reject a falsified ideology.
- Sometimes borrow from rejected ideologies.
- "Let a thousand flowers bloom!"

According to Feyerabend, science is an essentially anarchist enterprise: "theoretical anarchism is more humanitarian and more likely to encourage progress than its law-and-order alternatives" (Feyerabend 1975, p. 17). He criticizes the aims of scientific education to simplify science by simplifying its participants; the result is a uniform science separated from the rest of the world and held together by its strict rules. The students will obey the mental image of the professor, and he will conform to the standards of argumentation he has learned, and he will not be aware that this is only a result of the training he has received. Feyerabend refers to Kropotkin (1908) when he concludes by saying that such scientific education is in conflict with "the cultivation of individuality which alone produces, (...) well-developed human beings" (Feyerabend 1975, p. 20). There are always circumstances when it is advisable to break with the fundamental rules of science. His intention is not to replace one set of rules with another but rather to facilitate methodological diversity.

Feyerabend argued that it is always a good idea to ask counter questions to scientific theories. In other words we need a dream world if we are to discover the real world, and by developing utopia we become aware of the current ideology. Today's knowledge may well become the fairy-tale of tomorrow, and the most laughable myth today may turn into the firmest of solid facts of tomorrow.

There are myths, dogmas and metaphysics, and there are many ways to construct a worldview. According to Feyerabend, it is clear that a fruitful exchange between science and such "non-scientific" worldviews will be in ever greater need of anarchism than science is itself. Thus, "anarchism is not only possible, it is necessary both for the internal progress of science and for the development of our culture as a whole" (Feyerabend 1975, p. 180).

Ideology and utopia

In 1516, Thomas More coined and defined the word utopia as a combination of two parts: "no place" and a "good place". Utopia as method "is the imaginary reconstruction of society" (Levitas 2012, p. 336) that makes connections between "different policy spheres, different arenas of experience, and between present and future – and requires these to be addressed at the level of concrete institutions, rather than merely abstract principles" (Levitas 2007, p. 300).

Karl Mannheim published "*Ideology and Utopia*" in 1936, a period of chaos and upheaval in Europe. He defined utopia as a contrast to the existing ideology. Utopia should challenge the current dominating ideology. In opposition to ideology, as a conservative power in society, utopia expressed the radical, creative, and self-transcending processes in society. Mannheim argued that utopian thinking was essential to start a process of change.

> Ideologies i.e. those complexes of ideas which direct toward the maintenance of the existing order, and utopias – or those complexes of ideas which tend to generate activities toward changes of the prevailing order – do not merely deflect thought from the object of observation, but also serve to fix attention upon aspects of the situation which otherwise would be obscured or pass unnoticed.
>
> (Wirth in Mannheim 1936, p. xxi)

Mannheim's communitarian kinship becomes clear when he claims that it is incorrect to say that the single individual thinks; it is preferable to say that "he participates in thinking further what other men have thought before him" (Mannheim 1936, p. 3). All elements of meaning have reference to one another and derive their significance from the reciprocal interrelationship in a frame of thought. Ideology refers to the characteristics of the total structure of ideas in a concrete historical epoch. According to Guérin, the ideology is a reality:

> I am born into it, raised within it and I have my obligations to it, I owe it "loyalty and homage". It takes me under its sheltering wing and I live

by its grace (...) For instance, it teaches me to abide the laws, to refrain from trespasses against State property, to venerate a divine and earthly majesty, etc. (...) It prepares me to become a "useful tool", a useful member of society.

(Guérin 2005, p. 22)

Ideology plays an important role in the understanding of the society in which one is living. According to Westoby and Dowling, "people need a map, pattern, structure and organisation for thinking and acting" (Westoby and Dowling 2013, p. 91). Ideology provides people with a common world-view that is important because society cannot do without order and needs common rules. In the existing society the government is the guarantor of order. The government offers itself as the absolute and necessary condition for order. The idea is that "the stronger the government, the nearer perfect order" (Guérin 2005, p. 87). Ideas that are incongruous with the state of reality in which they occur, are utopian. Utopia shatters the order of things, partially or wholly.

Ideology, which describes the present from the inside

- Is important to create identity – individually and collectively
- Is rooted in the ideas of dominant social groups
- Refers to accepted common norms and values
- Justifies authorities

Utopia, which understands the present from outside

- Is somewhere else – is geared towards the future
- Should not be realized; we can only approach it, to work in that direction
- Contributes to change; society is unfinished, dynamic; it is always underway
- Challenges authorities

In contrast to political philosophy and ethics, both of which have a tendency to look at sustainable development as an abstract concept, utopia operates the concept at a concrete level and describes the institutional preconditions. Utopia is a description of a society different from the existing; it is outside Cell 1 (figure 2.1) (actuality) and it questions the existing paradigm and the negative heuristics in the existing hard core. It is a description of "a different set of social institutions and practices embedding different ethics and values" (Levitas 2017, p. 6). Realistic utopia is placed in Cell 3 (figure 2.1), and utopias based on wishful thinking are placed in Cell 2 (figure 2.1). Kropotkin rooted his utopian speculations in what he felt was the practically possible, "yet he was cautious in avoiding the overt determinism that this stance could entail" (Adams 2015, p. 143). Even if Kropotkin was against detailed descriptions of utopia, he wanted to enshrine flexibility into utopia, and he portrayed a relatively clear picture of the future social systems in his book, *The Conquest of Bread* (1892/2014). The development of realistic utopia is focused on in the following discussions.

The question of how to actualize the potential on the individual, organizational and social levels is most challenging. A holistic description of utopia "treats social arrangements, means of livelihood, ways of life, and their accompanying ethics as an indivisible system" (Levitas 2017, p. 6). In accordance with political philosophy, dictated by the tension between what is and what ought to be, rather than by one of the extremes, Colin Tudge asked, "What is and what could be" (Tudge 2016, p. 16). This is the core challenge in utopian thinking. Tudge maintains that everyone, everywhere, could have plenty to eat, and farming should have its rightful place at the center of human affairs. Today humanity could be at peace with itself and with our fellow creatures and the biosphere at large:

> All that stands between us and a long and glorious future is seriously bad strategy based on false ideas that happen to be convenient to the people with the most power: ideas rooted in a debased ideology that put short-term wealth and dominance above all else.
>
> (Tudge 2016, p. 16)

As we shall see later, anarchism represents a framework that differs from its predecessors, liberalism and Marxism (discussed in the next chapter). Anarchism could also be defined as a mediator between the two extremes.

To stimulate creative thinking it is relevant to elaborate on the structural relations between a society and its economic system. Anarchist political philosophy does not take the dominating system as established and permanent but challenges it by developing a political platform for a visionary society, one often referred to as utopian. The aim is not to create a new dominating ideology but rather to "create a transformational training space that enables participants and possibilitators-in-dialogue with others to imagine new possibilities for our world" (Westoby and Dowling 2013, p. 131).

Studying anarchist philosophy has helped to rescue the concept of utopia from its negative connotations following on from the connection to Cell 2 (figure 2.1) (false promises). Utopia often serves as a means to escape from the many imperfections of the world and create some visionary solutions that transcend the actuality. Contrary to this understanding, anarchism refers to a realistic utopian political platform that can contribute to releasing the true current potential on the micro, meso and macro levels (Cell 3, figure 2.1).

A fundamental challenge to utopian thinking is the objection that "the kinds of life sketched in these utopias are a bare improvement on the present" (Adams 2015, p. 155). Descriptions of utopia could also be coupled with paradigm shifts and deep changes in the current hard core. The power of utopianism is in thinking creatively about the future, expressing hopes, ambitions and objectives, and doing away with the restrictions of the present. Utopia based on anarchism is realistic because anarchism "is built on the assumption of propensities, values and tendencies which, it is argued, are already present in human social activity" (Suissa 2010, p. 5). And, as we will see later, Kropotkin and Reclus based their anarchist ideas on evolutionary theory and natural science.

Clarke maintains, "no ideology is pure ideology and elements of utopia are always embedded in ideology itself" (Clark 2013, p. 136). Anarchism is a kind of utopia because it questions many of the presuppositions of the current society and suggests radically different social and economic forms. Anarchism visualizes an alternative future based on autonomy, individuality, community, solidarity and a deep concern for the natural environment, by developing a just economic system that maintains peace between rival interests.

Implementation of deep changes presupposes a potent tension between what is (ideology) and what could be (utopia). The intention of utopia is to shatter the presented order. It is problematic to implement deep "change processes in the absence of visions or utopias" (Jakobsen and Storsletten 2017, p. 75). Utopian thinking can inspire change processes by offering a contrast, an alternative, to the existing order by asking what is actual and what is possible. All changes in history have contained a utopian dimension. Utopian thinking is not only about the future; it will always influence the present by projecting a community based on individual freedom, solidarity, peace cooperation, meaningful labour, economic sustenance and ecological responsibility as well as providing room for disagreement. "The most utopian of utopianisms is also the most practical one" (Clark 2013, p. 140). This is in accordance with the idea that anarchism has no possibility of realization unless its roots are developed on a realistic base, in other words, a possible impossibility. Thinking about how the political and economic structures can be different provides an important reminder that there are other ways of developing economic theory and practice in a direction where freedom, equality, solidarity and environmental and social responsibility are given priority. The utopia of the European bourgeois at the end of the 18th century was the idea of "freedom":

> It was in part a real utopia, i.e. it contained elements oriented towards the realization of a new social order which were instrumental in disintegrating the previously existing order and which, after their realization, did in part become translated into reality.
>
> (Mannheim 1936, p. 203)

All ideas which transcend the actual situation are utopian and have a transforming effect upon the existing order. The impossible gives birth to the possible while the absolute interferes with the world and influences actual events.

Utopian thinking is valuable because it has the imagination to visualize a society based on liberty, justice, peace and ecological sustainability, and this sets it apart from virtually all current thinking.

Today anarchism emerges in different guises in, amongst others, movements arguing for the necessity of local food production, peace movements, feminism, and, as focused on in this book, ecological economics. The challenge is to find the extent to which anarchist philosophy is relevant as a political platform to develop and implement ecological economics for quality of life integrated in sustainable nature. It is important to be aware that ecological economics is not a homogenous field of science (or practice), and, just as anarchism, it is open to interpretation in many different directions.

From this outlook we can go further in questioning the extent to which anarchism is a relevant and influential source of inspiration in the development of a political platform for ecological economics. In accordance with utopia as a method, the idea of anarchism is to inspire to form "the new society within the shell of the old" (Snyder 1961). I have referred to different eminent commentators who argue that anarchism becomes more and more relevant for the new century because it combines deep environmental concerns with a critique of modern culture. Marshall puts it this way: "anarchism is the only political ideology capable of addressing the challenges posed by our new green consciousness to the accepted range of political ideas" (Marshall 2008, p. 667). In other words, it gives method to our goal of moving in the direction of significant change.

Green economy and ecological economics

The difference between green economy and ecological economics represents an illuminating illustration of the creative tension between ideology (actuality) and utopia (potentiality), with relevance for both the difference between Cells 1 and 3 in Figure 2.1, and Lakatos' theory of research programs. Without doubting that representatives of both perspectives are seriously trying to solve the most pressing environmental and social problems, it is obvious that their approaches are quite different. Green economy focuses on reducing the negative symptoms of the dominating system, while ecological economics requires changes on the systems level. Green economy recommends changes in the protective belt of mainstream economics without questioning its hard core. Ecological economics questions the hard core of mainstream economics in order to change the whole research program. In other words, green economy represents an evolutionary approach to a change process based on minor adjustments to the theories in the protective belt, while ecological economics has a radical image, demanding a revolutionary paradigm shift and deep changes in the hard core of mainstream economics. Connected to Figure 2.1, green economy operates within the frames of Cell 1. That is, all changes are done without challenging the hard core of mainstream economy. Rather

than integrating nature, society and economy in a comprehensive understanding, the dispute is dominated by a discourse that "reduces everything
to exchange in price-making markets" (Spash 2017, p. 4).

The definition of "circular economy" is an illustrating example of a
successful change in the protective belt without disturbing the hard core of
the research program. "A circular economy is led by business for a profit
within the 'rules of the game' decided by an active citizenship in a flourishing democracy. (...) The business angle of a circular economy – higher
competitiveness, higher resource security and material efficiency" (Webster
2015, p. 90). Other examples are CSR (corporate social responsibility),
environmental management systems, and business ethics that make changes
in the protective belt without criticizing the hard-core principles. On a
general level, greening the economy is focused on reducing the most
criticized effects on the social and natural environment. The Brundtland
report, *Our Common Future* (1987), is an example of green economy,
partly because the report argues that environmental responsibility depends
on (green) growth. In order to reach the goal of sustainable development,
more resources are needed. *Our Common Future* supports "an economic
argument known as 'weak sustainability', an approach to the management
of natural capital that sees it as potentially interchangeable with or replaceable
by human capital" (Gerasimova 2017, p. 27). The implication is that putting
sustainability in place will not require much in the way of radical change.
Green economists also argue that greening the economy is an efficient marketing tool to enhance the reputation of market power. By these means green
strategy is presented as an effective instrument to increase a company's profits
and its competitive advantage. In a long-term perspective, they argue that
growth should be as green as possible.

Hard core of mainstream economy

- Growth
- Competition
- Egoism
- Strategy

Protective belt in green economy

- Green growth
- CSR as a marketing strategy
- Business ethics for better reputation
- Green strategy

It is fair to conclude that green economy represents the dominating
ideology, existing within the framework of Cell 1 (figure 2.1) and accepting the hard-core principles, and fails to challenge the existing system on

any hard-core principles. Green economy makes serious attempts to improve the dominating economic system by diminishing its most immediate symptoms while leaving the inherent underlying troubles set aside and entirely untouched. Green economy is based on the failing assumption that unlimited growth is possible because of human capacity to make technological innovations. (Cell 2, figure 2.1). The problem is that economic growth is unavoidably limited by biophysical constraints, "the limits of biological processes given by the laws of physics" (Marazzi 2017, p. 24).

Ecological economics belongs to Cell 3 (figure 2.1), indicating that its implementation requires deep changes in the hard core and a concrete realist description of a utopian society. This means that ecological economics accepts that the solution to the problems we are facing requires deep ideological changes. In other words, "instead of trying to solve problems by transforming reality to fit the model, it is more appropriate to change the model to fit in with reality" (Jakobsen and Storsletten 2017, p. 73). First of all, growth in the extraction and consumption of natural resources represents one of the core problems and must be rejected and replaced by qualitative development. Ecological economists start with a basic but crucial point, "an acknowledgement that the planet's natural resources are limited and those human societies are dependent on the Earth's capacity to regenerate resources" (Marazzi 2017, p. 18). In line with these arguments, Herman Daly and John B. Cobb, Jr. (Daly and Cobb, 1994) reason that ecological economics is based on acceptance of the necessity to implement a de-growth economy and shift the focus away from quantitative growth towards qualitative development. Further, ecological economists argue that competition must be replaced by cooperation in order to handle the serious anomalies connected with, for example, an increasing gap between rich and poor. The idea of rationality as egocentric maximization of utility must be substituted with solidarity, and a partnership approach must reject and replace strategic planning.

Hard core of mainstream economy

- Growth (quantitative)
- Competition
- Egoism
- Strategy

Hard core of ecological economics

- Development (qualitative)
- Cooperation
- Solidarity
- Partnership approach

Consequently, we can see that ecological economics offers a radical alternative to the hard core of the dominating economy; further, it is clear that ecological economics is not focused primarily on finding new answers to the old questions merely by making changes in the protective belt. Rather, ecological economics focuses on critical questions to be asked of the hard core. In the spirit of Feyerabend, the questions often challenge principles and theories accepted by most economists today. By asking, and answering, these critical questions it is possible to uncover new perspectives and develop a more life-enhancing economic theory and practice. Ecological economics, fundamentally, asks how we can develop an economy and a society based on peaceful relations between humans and nature, between humans, and within the individual human being. This is in accordance with the idea that utopia should challenge and disturb the dominating ideology to stimulate and create the change processes.

Concluding remarks

In this chapter I have presented and reflected on the connections between a mosaic of different perspectives on how to understand change processes in theory and practice, with a specific focus on the economy. The point of departure was an analytic scheme to differentiate between what is possible in different combinations and what could be done depending on actual and ideological characteristics. My conclusion was that ecological economics is possible in practice but requires a massive shift in ideology. Kuhn used the term paradigm to describe such deep systemic shifts. By introducing the distinction between hard core and protective belt, Lakatos made the understanding of scientific development easier. I established that changes in a research program could be introduced without disturbing the principles in the hard core. Paradigm shifts and deep changes in the hard core were compared with the contrast between ideology and utopia, as described by Mannheim, and the tension created between the two poles gives energy and direction to the process of change.

Last in this line of reasoning was the distinction between green economy and ecological economics. Green economy was defined as a kind of economic practice focused on reducing the negative symptoms within the existing economic system. Our existing economic system is described as belonging to actuality (Cell 1, figure 2.1), the dominating ideology characterized by hard-core doctrines. Derrida argues that once a particular view of reality becomes dominant, "then social and political processes regulate and discipline people into certain ways of ethical being, thinking and behaving that are consistent with such a view" (Westoby and Dowling 2013, p. 117) According to Spash,

> economics has been identified with (…) "formal economics", where a
> narrow market exchange model dominates, a model that misconstrues

the historical meaning of markets, trade and money, and is blind to the potential alternative forms of social integration and organisation.

(Spash 2017, p. 3)

Ecological economics asks questions of the dominating ideology, is often in conflict with scientifically accepted theories and aims to break through and develop realistic utopian solutions (Cell 3 in figure 2.1). According to Feyerabend, hypotheses which contradict well-confirmed theories give us evidence that cannot be obtained in other ways.

Following on from this position, the next chapter delves deeper into the following questions, which are relevant to the development of a philosophical platform for ecological economics.

- What kind of society do we want?
- What would the economy look like in this society?
- What kind of activities would best further the realization of this society?

Underlying these questions is a basic and driving scepticism that the dominating system can solve the problems we face or inspire a process towards a better world characterized by the good life in a good society. In other words, the focus is on possible impossibilities, asking critical questions of the hard core of the dominating ideology and putting forward realistic utopian solutions.

As a basis for the discussion I will offer some reflections on the main challenges the global society faces today by making a critical review of the UN's 8 Millennium Development Goals (MDGs), the UN's 17 Sustainable Development Goals (SDGs) and the 16 principles outlined in the Earth Charter. They all represent a qualified analysis and put in order of priority the most serious problems the global society has to solve. These reports address those issues that are of concern in the current society by projecting a utopian future in which they are resolved. All three declarations conclude that it is necessary to see deep changes on different levels; it is not enough to make minor changes in "the protective belt" of the existing system. One of the main arguments for the necessity of a paradigm shift is the deep understanding of how everything is interconnected.

It is encouraging to notice that the word crisis, from the Greek "krisis", referred to "that moment in the course of an illness when it decisively turns towards either health (...) or death" (Illich 2015, p. 13). The point is that today we have the opportunity to choose between two fundamentally different alternatives, either to follow mainstream capitalism or follow an ecological economic alternative. According to Mannheim (1936), this means that we need the energy that develops in the tension between actuality (ideology) and potentiality (utopia) in order to make deep changes.

3 Challenges facing today's society

Introduction

In this chapter I present and discuss the prioritized challenges in the current society based on the UN's Millennium Development Goals, the UN's Sustainable Development Goals and the Earth Charter. When the declarations are studied it becomes clear that global society, at the beginning of the 21st century, prioritizes the unfair distribution of wealth and all its environmental problems.

In 1950 Martin Buber wrote:

> For the last three decades we have felt that we were living in the initial phases of the greatest crisis humanity has ever known. It grows increasingly clear to us that the tremendous happenings of the past years, (...) can be understood only as symptoms of this crisis.
>
> (Buber 1996, p. 129)

> The crisis was not only connected to the political and economic systems, what was in question were "nothing less than man's whole existence in the world".
>
> (Buber 1996, p. 129)

Murray Bookchin expressed an important point when he argued that knowledge of history is important to the understanding of the current society. On a general level the society cannot be understood independently of the changing cultural and geographical conditions. He maintained the problem today is that "We normally live completely immersed in the present – to such a degree (...) that we often fail to see how much our own social period differs from the past" (Bookchin 2004, p. iii).

Even if the environmental and social challenges facing the global society today differ from what they were some epochs back in history, they are just as serious and threatening. Our interest in environmental responsibility is relatively new. Sustainable development became one of the catchphrases after the publication of the Brundtland report, *Our Common Future*, in 1987. This report is interesting not only because it focuses on environmental problems such as climate change, but it also gives priority to social justice and human well-being. Our world community has taken serious action to solve these problems without ever coming close to substantial solutions. Even if the majority of climate researchers are convinced that global warming over the last century is man-made and the politicians argue that reduction of greenhouse gases should have the highest priority, despite all this the global, environmental and social problems have become ever more challenging at both national and international levels. Temperatures are rising and the gap between rich and poor is increasing both within countries and between countries. One interesting question is why the Brundtland report has not had a more significant impact.

One explanation of why the actual measures taken have had little effect could be that today's society is trapped in an ideology opposed to, and indeed obstructing, deep change. Because the dominant utopia is characterized by "endless material progress, based on the fundamental utopian fantasy of infinite powers of production and infinite possibilities for consumption" (Clark 2013, p. 127), the existing ideology is threatening the future of humanity as well as the eco-systems. Another explanation is that the required actions are too fragmentary, "involving not just changes in behaviour of national governments and how they work together, but in the behaviour of individuals" (Gerasimova 2017, p. 64). A third explanation concerns "the ambiguity of the concept of sustainable development, and the complexity of the issues it covers" (Gerasimova 2017, p. 64). How serious the situation is could be described by referring to some "optimistic" climate scientists who warn that we are coming closer to the tipping point day by day, while others, more "pessimistic", argue that the tipping point has already been passed.

Operative solutions require both local action and international agreements. Up until today international collaboration has focused on reducing the negative symptoms of climate change, such as air quality, water shortages and soil problems, and on the fact that non-human life forms face extinction. The problem is, quite simply, that when environmental pollutants are released into nature, it is expensive and time consuming to clean up and the consequences of this strategy are extreme, and its negative impact on the environment has reached alarming dimensions. Because some of the most disastrous causes behind the problems are the increases in economic production and consumption, it seems unrealistic to solve all these massive problems within an economic system based entirely on endless growth. Based on this line of reasoning, it is rational to conclude that good intentions, as set out in the Brundtland report, are not enough if we are to bring in deep change and the bonds binding us to materialism and neoliberalism have to be broken.

Now, "we stand at a critical moment in Earth's history, a time when humanity must choose its future" (The Earth Charter). To understand and cope with the problems it is necessary to start from a valid description of reality. Feyerabend argued that if we really want to understand the nature of the world we are living in, we must use all ideas, "not just a small selection of them" (Feyerabend 1975). Unless we have a rich perspective to broaden our roots in contemporary life, our understanding of the world as it really is may be easily distorted and the rich potentialities for the future overlooked. So we can look at things again – if it is impossible to identify solutions within the existing ideology we will have to find utopian alternatives that provide the energy and direction to form the necessary change processes. Our global common destiny forces us to seek creative solutions that will be identified not only through our ability to ask challenging questions but also our skill to examine the answers in great detail. According to Feyerabend, deep change depends on our ability to ask questions which often go against the grain or are often inconsistent with the dominating ideology. We are in danger if we fail to realize that both the political and the economic systems have to adapt to the changes.

In the following paragraphs I look in greater detail at the UN's MDGs (1990–2015), the UN's SDGs (2015–2030) and the Earth Charter. Together these declarations give a detailed impression of the problems to which world society gives a high priority. It is a challenging task to give a valid interpretation of the different goals without being unfair to the ideas behind these declarations. Only by being explicit in the description and explanation of the preconditions can these problems be reduced.

These declarations indicate that the international community is facing a vast complex of challenges by way of the natural environment, poverty, war, terrorism and financial crises. We must accept that all these problems are interconnected and it is impossible to solve them in isolation, one by one. We need integrated solutions based on a holistic understanding.

Sustainable Development Goals

As a starting point I give a very short introduction by referring to the goals in the UN's MDGs, together with the UN's SDGs and the Earth Charter. Such an overview will give a relevant and informative picture of the challenges mentioned in the three declarations.

Box 3.1 The 8 Millennium Development Goals (MDGs) 1990–2015

1. Eradicate extreme poverty and hunger, 2. Achieve universal primary education, 3. Promote gender equality and empower women, 4. Reduce child mortality, 5. Improve maternal health, 6. Combat HIV/ AIDS, malaria and other diseases, 7. Ensure environmental sustainability, 8. Develop a global partnership for development.

Box 3.2 The 17 Sustainable Development Goals (2015–2030)

1. No Poverty – End poverty in all its forms everywhere, 2. Zero Hunger – End hunger, achieve food security and improved nutrition

and promote sustainable agriculture, 3. Good Health and Well-Being for People – Ensure healthy lives and promote well-being for all at all ages, 4. Quality Education – Ensure inclusive and equitable quality education and promote lifelong learning opportunities for all, 5. Gender Equality – Achieve gender equality and empower all women and girls, 6. Clean Water and Sanitation – Ensure availability and sustainable management of water and sanitation for all, 7. Affordable and Clean Energy – Ensure access to affordable, reliable, sustainable and modern energy for all, 8. Decent Work and Economic Growth – Promote sustained, inclusive and sustainable economic growth, full and productive employment and decent work for all, 9. Industry, Innovation and Infrastructure – Build resilient infrastructure, promote inclusive and sustainable industrialization and foster innovation, 10. Reduced Inequalities – Reduce income inequality within and among countries, 11. Sustainable Cities and Communities – Make cities and human settlements inclusive, safe, resilient and sustainable, 12. Responsible Consumption and Production – Ensure sustainable consumption and production patterns, 13. Climate Change – Take urgent action to combat climate change and its impacts by regulating emissions and promoting developments in renewable energy, 14. Life Below Water – Conserve and sustainably use the oceans, seas and marine resources for sustainable development, 15. Life on Land – Protect, restore and promote sustainable use of terrestrial ecosystems, sustainably manage forests, combat desertification, and halt and reverse land degradation and halt biodiversity loss, 16. Peace, Justice and Strong Institutions – Promote peaceful and inclusive societies for sustainable development, provide access to justice for all and build effective, accountable and inclusive institutions at all levels, 17. Partnerships for the Goals – Strengthen the means of implementation and revitalize the global partnership for sustainable development.

Box 3.3 The 16 goals of the Earth Charter

1. Respect Earth and life in all its diversity, 2. Care for the community of life with understanding, compassion, and love, 3. Build democratic societies that are just, participatory, sustainable, and peaceful, 4. Secure Earth's bounty and beauty for present and future generations, 5. Protect and restore the integrity of Earth's ecological systems, with special concern for biological diversity and the natural processes that sustain life, 6. Prevent harm as the best method of environmental

protection and, when knowledge is limited, apply a precautionary approach, 7. Adopt patterns of production, consumption, and reproduction that safeguard Earth's regenerative capacities, human rights, and community well-being, 8. Advance the study of ecological sustainability and promote the open exchange and wide application of the knowledge acquired, 9. Eradicate poverty as an ethical, social, and environmental imperative, 10. Ensure that economic activities and institutions at all levels promote human development in an equitable and sustainable manner, 11. Affirm gender equality and equity as prerequisites to sustainable development and ensure universal access to education, health care, and economic opportunity, 12. Uphold the right of all, without discrimination, to a natural and social environment supportive of human dignity, bodily health, and spiritual well-being, with special attention to the rights of indigenous peoples and minorities, 13. Strengthen democratic institutions at all levels, and provide transparency and accountability in governance, inclusive participation in decision-making, and access to justice, 14. Integrate into formal education and life-long learning the knowledge, values, and skills needed for a sustainable way of life, 15. Treat all living beings with respect and consideration, 16. Promote a culture of tolerance, nonviolence, and peace.

Even if the three declarations differ on many dimensions, there are many similarities. Firstly, there has been a change from the MDGs to the SDGs. Secondly, the Earth Charter differs from the official UN documents. The Earth Charter initiative is anchored in a global network of organizations and individuals which have defined a guide for transition towards a more just, sustainable, and peaceful world.

On the one hand, the MDGs mention some points that have reduced focus in the SDGs. For example, Goal 4 – "Reduce child mortality", Goal 5 – "Improve maternal health" and Goal 6 – "Combat HIV/AIDS, malaria and other diseases". These goals are now included under other headings in the SDGs. The reduced focus on the goals linked to health services could mean that they have been solved or at least reduced over the last decades.

On the other hand, the SDGs are much more detailed than the MDGs on some topics. To synthesize some problems that are relevant for the discussions on anarchism (Chapters 5, 6 and 7), and on ecological economics (Chapters 8 and 9), I have structured the next paragraphs as follows: 1. Poverty, 2. Environmental sustainability, 3. Economy, 4. Politics, 5. Education, and 6. Cooperation. I look closely into the challenges that are most focused on in all three reports.

Poverty is extended from Goal 1 in the Millennium Development Goals – "Eradicate extreme poverty and hunger" – to at least four goals in the SDGs – 1. "No Poverty", 2." Zero Hunger", 8. "Decent Work and Economic Growth" and 10. "Reduced Inequalities". This signifies that even if extreme poverty is reduced, the UN considers poverty to be one of today's most pressing challenges. Environmental sustainability is extended from Goal 7 in the MDGs – "Ensure environmental sustainability" – to five goals in the SDGs – 6. "Clean Water and Sanitation", 11. "Sustainable Cities and Communities", 13. "Climate Change", 14. "Life Below Water", and 15. "Life on Land". This is a signal that problems linked to degradation of the natural environment have increased in importance. Challenges connected to economy in the SDGs include Goal 7. "Affordable and Clean Energy", Goal 9. "Industry, Innovation and Infrastructure" and Goal 12. "Responsible Consumption and Production". Politics is mentioned in the SDGs' Goal 16. "Peace, Justice and Strong Institutions". The importance of education is described in the SDGs' Goal 4. "Quality Education – Ensure inclusive and equitable quality education and promote lifelong learning opportunities for all" and Goal 5. "Gender Equality – Achieve gender equality and empower all women and girls". The need for international cooperation is emphasized in both UN declarations: Goal 8 in the MDGs, "Develop a global partnership for development" and Goal 17 in the SDGs, "Partnerships for the Goals – Strengthen the means of implementation and revitalize the global partnership for sustainable development".

From this brief overview of the two UN declarations, it is reasonable to draw the following conclusions: the goals connected to the elimination of poverty have increased in focus and are given the highest priority. Environmental sustainability goals are much more detailed and focused. Other problem areas are economy, politics, education and cooperation. Both declarations portray cooperation as necessary to cope with these global challenges.

If we compare and contrast the declarations from the UN with the Earth Charter, there are several interesting variations: Poverty is mentioned in Goal 9, environmental sustainability in goals 2, 4, 5 and 15, economy in Goal 7, politics in goals 12 and 13, and education in goals 8 and 14. Cooperation is mentioned to a greater or lesser extent in all paragraphs. The focus on ethics in the Earth Charter is the most substantial difference from the UN reports. It has an eco-centric perspective that underlines the ethical duty we have to respect all life forms on earth, not only human. In addition, it speaks explicitly about feelings and emotions and takes indigenous people into account.

It can be meaningfully concluded that the two UN declarations are more rational, detailed and anthropocentric than the Earth Charter. While the Earth Charter refers to ethics and human rights, the UN declarations refer more to law and science.

A common trait in all three declarations is that they are written rather like holograms, which means that all paragraphs make reference to the general goal of sustainable development, and that general goal runs through all paragraphs.

Poverty

Poverty is mentioned in the first position in the MDGs and in the SDGs. This indicates that the increasing gap between rich and poor is the most challenging problem in the global society today. There is a change from Goal 1 in the MDGs, "Eradicate extreme poverty and hunger", to Goal 1. "No Poverty – End poverty in all its forms everywhere" in the SDGs. The change indicates that extreme poverty is reduced but poverty is still a serious problem for a great number of people. The Earth Charter mentions poverty as Goal 9, and it claims that the eradication of poverty is an ethical, social, and environmental imperative.

In the SDGs, problems concerning poverty are split into several goals, compared to what we find in the MDGs. The consequences of poverty are described in Goal 2. "Zero Hunger – End hunger, achieve food security and improved nutrition and promote sustainable agriculture" and Goal 8. "Decent Work and Economic Growth – Promote sustained, inclusive and sustainable economic growth, full and productive employment and decent work for all". Poverty is described in Goal 10 of the Earth Charter: "Ensure that economic activities and institutions at all levels promote human development in an equitable and sustainable manner". The following descriptions (in italics) of the UN's 17 SDG's are citations from the UN's home page: https://sustainabledevelopment.un.org/sdgs

SDG Goal 1: No Poverty – End poverty in all its forms everywhere

The goal is to ensure that all women and men, especially poor and vulnerable, have equal rights to financial resources as well as access to basic services, ownership and control of land and other forms of property, heritage, natural resources, appropriate technology and financial services, including microfinance.

Build the resilience of the poor and people in vulnerable situations so that they are less vulnerable to climate-related extreme events and other economic, social and environmental stresses and disasters.

Ensure significant mobilization of resources from many different sources, including through enhanced development cooperation, to provide developing countries, especially the least developed countries, with sufficient and predictable means to implement programs and policies aimed at eradicating all forms of poverty.

Create good political frameworks at national, regional and international levels based on development strategies that benefit the poor, with the aim of accelerating investment in poverty-alleviation measures.

Goal 2: Zero Hunger – End hunger, achieve food security and improved nutrition and promote sustainable agriculture

All people, especially the poor and people in vulnerable situations, including infants, should have access to safe, nutritionally healthy and adequate food

throughout the year. The productivity and income of small-scale producers – especially women, indigenous peoples, drivers of family farms, livestock communities and fishermen – should increase. Sustainable agriculture should be facilitated.

To reach this goal, secure and equal access to land and other production resources and input resources, such as knowledge, financial services, markets and opportunities for value added, are necessary.

Ensuring sustainable food production systems and introducing robust agricultural methods that increase productivity and production help maintain ecosystems and strengthen the ability to adapt to climate change, extreme weather, drought, floods and other disasters, which gradually leads to better soil quality. The genetic diversity of seeds, cultures, and livestock and related wildlife, including through well-known and rich seed and plant stocks, nationally, regionally and internationally, will maintain access to, and a fair and equal distribution of, the benefits resulting from use of genetic resources and associated traditional knowledge, in line with international unity.

Increase investments, including through better international cooperation, rural infrastructure, agricultural research and guidance services, technology development and establishment of plant and animal genetic banks, aimed at improving agricultural production in developing countries, especially in the least developed countries. Correct and impede trade restrictions and distortions on world agricultural markets, including through a parallel phasing out of all forms of export subsidies on agricultural products and all export measures with equivalent effect, in accordance with the mandate of the Doha Round.

Take measures to ensure that the markets for food products and their by-products work for their purpose, and facilitate rapid access to market information, including on food reserves, to help limit extreme fluctuations in food prices.

Goal 8: Decent Work and Economic Growth – Promote sustained, inclusive and sustainable economic growth, full and productive employment and decent work for all

Maintain economic growth per capita in accordance with the conditions in the respective countries and with a growth of at least seven percent per capita GDP per year in the least developed countries. Increase economic productivity through diversification, technological modernization and innovation, with emphasis on profitable and labour-intensive sectors. Promote a developmental policy that supports productive business, creating decent jobs, entrepreneurship, creativity and innovation, and stimulate the formalization and growth of the number of very small and medium-sized businesses, including by providing access to financial services.

Gradually improve the utilization of global resources in consumption and production, and work to eliminate the link between economic growth and environmental degradation, which allows developed countries an unfair advantage, in accordance with the ten-year Sustainable Consumption and Production Action Program.

Achieve full and productive employment and decent work for all women and men, including youth and people with disabilities, and achieve equal pay for equal work. Significantly reduce the proportion of young people who are neither employed nor under education or training. Take immediate and effective measures to abolish forced labour, end modern slavery and trafficking and ensure that the worst forms of child labour are banned and abolished, including recruitment and use of child soldiers, and abolish all forms of child labour by 2025.

Protect labour rights and promote a safe and secure working environment for all workers, including migrant workers and especially female immigrants, as well as workers in difficult working conditions. Develop and implement policies to promote a sustainable tourism industry that creates jobs and promotes local culture and local products.

Strengthen national financial institutions' ability to stimulate and expand access to banking and insurance services and financial services for all. Increase support for trade aid (Aid for Trade) to developing countries, especially the least developed countries, including through a better-integrated framework for trade-related technical assistance to LDCs. Develop and implement a global strategy for youth employment by 2020 and implement the Global Jobs Pact of the International Labour Organization.

Goal 10: Reduced Inequalities – Reduce income inequality within and among countries

Achieve a gradual and lasting revenue increase for the poorest 40 percent of the population. Ensure that everyone is empowered and promote their social, economic and political inclusion, regardless of age, gender, disability, race, ethnicity, national origin, religion or economic or other status. Ensure equal opportunities and reduce discrimination, inter alia by eliminating discriminatory laws, policies and practices, and by promoting legislation, policies and measures that are suitable for achieving this goal. Adopt policies, particularly with regard to taxes and fees, payroll and social care, with a view to achieving gradual equalization of differences. Improve the regulation and supervision of global financial markets and financial institutions, and strengthen the implementation of the regulatory framework.

Ensure that developing countries become better represented and receive greater participation in decision-making processes in global financial institutions, so that institutions become more efficient, trustworthy, responsible and legitimate. Provide for migration and mobility in orderly, safe, regular and responsible forms, including by implementing a planned and well-managed migration policy.

Implement the principle of special treatment and differentiated treatment of developing countries, especially the least developed countries, in accordance with agreements with the World Trade Organization. Stimulate public development assistance and capital flows, including foreign direct investment, to the states where the need is greatest, especially the least developed countries, African countries, small developing countries and coastal developing countries, in accordance with their own plans and programs. Reduce transaction fees to less than three percent in the case of transfers from immigrants to their home countries, and abolish transfer schemes where fees exceed five percent.

Prioritized objectives:

- End poverty in all its forms everywhere
- End hunger; all people should have access to healthy food
- Increase income of small-scale producers and sustainable food production systems
- Equal right to natural and economic resources, ownership of land, appropriate technology
- Enable the poor to develop their own capacities
- Decent work and economic growth
- Ensure that the markets for food products work
- Eliminate the link between economic growth and environmental degradation
- Reduce income inequalities within and among countries
- Focus on the needs of developing nations
- Make knowledge about human health and environmental protection publicly available
- Support international scientific and technical cooperation on sustainability

The Earth Charter on poverty

The Earth Charter states that the eradication of poverty is an ethical, social and environmental imperative. All people should be guaranteed the right to clean water, clean air, food security, uncontaminated soil shelter, and safe sanitation, allocating the national and international resources required. In addition, it states that it is an ethical duty to recognize the ignored, protect the vulnerable, serve those who suffer, and enable them to develop their capacities and to pursue their aspirations. (The following descriptions of the 16 goals in the Earth Charter (written in Italics) are citations from the Earth Charters home page: http://earthcharter.org/discover/the-earth-charter/

Goal 9: Eradicate poverty as an ethical, social, and environmental imperative

a. *Guarantee the right to drinkable water, clean air, food security, uncontaminated soil, shelter, and safe sanitation, allocating the national and international resources required.*

b. *Empower every human being with the education and resources to secure a sustainable livelihood, and provide social security and safety nets for those who are unable to support themselves.*

c. *Recognize the ignored, protect the vulnerable, serve those who suffer, and enable them to develop their capacities and to pursue their aspirations.*

The Earth Charter does not explicitly mention anything about producing healthy food, but it asserts that it is necessary to support international scientific and technical cooperation on sustainability, with special attention to the needs of developing nations. It also says that information of vital importance to human health and environmental protection, including genetic information, should remain available and in the public domain. At all levels sustainable development plans should be adopted. In the same spirit, the traditional knowledge and spiritual wisdom which exists in all cultures, and contributes greatly to environmental protection and human well-being, should be recognized and preserved.

Instead of discussing economic growth and full employment, the Earth Charter speaks about ensuring that economic activities and institutions at all levels promote human development in an equitable and sustainable manner. There are two goals: One is to promote equitable distribution of wealth within and among nations. The second is to empower every human being with education and resources to secure a sustainable livelihood and provide social security and safety nets for those who are unable support themselves.

Prioritized objectives:

- The eradication of poverty is an ethical, social and environmental imperative.
- It is an ethical duty to recognize the ignored and protect the vulnerable.
- It is a right to have access to clean water, clean air, food security, uncontaminated soil, shelter and safe sanitation.
- Traditional knowledge and spiritual wisdom in all cultures that contribute to environmental protection and human well-being should be recognized and preserved.
- Promote human development in an equitable and sustainable manner.
- Promote equitable distribution of wealth within nations and among nations.

Comments on poverty

Both the UN's SDGs and the Earth Charter point out that the global community should contribute to give all people security regarding satisfaction of basic needs. A high quality of life not only requires having access to healthy food, satisfactory housing and reasonable clothes, but also includes good social and environmental relations. The Earth Charter goes a step further than the SDGs and states that it is an ethical duty to enable all people to develop their own potential. A system that allows a minority of the world's population to have control over most of the world's resources is not fair. Because of the dominating global economic system, the need for foreign currency is almost unlimited in poor countries. The consequence is that large multinational companies can establish themselves in poor countries and disregard all forms of social and environmental regulations. In addition, the state accepts minimal taxation of the companies. Because of low incomes within the local community, schools and health care systems operate on a very basic level.

The global financial crisis has exposed several significant weaknesses in the existing financial system: a significant drop in the level of public trust and confidence in financial institutions is among them. To solve problems connected to the imbalance between finance and the real economy, it is necessary to focus more on developing real economy than on stimulating growth in finance. In addition the financial system must be changed to be more resilient and able to withstand quakes in the market.

Within the existing economic system there is, perhaps surprisingly, a positive correlation between economic growth and the increasing gap between rich and poor which, in most OECD countries, is at its highest level in 30 years. A plausible explanation why inequality and growth are correlated is that small farms and firms lose in competition with big multinational companies in almost all areas. Small-scale local production in poor countries has no chance in competition with the powerful global companies. This explanation is relevant on a national level and even more relevant on a global level. Economic justice is about sharing the world's resources based on fairness. In addition, lasting peace between people depends on a global economic system based on fairness and equity. Peacebuilding is a question of ensuring the fundamental rights of people. One suggestion is to replace competition with cooperation as the fundamental principle in economics.

The SDGs are explicit in stressing how necessary it is to stimulate production systems and production methods which encourage growing more healthy food. The Earth Charter stresses that the loss of biodiversity has negative consequences for life on Earth because of the disturbance in the food chains connecting all kinds of life in the eco-systems. A dramatic increase in production of all kinds of products has resulted in high rates of pollution in the air, water and soil, and this causes serious interruption to many global eco-systems, e.g., lakes without fish and a dramatic reduction in rainforests. Most of the pollution is a by-product of our modern lifestyle.

Plastic is one of the most problematic forms of pollution, as it spreads both through soil and sea as micro substances which disturb all kinds of life forms. The shortage of potable water is already a fast-growing global problem, with one-third of humans having inadequate access to clean, fresh water. Pollution reduces the opportunity to cultivate the soil and produce healthy food for increasing numbers of people. This can lead to food shortages and more famines.

Today billions of people worldwide are unemployed or underemployed. Because "full" employment is no longer thought to be achievable, the solution is to find measures to share work in a fair way and distribute resources in accordance with the needs.

From the time of the publication of the Brundtland report, the idea that economic growth is a prerequisite for the protection of the environment has been part of the hard core of the dominating economic system. Economists and politicians thought that all kinds of problems could be solved through economic growth. Growth in production is accompanied by rising consumption. Despite economic growth, there is evidence that our current social, political and economic systems are intensifying inequalities, rather than reducing them. This is in contradiction to the Brundtland report, which referred to the benefits of the trickle-down effect.

Continued economic growth should provide the financial opportunities for money to be spent on environmental protections and technologies designed to reduce pollution. In this perspective, it is emphasized how necessary it is to transfer modern technology and money from rich to poor countries to allow poor countries to industrialize without harming the eco-systems and the life quality of the workers and the population. Any solutions to the problems connected with the interplay between economy, nature and society presuppose that the available resources are used in a sensible manner. Today, an increasing number of scientists and economists agree that there is a positive connection between economic growth and environmental problems. In other words, economic growth is not part of the solution; rather it is part of the problem.

Environmental sustainability

Environmental sustainability is described in much more detail in the SDGs than in the former UN reports. Aims connected with sustainable environmental development are outlined in six different goals concerning the interplay between the economy, society and nature. In contrast to the UN's anthropocentric perspective, the Earth Charter has an eco-centric understanding, including nature's inherent value.

Goal 6: Clean Water and Sanitation – Ensure availability and sustainable management of water and sanitation for all

Provide universal and equal access to safe drinking water at an affordable price for all. Provide access to adequate and equitable sanitation, hygiene and toilet conditions for all, with particular emphasis on the needs of girls and women as well as persons in vulnerable situations. Provide better water quality by reducing contamination, abolishing waste dumping, minimizing emissions of hazardous chemicals and materials, halving the proportion of untreated waste water and significantly increasing recovery and safe consumption worldwide.

Significantly improve the utilization of water in all sectors and ensure sustainable extraction of and access to fresh water to deal with scarcity of water and significantly reduce the number of people affected by water shortage. An integrated management of water resources at all levels, including through cross-border cooperation where applicable. Protect and restore water-related eco-systems, including mountains, forests, wetlands, rivers, water-borne rocks and lakes.

Expand international cooperation and support capacity building in developing countries in terms of water and sanitation activities and programs, including water collection, desalination, efficient use of water resources, waste water treatment and recycling. Support and strengthen community involvement in order to improve the management of water and sanitation.

Goal 3: Good Health and Well-Being for People – Ensure healthy lives and promote well-being for all at all ages

Maternal mortality rates around the world should be reduced dramatically. Reduce premature mortality caused by non-communicable diseases by one-third through prevention and treatment, and promote mental health and quality of life.

Strengthen prevention and treatment of substance abuse, including narcotics and harmful use of alcohol. Halve the number of deaths and injuries in the world caused by traffic accidents. Ensure universal access to services related to sexual and reproductive health, including family planning and related information and training, and ensure that reproductive health is incorporated into national strategies and programs.

Achieve general healthcare coverage, including protection against financial risk, and universal access to basic and good healthcare, as well as safe, effective and necessary medicines and good-quality vaccines, at an affordable price. Significantly reduce the number of deaths and illnesses caused by hazardous chemicals and polluted air, water and soil.

Goal 11: Sustainable Cities and Communities – Make cities and human settlements inclusive, safe, resilient and sustainable

Ensure public access to satisfactory and safe housing and basic services at an affordable price, and better conditions in slums. Ensure that everyone has access to safe, accessible and sustainable transport systems at an affordable price, and improve road safety, especially through the development of public transport, with particular emphasis on the needs of people in vulnerable situations, women, children, persons with disabilities and older people. Achieve more inclusive and sustainable urbanization with the possibility of an integrated and sustainable settlement planning and management that provides co-determination in all countries.

Strengthen efforts to protect and secure the world's cultural and natural heritage. Achieve a significant reduction in the number of deaths and the number of people affected by disasters, including water-related disasters, and significantly reduce the direct economic losses in the world's total gross national product as a result of such disasters, with emphasis on the protection of the poor and people in vulnerable situations. Reduce the negative impacts on the environment in the metropolitan areas, per capita, in particular by paying close attention to air quality and public and other forms of waste management.

Provide public access to safe, inclusive and easily accessible green spaces and public spaces, especially for women, children and the elderly, as well as disabled persons. Support positive economic, social and environmental relations between urban, surrounding and scattered areas by strengthening national and regional development plans. Achieve a significant increase in the number of cities and settlements that adopt and implement an integrated policy and plan aimed at inclusion, better use of resources, combating and adaptation to climate change, and ability to withstand and manage disasters, as well as to develop and implement comprehensive and comprehensive risk management in the event of disasters. Assist the least developed countries to build sustainable and solid buildings using local materials, including through economic and technical assistance.

Goal 13: Climate Change – Take urgent action to combat climate change and its impacts by regulating emissions and promoting developments in renewable energy

Strengthen the ability to resist and adapt to climate-related hazards and natural disasters in all countries. Initiate action against climate change in politics, strategies and planning at the national level. Strengthen individuals and institutions' ability to counteract, adapt to and reduce the impact of climate change and their ability to achieve early warning, as well as enhance knowledge and awareness of this.

Promote schemes to enhance the ability for effective planning and management related to climate change in the least developed and small developing countries, with emphasis on women and youth as well as local and marginalized societies. Recognize that the UN Framework Convention on Climate Change is the most important international and intergovernmental forum for negotiations on global action against climate change.

Goal 14: Life Below Water – Conserve and sustainably use the oceans, seas and marine resources for sustainable development

Prevent and significantly reduce all forms of marine pollution, especially from land-based activities, including pollution caused by marine sedimentation and nutrients. Manage and protect eco-systems in the ocean and along the coast in order to avoid major damage, including by strengthening the systems' resilience and implementing restorative measures to make the seas healthy and productive. As far as possible, limit and handle the consequences of marine acidification, including through increased scientific cooperation at all levels.

Introduce effective measures to regulate harvesting and end overfishing and illegal, unreported and unregulated fishing, as well as destructive fishing practices, and implement scientifically based management plans to restore fish stock as quickly as possible to a level that can deliver the best sustainable yield from the biological characteristics of the stock.

Prohibit certain types of fisheries subsidies that contribute to overcapacity and overfishing, abolish subsidies that contribute to illegal, unreported and unregulated fishing and avoid introducing new equivalent subsidies while recognizing that appropriate and effective special treatment and differentiated treatment of developing countries and the least developed countries should be an integral part of the World Trade Organization's negotiations on fisheries subsidies. The economic benefits for small developing countries and the least developed countries will increase as a result of sustainable use of marine resources, including through sustainable management of fisheries, aquaculture and tourism.

Strengthen scientific knowledge; build up research capacity and transfer marine technologies while taking into account the criteria and guidelines of the Intergovernmental Oceanographic Commission for the Transfer of Marine Technology. Improve the state of the sea and increase the contribution of marine species diversity to development in developing countries, especially in small developing countries and the least developed countries.

Give fishermen who operate small-scale fishing with simple tools access to marine resources and markets. Increase conservation and sustainable use of the seas and oceans by implementing international law as laid down in the UN Convention on the Law of the Sea, which provides the legal basis for the conservation and sustainable use of the sea and marine resources, as also stated in paragraph 158 of the UN report entitled *The Future We Want*.

Goal 15: Life on Land – Protect, restore and promote sustainable use of terrestrial ecosystems, sustainably manage forests, combat desertification, and halt and reverse land degradation and halt biodiversity loss

Conservation, restoration and sustainable use of freshwater-based eco-systems and services using these eco-systems, on land and inland areas, in particular forests, wetlands, mountains and dry areas, in accordance with obligations under international agreements. Promote the implementation of sustainable management of all forests by 2020, stop deforestation, restore deteriorated forests and significantly increase forestry and new planting at the global level.

Conservation of eco-systems in mountain areas, including their biological diversity, will ensure that they are better able to make important contributions to sustainable development. Implement immediate and comprehensive measures to reduce the destruction of habitats, stop biodiversity loss and protect endangered species and prevent them from dying out. Promote a fair and equal sharing of the benefits associated with the use of genetic resources, and promote an appropriate approach to such resources in line with international agreements. Take immediate action to stop the shooting and illegal trafficking of protected plant and animal species and handle both the supply *and demand side of the trade in illegal products from wildlife. Take measures to prevent the introduction and spread of alien species and to significantly reduce the impact of alien species on land and water-based eco-systems, as well as control or eradicate priority environmentally polluted species.*

Incorporate principles of eco-systems and biodiversity in national and local planning and development processes, poverty reduction strategies and accounts. Provide and achieve a significant increase in financial resources from all sources with a view to conservation and sustainable use of biological diversity and eco-systems. Provide substantial resources from all sources and at all levels to finance sustainable forest management and provide appropriate means to promote such management in developing countries, including for the conservation and new planting of forests. Increase global support for measures to combat poaching and illegal trafficking of protected species, including by strengthening local communities' ability to avail themselves of the opportunities available to maintain a sustainable life basis.

Prioritized objectives:

- Initiate action against climate change
- Counteract, adapt to and reduce impact of climate change
- Expand international cooperation
- Good health and well-being for all people
- Safe housing and basic service at an affordable prize
- Access to safe and sustainable transport system at an affordable price
- Positive economic, social and environmental relations between urban and rural areas
- Access to clean drinking water and sanitation
- Easily accessible green spaces and public spaces in sustainable cities
- Protect eco-systems in the ocean
- Give small-scale fishing with simple tools access to marine resources and markets
- Provide everybody with educational (arts, humanities and sciences) opportunities, empower everybody to actively contribute to sustainable development

The Earth Charter on environmental sustainability
The Earth Charter says

> manage the use of renewable resources such as water, soil, forest products, and marine life in ways that do not exceed rates of regeneration and that protect the health of ecosystems. Manage the extraction and use of non-renewable resources such as minerals and fossil fuels in ways that minimize depletion and cause no serious environmental damage. Promote recovery of endangered species and ecosystems.
>
> (The Earth Charter)

Goal 1. Respect Earth and life in all its diversity

a. Recognize that all beings are interdependent and every form of life has value regardless of its worth to human beings.
b. Affirm faith in the inherent dignity of all human beings and in the intellectual, artistic, ethical, and spiritual potential of humanity.

Goal 4. Secure Earth's bounty and beauty for present and future generations

a. Recognize that the freedom of action of each generation is qualified by the needs of future generations.
b. Transmit to future generations values, traditions, and institutions that support the long-term flourishing of Earth's human and ecological communities.

Goal 5. Protect and restore the integrity of Earth's ecological systems, with special concern for biological diversity and the natural processes that sustain life

a. Adopt at all levels sustainable development plans and regulations that make environmental conservation and rehabilitation integral to all development initiatives.
b. Establish and safeguard viable nature and biosphere reserves, including wild lands and marine areas, to protect Earth's life support systems, maintain biodiversity, and preserve our natural heritage.
c. Promote the recovery of endangered species and eco-systems.
d. Control and eradicate non-native or genetically modified organisms harmful to native species and the environment, and prevent introduction of such harmful organisms.
e. Manage the use of renewable resources such as water, soil, forest products, and marine life in ways that do not exceed rates of regeneration and that protect the health of eco-systems.
f. Manage the extraction and use of non-renewable resources such as minerals and fossil fuels in ways that minimize depletion and cause no serious environmental damage.

Goal 15. Treat all living beings with respect and consideration

a. Prevent cruelty to animals kept in human societies and protect them from suffering.
b. Protect wild animals from methods of hunting, trapping, and fishing that cause extreme, prolonged, or avoidable suffering.
c. Avoid or eliminate to the full extent possible the taking or destruction of non-targeted species.

The Earth Charter mentions water in two different contexts: firstly, under the heading of "Protect and restore the integrity of Earth's ecological systems, with special concern for biological diversity and the natural processes that sustain life." Here it says that renewable resources such as water, soil, forest products, and marine life should be managed in ways that do not exceed rates of regeneration and that protect the health of eco-systems. Secondly, to secure the right to drinkable water, clean air, food security, uncontaminated soil, shelter, and safe sanitation, national and international resources should be reallocated in a fair and equitable manner.

The Earth Charter mentions human health explicitly once, under the heading "Adopt patterns of production, consumption, and reproduction that safeguard Earth's regenerative capacities, human rights, and community well-being". Universal access to health care fosters reproductive health and responsible reproduction. Health could be connected indirectly to the claim that all people, especially children and young people, should be provided with educational opportunities that empower them to contribute actively to sustainable development. The contribution of the arts, humanities and sciences should be promoted in sustainability education.

The Earth Charter states that communities on all levels should guarantee human rights and fundamental freedoms, provide everyone with an opportunity to realize their full potential and enable all to achieve a secure and meaningful livelihood that is ecologically sustainable. The Earth Charter wants to ensure that information of vital importance to human health and environmental protection, including genetic information, remains available in the public domain. Decision-making must address the cumulative, long-term, indirect, long-distance, and global consequences of human activities. The burden of proof should be placed on those who argue that a proposed activity will not cause significant harm, and the responsible parties should be made liable for the cost of any environmental harm they cause.

Prioritized objectives:

- Protect and restore the integrity of Earth's ecological systems
- Special concern for biological diversity and the natural processes that sustain life
- Resources should be reallocated based on fairness
- Safeguard Earth's regenerative capacities, human rights, and community well-being
- Provide everyone with an opportunity to realize their full potential

Comments on environmental sustainability

Both the UN declaration and the Earth Charter agree that access to clean water is of the greatest importance both for humans and for life in general. Even if today many leaders in politics and economics are working actively for environmental and social responsibility, the problems are still increasing both in number and severity. Waste from human activities is spread as poison in soil and water. As an example, large amounts of mercury have been detected in many different life forms. Greenhouse gases and contaminants are other examples of problems that relate to our lifestyle. Environmental problems requiring international cooperation are difficult to solve because it takes time to ratify the agreements and start up concrete change processes.

The UN's SDGs are focused on how to cure different kinds of illness, stop infant mortality and reduce the negative consequences of drug and alcohol abuse. The Earth Charter is more focused on measures that contribute to a sustainable and meaningful life. Moral and spiritual education are important elements.

Both declarations focus on the requirement to develop sustainable cities. While the SDGs are more concrete and focused on physical conditions such as transport, construction and adaptation to climate change, the Earth Charter talks more about human rights and quality of life in the context of cultural and political dimensions.

The most recognized environmental problem today is climate change caused by emissions of greenhouse gases, such as CO_2 and methane. There is a global warming due to the increasing amount of greenhouse gases in the atmosphere, and it is likely that we will see dramatic changes in the climate in the future. The planet is getting warmer and we will probably get more extreme weather, more rain and more storms. Insects carrying infectious diseases will spread due to increases in temperature.

Loss of biodiversity, which may well be the most serious problem, is directly related to the combination of economic growth and human expansion. Because of the interconnectedness in the global eco-systems, extinction of one species has an extremely negative effect on the global natural environment. Today the habitats of an increasing number of species, animals and plants, are threatened. Hundreds of species of plants and animals disappear from Earth every day. Species that require large areas experience tough living conditions when their habitats are destroyed by human activities. The situation gets even more serious when we know that pollutants spreading through the air and the oceans may lead to a reduction in the reproductive capacity of both animals and plants. Accepting that nature is the context for all life, including humans, the consequence of extinguishing other forms of life at an ever-increasing rate could be characterized as a form of suicide.

Economy

In the SDGs, the goals' references to economics are set out in three different sections concerning production, distribution, consumption and reprocessing of different fractions of waste products. The Earth Charter puts more focus on responsible consumption and argues that quality of life is more important than increasing consumption rates.

Goal 7: Affordable and Clean Energy – Ensure access to affordable, reliable, sustainable and modern energy for all

Ensure universal access to reliable and modern energy services at an affordable price. Significantly increase the share of renewable energy in the world's total energy consumption. Double the energy efficiency rate worldwide. Strengthen international cooperation to facilitate access to clean and renewable energy research, technology, energy efficiency and advanced and cleaner fossil fuels technologies, and also promote investment in energy infrastructure and clean energy technology. Develop infrastructure and upgrade technology to provide modern and sustainable energy services to all residents of developing countries, especially the least developed countries, small developing countries and coastal developing countries, in accordance with their respective support programs.

Goal 9: Industry, Innovation and Infrastructure – Build resilient infrastructure, promote inclusive and sustainable industrialization and foster innovation

Develop reliable, sustainable and solid infrastructure, including regional and cross-border infrastructure, to support economic development and quality of life with affordability and equal access for all. Promote inclusive and sustainable industrialization, and significantly increase the business sector's share of employment and gross domestic product, in line with the conditions in the respective countries, and double this share in the least developed countries. Increase access to financial services, including affordable credit, for small industrial companies and other businesses, especially in developing countries, and strengthen these companies' integration into value chains and markets.

Upgrade infrastructure and transform business to become more sustainable, with more efficient use of resources and greater use of clean and environmentally friendly technologies and industrial processes where all countries make an effort according to their own ability and capacity. Strengthen scientific research and upgrade the technological capabilities and capacity of business sectors in all countries, especially developing countries, including through stimulating innovation and significantly increasing the number of employees in research and development activities per million inhabitants, as well as increasing grants to public and private research and development.

Facilitate sustainable and robust development of infrastructure in developing countries by increasing financial, technological and technical assistance to African countries, the least developed countries, coastal developing countries and small developing countries. Support national development of technology, research and innovation in developing countries, including by ensuring political framework conditions that promote, among other things, diversity in business and provide merchandise with added value. Increase access to information and communications technology significantly and work towards ensuring that the least developed countries get universal and affordable access to the Internet by 2020.

Goal 12: Responsible Consumption and Production – Ensure sustainable consumption and production patterns

Implement the ten-year Action Program for Sustainable Consumption and Production, with participation from all countries and in developed countries, while taking into account developing countries' development and opportunities. Achieve sustainable management and efficient use of natural resources.

In accordance with internationally agreed-upon framework, achieve more environmentally sound management of chemicals and all types of waste throughout their life cycle, and significantly reduce emissions of chemicals and waste to air, water and soil to minimize the harmful effects on human health and the environment. Significantly reduce waste through bans, reductions, recycling and reuse. Encourage companies, especially large and multinational companies, to implement sustainable working methods and integrate information about sustainability in their reporting routines. Promote sustainable procurement systems, in accordance with the policies and priorities of each country.

Ensure that everyone in the world has relevant information about consciously sustainable development and a lifestyle that is in harmony with nature. Support developing countries in their efforts to strengthen their scientific and technical capacities to gradually introduce more sustainable consumption and production patterns. Develop and implement methods to monitor the consequences of sustainable development on a sustainable tourism industry, create jobs and promote local culture and local products.

Reduce ineffective subsidies to fossil fuels by eliminating market distortions that encourage excessive consumption, in accordance with the conditions in each country, including by revising taxes and fees and eliminating harmful subsidies where they exist so that environmental impacts are revealed, while fully taking into account the special needs and situations of developing countries, and minimize any harmful consequences of their development in a manner that protects the poor and the affected communities.

Prioritized objectives:

- Increase the share of renewable energy
- Double the energy efficiency rate worldwide
- Strengthen international cooperation
- Develop reliable, sustainable and solid infrastructures
- Promote inclusive and sustainable industrialization
- Increase the business sector's share of employment and gross domestic product
- Increase access to financial services for small industrial companies and other businesses
- Strengthen small companies' integration into value chains and markets
- Greater use of environmentally friendly technologies
- Ensure sustainable consumption and production patterns

The Earth Charter on economy

The Earth Charter attests that we should act with restraint and efficiency when using energy and should turn increasingly to renewable energy resources such as solar and wind.

Goal 7: Adopt patterns of production, consumption, and reproduction that safeguard Earth's regenerative capacities, human rights, and community well-being

a. *Reduce, reuse, and recycle the materials used in production and consumption systems, and ensure that residual waste can be assimilated by ecological systems.*
b. *Act with restraint and efficiency when using energy, and rely increasingly on renewable energy sources such as solar and wind.*
c. *Promote the development, adoption, and equitable transfer of environmentally sound technologies.*
d. *Internalize the full environmental and social costs of goods and services in the selling price, and enable consumers to identify products that meet the highest social and environmental standards.*
e. *Ensure universal access to health care that fosters reproductive health and responsible reproduction.*
f. *Adopt lifestyles that emphasize quality of life and material sufficiency in a finite world.*

The declaration details how to enhance the intellectual, financial, technical and social resources of developing nations, and relieve them from onerous international debt. In addition it is important to ensure that all trade supports sustainable resource use, environmental protection and progressive labour standards.

Prioritized objectives:

- Act with restraint and efficiency when using energy
- Ensure that all trade supports sustainable resource use, environmental protection and progressive labour standards

Comments on economy

From a historical perspective, trade has been part of the culture of every society. Connections with other people through local, regional and global markets have been an important source of inspiration to social development. The trade routes opened exchange of not only commodities, but also of ideas, knowledge and philosophy. Today the picture is more complex, and international trade has resulted in great prosperity for many people and countries, but it has also resulted in increased poverty. The connection between economy and nature has been essential for social development in a wider perspective. The extent to which trade creates prosperity or poverty depends on the systemic conditions for trade and human consciousness. Cheap products for people in the West are very often produced by people earning an extremely low salary, many of them children, who work under horrible conditions. In other words, the global economic system is based on slavery in a very clever disguise.

The Earth Charter asks for action to avoid the possibility of serious or irreversible environmental harm caused by incomplete or inconclusive scientific knowledge.

The SDGs' focus is on increasing the production of renewable energy while the Earth Charter talks about reduction in the consumption of energy, a combination which represents synergy. One consequence of the increasing number of people on Earth is that human beings exploit more land and reduce the space for all other species, plants and animals. The negative side effects of humans taking over the global eco-systems are many, varied and extremely hard to solve. Loss of biodiversity, pollution of soil, water and air, and climate change are problems all traceable back to the modern lifestyle. To solve the problems, we have to search for alternatives which differ radically from the dominating economic system.

An increasing number of distinguished researchers (Schumacher 1973/ 1993; Boulding 1981; Rees 2008; Spash 2013) argue that it is not enough to reduce the negative symptoms of the existing economy; the only thing that can save the environment is a paradigmatic shift towards a society based on simplicity in means and richness in ends – in other words a dramatic change in the hard core of mainstream economy. Exponential growth in production and consumption is incompatible with peaceful coexistence between humans and nature, between humans and within the individuals. Numerous contributors to ecological economics, such as Herman Daly and Robert Costanza, argue that economic growth in rich countries is a significant cause of the major environmental problems. Nevertheless, there is an important distinction to be made between ecological economists (utopian) who believe that economic growth must stop (steady-state economy), and those green economists (ideology) who believe that a sustainable economic growth is needed (green growth). Several international NGOs are in harmony with steady-state economy and emphasize that it is necessary if we are to make fundamental changes at a deeper systemic level to solve the problems.

Politics

A living democracy, open to the participation of all, is declared an important condition for sustainable development in Goal 16 in the SDGs. The Earth Charter gives priority to politics and describes three different goals, focusing on the importance of participation in democratic processes as a prerequisite for sustainable development.

Goal 16: Peace, Justice and Strong Institutions – Promote peaceful and inclusive societies for sustainable development, provide access to justice for all and build effective, accountable and inclusive institutions at all levels

Achieve a significant reduction in all forms of violence and the proportion of violence-related deaths worldwide. Stop abuse, exploitation, trafficking in human beings and all forms of violence against and torture of children. Promote the rule of law nationally and internationally, and ensure equal access to justice for all. Achieve a significant reduction in illegal financial and weapon flows, and make it easier to track down and return stolen assets as well as combat all forms of organized crime. Achieve a significant reduction in all forms of corruption and bribery.

Develop well-functioning, responsible and open institutions at all levels. Ensure responsive, inclusive, co-determined and representative decision-making at all levels. Expand and strengthen developing countries' participation in institutions for global governance. Ensure legal identity for all, including birth registration.

Secure public access to information and protect fundamental freedoms, in accordance with national laws and international agreements. Strengthen relevant national institutions, inter alia through international cooperation, with a view to building capacity at all levels, and especially in developing countries, to prevent violence and fight terrorism and crime. Promote and enforce non-discriminatory laws and policies for sustainable development.

Prioritized objectives:

- Promote peaceful and inclusive sustainable societies
- Protect fundamental freedoms
- Provide access to justice for all people
- Reduction in all forms of violence
- Stop abuse, exploitation, trafficking in human beings and all forms of violence against and torture of children
- Reduce all forms of corruption and bribery
- Develop well-functioning, responsible and open institutions at all levels
- Promote and enforce non-discriminatory laws
- Promote policies for sustainable development

The Earth Charter on politics

Support local, regional and global civil society, and promote the meaningful participation of all interested individuals and organizations in decision-making. Protect the rights to freedom of opinion, expression, peaceful assembly, association, and dissent. Institute effective and efficient access to administrative and independent judicial procedures, including remedies and redress for environmental harm and the threat of such harm.

Goal 3: Build democratic societies that are just, participatory, sustainable, and peaceful

a. Ensure that communities at all levels guarantee human rights and fundamental freedoms and provide everyone an opportunity to realize his or her full potential.
b. Promote social and economic justice, enabling all to achieve a secure and meaningful livelihood that is ecologically responsible.

Goal 12: Uphold the right of all, without discrimination, to a natural and social environment supportive of human dignity, bodily health, and spiritual well-being, with special attention to the rights of indigenous peoples and minorities

a. Eliminate discrimination in all its forms, such as that based on race, colour, sex, sexual orientation, religion, language, and national, ethnic or social origin.
b. Affirm the right of indigenous peoples to their spirituality, knowledge, lands and resources and to their related practice of sustainable livelihoods.
c. Honour and support the young people of our communities, enabling them to fulfill their essential role in creating sustainable societies.
d. Protect and restore outstanding places of cultural and spiritual significance.

Goal 13: Strengthen democratic institutions at all levels, and provide transparency and accountability in governance, inclusive participation in decision making, and access to justice

a. Uphold the right of everyone to receive clear and timely information on environmental matters and all development plans and activities which are likely to affect them or in which they have an interest.
b. Support local, regional and global civil society, and promote the meaningful participation of all interested individuals and organizations in decision-making.
c. Protect the rights to freedom of opinion, expression, peaceful assembly, association and dissent.
d. Institute effective and efficient access to administrative and independent judicial procedures, including remedies and redress for environmental harm and the threat of such harm.
e. Eliminate corruption in all public and private institutions.
f. Strengthen local communities, enabling them to care for their environments, and assign environmental responsibilities to the levels of government where they can be carried out most effectively.

Goal 16: Promote a culture of tolerance, nonviolence, and peace

a. *Encourage and support mutual understanding, solidarity and cooperation among all peoples and within and among nations.*
b. *Implement comprehensive strategies to prevent violent conflict and use
   collaborative problem solving to manage and resolve environmental
   conflicts and other disputes.*
c. *Demilitarize national security systems to the level of a non-provocative
   defense posture, and convert military resources to peaceful purposes,
   including ecological restoration.*
d. *Eliminate nuclear, biological, and toxic weapons and other weapons of
   mass destruction.*
e. *Ensure that the use of orbital and outer space supports environmental
   protection and peace.*
f. *Recognize that peace is the wholeness created by right relationships
   with oneself, other persons, other cultures, other life, Earth, and the
   larger whole of which all are a part.*

Strengthen local communities, enabling them to care for their environment,
and assign environmental responsibilities to the levels of government where
they can be carried out most effectively. Encourage and support mutual
understanding, solidarity, and cooperation among all peoples, within and
among nations. Implement comprehensive strategies to prevent violent conflict
and use collaborative problem solving to manage and resolve environmental
conflicts and other disputes. We have to recognize that peace is the wholeness
created by right relationships with oneself, other persons, other cultures, other
life, Earth and the larger whole of which all are a part.

Prioritized objectives:

• Promote meaningful participation in decision-making
• Protect the rights to freedom of opinion, expression, peaceful assembly,
  association, and dissent.
• Strengthen local communities, enabling them to care for their environment.
• Encourage and support mutual understanding, solidarity, and cooperation among all peoples, within and among nations.
• Recognize that peace is the wholeness created by right relationships
  with oneself, other people, other cultures, other life, Earth and the
  larger whole of which all are a part.

Comments on politics

Johan Galtung (1996) draws a distinction between negative peace and positive
peace. Negative peace refers to a reduction of violence realized by the use of
power (something bad is reduced). Negative peace is not true peace because it
does not mean absence of any conflict; it is only the absence of violence in all

forms. It is negative because something undesirable was stopped from happening (e.g., the violence is reduced, decline in oppression). Positive peace means that the reasons behind the conflict are eliminated or reduced (something good starts to happen). It could be the revitalization of relationships or the creation of fair social systems that serve the needs of the whole population. Peace therefore exists where people are interacting in a positive way and solving the causes behind the conflict by going to the core of problems.

The SDGs focus on both negative and positive peace. By implementing fair laws and institutions, the idea is that the disagreements behind conflicts can be solved. The Earth Charter is more explicit and deals with democratic participation by encouraging cooperation and solidarity between all people. In other words, a clear focus on positive peace.

Education

The goal is to give all people high-quality education which embraces not only knowledge relevant for employment but also knowledge to bring about sustainable development and the promotion of peace and equality between men and women. Lifelong learning is integrated as a goal in both the SDGs and the Earth Charter.

Goal 4: Quality Education – Ensure inclusive and equitable quality education and promote lifelong learning opportunities for all

Ensure that all girls and boys complete free and equivalent primary and secondary education that can provide them with relevant and real learning outcomes. All girls and boys will have access to good and early care and preschool so that they are prepared to begin primary school. Women and men are ensured equal access to good technical and vocational education and higher education, including university education, at an affordable price.

A significant increase in the number of young people and adults with competence, including in technical subjects and vocational subjects, relevant to employment, decent work and entrepreneurship. Abolish gender differences in education and training and ensure equal access to all levels of education and vocational education for vulnerable persons, including people with disabilities, indigenous peoples and children in vulnerable situations. Ensure that all youth and a significant proportion of adults, both women and men, learn to read, write and calculate. Ensure that all pupils and students acquire the skills necessary to promote sustainable development through education in sustainable development and lifestyle, human rights, equality, promotion of a peace and non-violence culture, global bourgeoisie and appreciation of cultural diversity and the contribution of culture to sustainable development.

Establish and upgrade education services that take care of children, people with disabilities and gender differences, and ensure a safe, non-violent, inclusive and effective learning environment for all. A significant increase worldwide in the number of grants available to students from developing countries, especially the least developed countries, small developing countries and African countries, to provide access to higher education, including vocational education and training programs for information and communication technology, engineering and science, in developed countries and in other developing countries. A significant increase in the number of qualified teachers, including through international cooperation on teacher education in developing countries, especially in the least developed countries and in small developing countries.

Goal 5: Gender Equality – Achieve gender equality and empower all women and girls

End all forms of discrimination against girls and women around the world. Abolish all forms of violence against all girls and women, both in public and private spheres, including trafficking in human beings, and sexual and other forms of exploitation. Abolish all harmful practices, such as child abuse, early marriages and forced marriage, as well as female circumcision. Recognize and appreciate unpaid care and household work through the provision of public services, infrastructure and social policy, and promote shared responsibility in the household and family, as appropriate in each country. Ensure full and effective participation of women in equal opportunities for senior positions at all levels of political, economic and public life. Ensure public access to sexual and reproductive health as well as reproductive rights, as agreed in accordance with the Action Program of the International Conference on Population and Development, Beijing Action Plan and the decisions of their respective supervisory conferences.

Implement reforms to give women equal rights to financial resources as well as access to ownership and control of land and other forms of property, financial services, heritage and natural resources, in accordance with national legislation. Strengthen the use of custom technology, especially information and communication technology, to strengthen women's position. Adopt and strengthen good policies and enforceable legislation to promote equality and strengthen the position of girls and women at all levels.

Prioritized objectives:

- Complete free and equivalent primary and secondary education, relevant to employment, decent work and entrepreneurship.
- Ensure that all students acquire the skills necessary to promote sustainable development and lifestyle, human rights, equality, promotion of peace and non-violent culture.
- Ensure full and effective participation of woman in equal opportunities for senior positions at all levels of political, economic and public life.
- Increase the number of qualified teachers, training programs for information and communication technology, engineering and science.

The Earth Charter on education

The Earth Charter integrates formal education and life-long learning in order to develop the knowledge, values and skills that are needed for developing a sustainable way of life. The goal is to empower all people to participate in the development of their societies for the common good. As mentioned in the last paragraph, the arts and humanities are to be considered just as important as science.

Goal 8: Advance the study of ecological sustainability and promote the open exchange and wide application of the knowledge acquired

a. *Support international scientific and technical cooperation on sustainability, with special attention to the needs of developing nations.*
b. *Recognize and preserve the traditional knowledge and spiritual wisdom in all cultures that contribute to environmental protection and human well-being.*
c. *Ensure that information of vital importance to human health and environmental protection, including genetic information, remains available in the public domain.*

Goal 11: Affirm gender equality and equity as prerequisites to sustainable development and ensure universal access to education, health care, and economic opportunity

a. *Secure the human rights of women and girls and end all violence against them.*
b. *Promote the active participation of women in all aspects of economic, political, civil, social, and cultural life as full and equal partners, decision-makers, leaders, and beneficiaries.*
c. *Strengthen families and ensure the safety and loving nurture of all family members.*

Goal 14: Integrate into formal education and life-long learning the knowledge, values, and skills needed for a sustainable way of life

a. *Provide all, especially children and youth, with educational opportunities that empower them to contribute actively to sustainable development.*
b. *Promote the contribution of the arts and humanities as well as the sciences in sustainability education.*
c. *Enhance the role of the mass media in raising awareness of ecological and social challenges.*
d. *Recognize the importance of moral and spiritual education for sustainable living.*

The Earth Charter attaches great importance to the necessity of eliminating discriminating gender differences. First of all it stresses that the human rights of women and girls should be secured. Active participation in all aspects of economic, political, civil, social and cultural life as full and equal partners, decision-makers, leaders, and beneficiaries should be promoted. In addition it says that discrimination in all forms, based on race, colour, sex, sexual orientation, religion, language, and national, ethnic or social origin should be eliminated. Indigenous people should have the right to practise their spirituality and knowledge, and use their lands and resources to practice sustainable living.

Prioritized objectives:

- Integrate formal education and life-long learning.
- Empower all people to participate in the development of their societies.
- Develop knowledge, values and skills that are needed for developing a sustainable way of life.
- Active participation in all aspects of economic, political, civil, social and cultural life.

Comments on education

Both declarations agree on the necessity of education, but the SDGs, more than the Earth Charter, are more concrete on instrumental learning goals, such as learning to read, write and calculate, and the means to reach these ends. The Earth Charter puts more focus on the importance of moral and spiritual values.

Even if both declarations give gender equality a high priority, there are some minor differences. The Earth Charter is more focused on moral and spiritual values and the SDGs are more concrete in describing specific measures.

Cooperation

Both the SDGs and the Earth Charter maintain that cooperation and participation in democratic processes at all levels are of vital importance in order to reach all the other sustainability goals.

Goal 17: Partnerships for the Goals – Strengthen the means of implementation and revitalize the global partnership for sustainable development

Strengthen the mobilization of national resources, including through international support to developing countries, with a view to improving countries' ability to claim taxes and other charges. Ensure that the developed countries fully implement their official development assistance obligations towards developing countries.

Mobilize additional financial resources to developing countries from multiple sources. Assist developing countries in achieving long-term and sustainable debt conditions through a coordinated policy to promote debt financing, debt relief or debt restructuring, and treat the debt of the poorest and most indebted countries in a way that reduces debt-related distress. Adopt and implement investment-promoting schemes for the least developed countries.

Improve access to and strengthen cooperation between North and South, and South and South, and the regional and international cooperation across science, technology and innovation, and improve knowledge sharing on mutually agreed terms, including through better coordination of existing schemes, in particular UN-level, and through a global system for technology availability. Promote development, transfer, and dissemination of environmentally friendly technology to developing countries on favourable terms, including on concessions and preferential terms, by mutual agreements. Fully launched technology bank and capacity building in science, technology and innovation for the least developed countries, and increase the use of custom technology, especially information and communication technology.

Increase international support for implementing effective and targeted capacity building in developing countries, thereby supporting national plans for implementing all sustainability goals, including through cooperation between North and South, South and South and triangular.

Promote a general, rule-based, open, non-discriminatory and equal multilateral trading system governed by the World Trade Organization, including finalizing the negotiations during the Doha Round. Significantly increase developing countries' exports, especially with the aim of doubling the least developed countries' share of world exports.

In practice, all the least developed countries provide timely and sustainable quota-free market access, in accordance with the decisions of the World Trade Organization, inter alia by ensuring that clear and simple preferential rules are applied on imports from the least developed countries that help to facilitate market access.

Prioritized objectives:

- International support to developing countries.
- Assist developing countries in achieving long-term and sustainable debt conditions.
- Adopt and implement investment-promoting schemes for the least developed countries.
- Strengthen cooperation between North and South, South and South.
- Promote a general, rule-based, open, non-discriminatory and equal multilateral trading system governed by the World Trade Organization.

The Earth Charter on cooperation

Sustainable societies depend on collaboration on all levels. Men and women should be empowered equally through education to participate as equal partners in all kinds of local, regional and global forums for decision-making.

Prioritized objectives:

- Cooperation among all peoples within and among nations.
- Meaningful participation in decision-making.
- Active participation of women as equal partners.
- Scientific and technical cooperation on sustainability.

Comments on cooperation

Both declarations agree that international cooperation is a necessary precondition for solving problems connected to poverty and sustainable environment. The UN's SDGs are more focused on international cooperation and the Earth Charter is more focused on individual participation through the empowerment of both men and women.

In addition to mentioning cooperation explicitly as the last goal, both declarations refer to cooperation in several of the other goals too. This is an example of the holographic design: the parts are in the whole, and the whole includes all parts.

Concluding remarks

From this systematic overview of the UN's MDGs and SDGs and the Earth Charter, the main problems, challenges and goals for the global society are highlighted and put in context. It is obvious that it is impossible to reach the goals without making deeper changes in the dominating political and economic ideology, and it is not enough to make changes in the protective belt, as we must have changes in the hard core or, in other words, a paradigm shift. The reason is that an atomized economy based on exponential growth is simply incapable of solving the integrated and dynamic problems that have been outlined in the various documents. In describing them under the different headlines of poverty, sustainability, education, economy, politics, and cooperation, many of the same measures are mentioned. A focus on small-scale businesses is one example; reducing inequality is another example. In order to develop integrated solutions, transdisciplinary knowledge is needed.

In the following chapters, I reflect on the extent to which anarchist political philosophy could be a source of inspiration for implementing radical changes in accordance with the principles of ecological economics. Within the existing political and economic system it is only possible to reduce the *symptoms* of the conflict between the mainstream economy and the social and ecological systems, but not the *cause*.

Eradication of poverty is mentioned as the most important task for the coming decades. The solutions are focused on measures to help developing countries and the poor to develop their own capacities without degrading the environment. To reach these goals, ownership of land is a prerequisite to increased income from small and family farms. Connected to this goal is the need to reduce the gap between rich and poor in developed countries as well. The Earth Charter points out that we have an ethical obligation to empower every human being with the education and the resources to secure a sustainable livelihood. Political, scientific and technical cooperation is essential if these goals are to be reached.

Environmental sustainability is given priority in the UN documents and the Earth Charter. Natural and social sustainability are connected, and the measures to reach these goals need to focus on reducing the negative impact on nature and society and to prepare for the changes to come. Reducing the gap between rich and poor and between urban and rural areas is mentioned as a necessary means. It is essential to stimulate initiatives to develop methods for measuring progress towards sustainable development. The UN reports are more focused on anthropocentric values while the Earth Charter pays attention to eco-centric values as well.

The economy is to be handled by focusing on both international cooperation and decentralized small-scale business and industry. Eco-friendly energy and the associated technology should be available for everybody. Justice and peace are mentioned as the most important tasks in politics. Politics should promote sustainable development and peaceful societies without corruption and bribery. In addition politics should encourage and promote well-functioning public-sector partnerships, between public, private and civil society, based on partnership experiences and resource strategies. It is a prerequisite to respect each individual country's policies to establish and implement the elimination of poverty and the implementation of measures to promote sustainable development.

Education for all has to be implemented within the next few decades. In addition to offering free education to all young people – irrespective of gender – education must be relevant for employment, but it is also said that students should acquire skills that promote sustainable development, peace and a non-violent culture. Education should focus on sustainable production and consumption. Education should also empower all people to participate in political and social life. To reach these goals, active participation in decision-making is a necessary condition. It is also important to strengthen the relationships local communities have with other humans and all of nature.

The UN declarations and the Earth Charter maintain that cooperation between countries and within countries is of great importance to promote all the other goals mentioned. It is therefore important to strengthen the global partnership for sustainable development. Partnerships between economic and political actors with the aim of sharing knowledge, technology, and financial resources are essential to help developing countries achieve sustainability goals. The SDGs list cooperation as the 17th goal, but cooperation is mentioned in almost all the other goals as well. The Earth Charter comments on the need for cooperation in almost every goal.

Some commentators have pointed out that the SDGs might be contradictory. For example, giving priority to growth in the global GDP might challenge ecological objectives. Similarly, increasing employment and wages can work against implementing a simpler lifestyle in rich countries. The critics argue that it should be enough to eradicate poverty. Three sectors – the economic, social and environmental sectors in their broadest sense – need to come together in order to achieve sustainable development. This will require the promotion of multidisciplinary and transdisciplinary research across different fields of science, and this can be difficult. Other critics have argued that the SDGs ignore, or place little value on, the local context.

Other commentators are more optimistic and argue that the development from the MDGs to the SDGs is positive because it puts more focus on the causes behind the problems. Both environmental challenges and economic inequity lead to a conclusion that "we need a radical change in our social systems, means of livelihood and ways of life" (Levitas 2017, p. 6). In the next chapter I will give an overview of the two dominating political and economic systems that represent the political platform for solutions within the dominating ideology – Cell 1 (Figure 2.1), possible possibilities. Where there is no vision, there will be no change. If utopia is understood as "the expression of the desire for a better way of being, then it is perhaps a (sometimes) secularized version of the spiritual quest to understand who we are, why we are here and how we connect to each other" (Levitas 2007, p. 290). Levitas concludes that it is a "quest for wholeness".

4 Liberalism and Marxism as political platforms

Introduction

As a context for the discussion of anarchism, it is essential to refer to liberalism and Marxism. Political philosophy operates on different levels of generality and abstraction, from the concrete and specific recommendations for policy and economy to abstract discussions aimed at a global interpretation of political reality. As the dominant political ideologies of the recent centuries have been liberalism and Marxism, they are introduced and examined. The question is "Do we need a new political platform to find solutions for the problems the global society is facing?"

If the answer is yes, then we will have to rethink our context of understanding and try out new solutions – solutions that will often seem strange and which go against currently accepted knowledge.

In most countries, liberalism and Marxism are mixed; in some countries Marxism dominates and in other countries liberalism dominates. In practice, political philosophy has developed a middle path between market liberalism and Marxism. The role of the State is indeed a major issue in social and political economy. The tendency today is that "neoliberalism as actualised has made the State a support for corporate, rather than public, interest, but at the same time the hope of many is that the State will be an environmental protector and enforcer of justice" (Spash 2017, p. 10).

Political philosophy concerns the actual and proper organization of individuals into societies and the discussion of those ideas. A distinctive characteristic of political philosophy is that the interest is a response to some particular events or challenges in the current society. Ethics has always had a powerful influence on the view of political philosophy. Political philosophy also focuses on ontology and epistemology and a systematic criticism of different visions of the world. Finally, political philosophy is confronted with a theory of human interests which furnishes criteria for the general appraisal of social institutions. My intention is not to give a comprehensive account of these political philosophies but to place anarchist philosophy within a comparative framework.

Liberalism

First let me clarify that liberalism is not a coherent political philosophy but rather a diverse collection of ideas and visions. In the following paragraphs I identify a few basic ideas that are relevant as a context for understanding anarchism.

Liberalism is a political philosophy that highlights the value of individual human freedom and points out that the State's primary task is to protect the freedom of individuals. Classic liberalism was developed in England and Germany in the late 17th and 18th centuries. Important representatives of classical liberalism are John Locke (1632–1704), Immanuel Kant (1724–1804), Adam Smith (1723–1790) and Jeremy Bentham (1748–1832). What first and foremost characterizes classical liberalism is its emphasis on the individual and the individual's inherent value. Smith believed that humans had a natural tendency to "'truck, barter and exchange', and that if individuals pursued their own interest in a market context, society as a whole would be served" (Miletzki and Broten 2017, p. 20). The image of man in liberalism is positive, that is, if the individual develops freely, humans are good by nature. Humans have enough reason to know what is for their own good. By cultivating individualism, we get a good society, and society is no more than the sum of single individuals. So, liberalism is based on ontological individualism and consequentialist ethics.

Two features characterize liberalism. Firstly, in liberalism the number one value is to give individuals the opportunity to develop freely. The main task of the State is to prevent individuals from disrupting each other's freedom, so the State is of some value as it guarantees individuals the opportunity to develop freely. Secondly, freedom is defined as negative freedom, that is, freedom from external force. When people who subscribe to the political philosophy of libertarianism discuss freedom, they are, on the one hand, likely to refer to "specific economic rights such as the ability to enter into market exchanges" (Miletzki and Broten 2017, p. 11). Political freedom, on the other hand, refers to the right to vote.

Clark and Martin criticize the focus on negative freedom and argue that positive freedom, which includes the freedom to express thoughts in every area including "science, politics, and morals, without any condition other than (...) respect for others" (Clark and Martin 2013, p. 144), is important.

An important motivation for the development of liberalism was to make sure that the obstacles created by the feudal society for innovation were eliminated. In order to ensure the citizens' safety by enforcing the adopted laws and ordinances of society, the State had to be allowed to use power to enforce order. To reduce the use of power, the State is bound by a number of laws and regulations adopted by the government.

Economic liberalism

The basic principle of economic liberalism is, according to Adam Smith, that the State should not interfere with the economy, as the State's only role is to ensure that the criteria for free competition are respected by the economic actors.

Resource allocation would be optimal if all economic activities were based on free competition between autonomous actors. As an example, freedom refers to the ability to enter into market exchanges without any restrictions. The goal was to increase national power without violating laws and regulations. It is taken for granted that egocentric decisions should represent the basis for decisions within the economy. Liberalistic market economy defines *homo economicus* as a maximising machine anchored in predefined preferences, whose decisions "leave no room for emotion, psychology or social embeddedness" (Spash 2017, p. 5). The reason was that egocentric action was supposed to make sure that energy was channelled in the direction of increased production and increased consumption. The dynamics in a liberalist economy are rooted in an idea that everyone is motivated when the smartest get the opportunity to acquire more value than the less smart ones. Thus, the large gap between rich and poor in society is legitimate and legitimised.

The key principles in economic liberalism are free trade in domestic business and free trade between countries. Free trade is based on an assumption that the relationship between supply and demand determines price, quantity and quality of goods. The idea is that if everyone is concerned only about increasing their own benefit, they will contribute more to the benefit of society than if they tried to do it directly. According to Adam Smith, "It is not from the benevolence of the butcher, the brewer, or the baker that we expect our dinner, but from their regard to their own interest" (Smith 1776/2007 p. 15). The explanation is that the economic actors who produce and distribute goods at the lowest price will succeed in the market.

Free trade was also a guarantee that consumers had a great amount of influence in the decision of what to produce and what prices are right. The idea is anchored in, on the one hand, a positive connection between the price of goods and demand, and, on the other hand, an acceptance that demand is determined by need. Consequently, the competitive market is the best instrument to make sure that the economy meets human needs. The problem is that demand is connected to payment, so the buyer with the money determines demand. People with vital needs but who lack purchasing power have no influence in liberalistic economic processes. In addition to the fact that the needs of people with minimal purchasing power have no influence whatever on the market, the connection between vital needs and buying behaviour is to a great extent affected by the controlling forces of advertising and other promotional measures. If the consumers' will is manipulated by market communication, mass media and social media, then freedom becomes fictional.

Free competition in the world market means that each country produces what it has the best prerequisites for producing. In this way, the idea is that the world's resources are used efficiently in order to maximize the total utility. Interrupting economic life with regulations would be like trying to change the laws of nature. In this all-encompassing competitive market, everything, at least in principle, can be bought and sold, including human labour. When a worker sells his labour, the salary is the price. The link between liberalism and utilitarian ethics makes it clear that the liberalist economy focuses on maximizing utility. The goal is to use the accessible (natural and human) resources in a way that provides maximum aggregated utility.

Box 4.1 Principles characterizing liberalist economy (hard core)

- Free trade
- Competition
- Growth in production and consumption
- Private property rights
- Utilitarianism
- Ontological individualism
- Methodological individualism
- Egocentrism

As the liberalist economy was developed further during the 19th century, it was found that the removal of regulations and state intervention did not have purely positive effects. It was all very good for the richest, the most prosperous and the lucky, but it came at a price – social distress and poverty, especially in the emerging working class. The wealth tended to gather in a small group while the rest lived in poverty. Since utilitarianism never concerned itself with fair distribution, it is not surprising that the liberalist economy was unable to deal with problems associated with the gap between rich and poor. Criticism of the liberalist economy is based on arguments that it fails to notice the economy's impact on nature and society because it is far too abstract – everything is decoupled from society and nature. If the economy is to survive, it must grow and create ever-increasing profits. This leads to irrational environmental side effects. Speculation and success on the stock market also leads to unintended negative side effects such as an unfair distribution of wealth. In addition, a liberalist economy is inherently anti-ecological because nature is treated as an economic resource (with no inherent value), just there to be exploited. Ward concludes that "capitalism roams the globe, seeking the least protected labour markets and the least protected physical environments, in order to stimulate, and to win, an ever growing market for its goods" (Ward 2004, p. 90). Emma Goldman went a step further and argued that capitalism dehumanized workers, "turning the producer into a mere particle of a machine, with less will and decision than his master of steel and iron" (Goldman 2017, p. 54).

Social liberalism

However, Smith was aware that the free games of market forces would lead to unintended side effects that could only be corrected through public regulations.

In the late 1800s, Smith's teachings were further developed in different directions. One direction was led by critics who claimed that the liberalist economy served particular interests in society and built on implicit value priorities. This understanding provided the basis for the development of social liberalism, which wanted the State to play an important role in society, especially in the economy. Social liberalism was a reaction to the individualism of classical liberalism, which claimed that individuals alone had responsibility for their development and that society should only intervene to protect individuals against each other. Individualism as the fundamental feature of liberalism was modified by the fact that society and social science thinking were incorporated into liberalism.

The principle of absolute freedom was moderated by the force of many unfortunate side effects. Without the community defining laws and regulations, individuals will develop unilaterally in an ever-more-selfish direction, with the consequence that the winner takes all and the weak go into the slums, into poverty and disease. The State can perform certain service functions and redeployment policies if it can do better than the free market.

To provide all reasonable opportunities, laws were required to ensure that the goods were distributed in a fairer way than the free market could achieve. John Stuart Mill (1806–1873) was particularly important in the development of social liberalism. In the area of social liberalism, the State has a significant responsibility for the welfare of citizens and for economic development. New theories argued that profitability went up if workers got higher wages. The State is a necessary evil to ensure law and order and to protect against external enemies.

Comments

Anarchism could have been placed under the liberal camp were it not for its commitment to society. Because the anarchists are closely connected to process philosophy, they differ from liberals, who "think that the self-seeking and deceitful element in human nature will remain statistically about as they are", while anarchists "believe in a moral progress such that the social casing of coercion may eventually be discarded" (Ritter 2010, p. 113). Another difference is that anarchists give community a higher status than the liberals. Their project is to organize society in order to reinforce the positive synergy between individuality and community. The liberals put more focus on the State, to which the anarchists are opposed. The disagreement could be explained by referring to the anarchists' communitarian commitment and the liberal idea that the society is nothing more than the sum of its individuals. The neoliberal economic system –

> An economic system defined by unhindered free trade – is inherently flawed because it encourages the accumulation of material wealth and overconsumption by a relatively small number of people while the

majority of the world's population has resources that are relatively scarce and too often unable to meet basic human needs.

(Wackernagel and Rees 1996, p. 18)

Costanza criticized the neoliberal economic model in which markets, entirely free from governmental interference, can allow unlimited economic growth; he argued that it is not physically possible for the economy to grow indefinitely, especially with a shrinking stock of natural resources (Wackernagel and Rees 1996, p. 25).

Spash argues that economics defines itself by its methodology rather than its content or object of study, the socio-economic system, and has become a narrow prescriptive field with no input and no output of either materials or energy. The consequence is that to be an economist today means "being able to abstract from reality using mathematical symbols to represent loosely defined concepts such as goods, services, labour, land, capital, prices, money, markets, trade, employment and utility" (Spash 2017, p. 5).

In capitalism, maximizing profits may be used as a means of achieving the highest goal: promoting the common good. The imperative, started 250 years ago by Adam Smith, that we should compete in business and "pursue the largest possible amount of personal financial gain (i.e. behave egoistically) stems from the paradoxical hope that the good of all will result from the egoistic behaviour of the individual" (Felber 2012, p. 2). Smith argued that an "invisible hand" guides the egoism of individuals for the maximum welfare of all. Felber points out that "Today we know that the invisible hand does not exist. It is a pure hope, and neither economics nor economic policy operates on the basis of hopes" (Felber 2012, p. 3).

The fact is that the competitive growth economy, which requires natural and human resources on an ever-increasing scale, leads to the destruction of all on which it depends. This kind of economy leads to conflict with nature, and between humans, and it also leads to individual conflicts. According to Westoby and Dowling, modern capitalism has produced (Westoby and Dowling 2013, p. 96).

1. A form of consumerism that has resulted in children becoming more dependent on the things they own rather than on one another, thereby undermining the possibilities of strong social relationships.
2. Capitalist logic, which diffused into workplaces, also undermines honour and responsibility, and
3. Contemporary culture, which produces the uncooperative self.

They conclude that this all adds up to a social dynamic that reduces cooperative capacities and weakens dialogue. Spash deepens these arguments and explains other conflicts by maintaining that

Industrialised economies did not get rich through fair trade but unequal exchange, and modern economies persist in exploitation of others in order to maintain their populations in an imperial mode of living, or at least enough of the population to keep the lid on social unrest.

(Spash 2017, p. 12)

A utopian approach is one way of thinking about a potentially better society. It has been pointed out that capitalism is justified on the basis that it is "an expression of the survival of the fittest and the survival of the good" (Bryson and Msindai 2017, p. 48). By doing so, we commit the naturalistic fallacy, because good has been defined as something other than itself, as the survival of the fittest. According to Piketty, "capitalism has an inbuilt tendency to ever-greater levels of inequality" (Levitas 2017, p. 5). The capitalist wants to give the customer as little as possible and take as much as possible. The larger the margin of profit one is able to make, the more successful one is considered as a businessman or as an industrialist. Levitas continues by arguing that what we currently "measure as growth is not very useful except within the framework of constantly-expanding capitalism" (Levitas 2017, p. 9).

Marxism

Communism is based on the ideas and theories of Karl Marx. He was one of "the loudest of voices critiquing the economic system of capitalism, in which trade and industry are held in private hands and conducted for the sake of private profit" (Miletzki and Broten 2017, p. 21). He tried to answer the following questions: What is wrong with the capitalist society? What causes society to change and in what direction will society change? Marx was in many ways an early representative of transdisciplinary science since he crossed the usual divisions between different sciences and between science and practice. The doctrine of society's superstructure over the production conditions was more important than judicial laws, dominant positions in philosophy, religion, and art.

Marx suggested that the capitalist system would lead to the accumulation of wealth in fewer and fewer hands, eventually collapsing on itself" (Miletzki and Broten 2017, p. 21). An economic system defined by unrestricted free trade is fundamentally unsound because it "encourages the accumulation of material wealth and overconsumption by a relatively small number of people, while the majority of the world's population has resources that are relatively scarce and too often unable to meet human needs" (Marazzi 2017, p. 18).

Although Marx believed he was able to prove that capitalist economy was self-destructive and would exterminate itself, he was open to the fact that capitalism had "achieved miracles that far exceed Egyptian pyramids, Roman aqueducts and Gothic cathedrals" (Bregman 2017, p. 42). However, capitalism also led to a growing working class, and the workplaces were often dangerous and unhealthy. The workers had long working days and no holidays. Competition between companies caused wages to be as low as possible. As a result, ever fewer people gathered more and more wealth at the expense of a rapidly growing number of poor workers. According to Marx, the value of labour is the value of the goods the workers produce. The added value is the difference between the value of the production and the salary the worker receives; the problem is that the capitalists steal the added value in terms of profit.

Marx criticized liberalist capitalism and went much further than social liberalism by claiming that the class divorce system must be terminated, not regulated. In addition, he believed that production should be adjusted to supply everyone's vital needs and not just go to the consumers who had money. Instead of regulating, or rather not regulating, the economy through the free market, the economy should be organized in the interests of the whole community. Marx suggested that the liberalist economy would lead to the accumulation of wealth in fewer and fewer hands and companies would exploit the workers and nature in order to increase profits.

It is the struggle between classes and the emergence of new classes that lead to a transition from one type of society to another. The class struggle has changed from epoch to epoch, but the basic principle is the same – the conflict and controversy between the haves and have nots. According to Marx, a transformation in the conditions of production leads to social change. One consequence of industrialization in Europe at the beginning of the 19th century was the development of the working class. Based on the idea that history is the result of class struggle, Marx argued that because of conflicting interests, the clash between the capitalists and the proletariat would result in deep changes in the society. The problem is that the State always defends the interests of the dominant class.

Marxism has a close connection to Durkheim's philosophy of science's perspectives. He argued, based on methodological collectivism, that social phenomena could only be explained by referring to other social phenomena. Despite social phenomena existing outside the minds and perceptions of individuals, they affect individual behaviours. Explanations based on methodological collectivism often contain concepts such as social scalability, economic system, public governance systems and cultural differences. Such explanations indicate that the individual's actions are more or less reasonable in the overall system. The point is that the explanation refers to phenomena outside the individual.

Marxist economy

Marx's division between capitalists and the proletariat represented one of the most important parts of his economic theory. He defined labour as a commodity that has the same value as the goods being produced. Work is the use of labour. When a capitalist buys labour for less than the value of production, there is an added value in terms of profit. In order to strengthen the capitalist in the competition, part of the profits must be reinvested in the company, which in turn leads to more workers, more profits and new investments. This creates an expansive economic system, with corporate goals as a management tool at corporate level and without any kind of management at the macro level. Economic growth can give either more leisure time or increased consumption. "From 1850 to 1980 we had both, but then it is largely the consumption that has increased" (Bregman 2017, p. 111). The big companies will create overproduction, and competition is weakened through market concentration. This development leads to crises that cannot be solved within the system, so another system will take over, according to Marx. Capitalist economy is self-destructive and will therefore be subject to social control at any given time.

The capitalists tried to control the workers by making them believe that the capitalists' norms and values were universal, for example, that free competition serves the community and that everybody is responsible for their own success. An important point in Marxist reasoning is that the conditions under capitalism are untenable for both capitalists (owners) and workers (labour). The workers are alienated from their own work and capitalists by the captivity of their own exploitation. In a sense, therefore, everyone will be better off when the capitalist system is dead.

In order to achieve a communist change in society, private ownership of the means of production must be terminated so that all property is owned by society in common. There is thus no upper class that has the opportunity to steal the socially created surplus.

Human creativity depends on whether it is given the opportunity to use and develop its abilities and skills. Within capitalism, workers were subject to machines and owners. Instead of developing jobs that secured variety and diversity, work was atomized and routinized. The consequence of reduced contact and interaction was increased isolation. An important point in Marxist thinking is that in the capitalist system workers are objectified and reduced to economic resources.

Revisionism

As an alternative to the revolutionary direction within communism, a reformist direction developed. Within revisionism, the understanding differs from that of the Marxist revolutionary. When the workers organize and form political parties, they will have more power to define the working conditions and their salary. The result is that capitalism does not collapse; on the contrary it will develop in a social direction and prove to be viable. In order to achieve positive results, it may even be necessary to cooperate with the capitalists. While liberalism has clear links to utilitarian ethics, where utility maximization is central, communism is connected to heteronomous deontological ethics where compliance with external values and norms is central. According to revisionist understanding, communitarianism is a fundamental understanding of society.

Box 4.2 Principles characterizing communist economy (hard core)

- Government management
- Government planning
- Growth in production and consumption
- The State as owner
- (Heteronomic) duty ethics
- Ontological collectivism
- Methodological collectivism
- Collectivism

Comments

Communism looks upon individuals as only living for the State, while liberalism is focused on the individual. Stirner accepted many of the premises of communism, but he argued that the people could only be able to develop their individuality by advancing beyond communism. One problem is that the communists focus solely on human beings as workers and forget the whole person. Another problem with communism is that the individual is completely subordinate to the State. According to Ritter, if it were not for the anarchist's commitment to society and the communist's commitment to the State, anarchists would have been placed in the communist camp:

> Each government, for the Marxists, gets its most causally significant attributes from the relations of production which it reflects. Anarchists, on the other hand, while they certainly appreciate how the particular effects of each state are shaped by its changeable attributes, also emphasize, in contradiction to the socialists, how its legality and coerciveness, which are inherent in its nature, cause more serious effects.
>
> (Ritter 2010, p. 127)

The anarchist denies the socialist's idea that leaders can be trusted to build the good society if they occupy a public office. Therefore, it is not possible to claim that anarchists are socialists at heart. Still, Chomsky reasons that anarchism could be seen as a part of the "libertarian wing of socialism" (Ritter 2010, p. 130).

Concluding reflections

From the previous paragraphs, it is clear that anarchism has much in common with both liberalism and socialism. In common with liberalists, anarchists give priority to freedom, and like socialists, they want equality. Anarchism was developed in the tension between these two political doctrines, and in a certain sense, "the tensions between liberal and socialist principles are reflected in the contradictions often to be found within the anarchist tradition" (Suissa 2010, p. 9). According to anarchism, freedom and equality are not contradictory; they are complementary. In the following chapters we will see that anarchists argue that freedom and equality, on a deeper level, are the same thing.

Economy treats money and utility as identical measures, and connects material welfare with overall well-being. If development is seen merely as the raising of income, then the aim of policies should be to increase gross domestic product per capita. "If the true meaning of development is broader, including such elements as education and health, then development policy should incorporate those aspects" (Miletzki and Broten 2017, p. 26).

In terms of the Sustainable Development Goals reflected on in the former chapter, liberalism and Marxism connect to different challenges. Liberalism discusses individual rights and democratic principles but have weak solutions, to say the least, concerning fair distribution of wealth. Marxism puts massive focus on equality and fairness and tends to give priority to collective over individual rights. Both of them define nature as a human or economic resource, and their worldview is mechanical.

5 History of anarchist philosophy

Introduction

The anarchists present a political and economic framework that could be characterized as utopian because it represents a standpoint that is distanced from what we find today. This brief overview of the history of anarchist philosophy ranges from Goodwin to Chomsky.

Anarchism distances itself from both liberalism and Marxism by arguing that liberalism is too focused on the individual and forgets the collective, while the Marxists are too focused on the collective and forget the individual. Anarchism gives priority to individual freedom in solidarity. In other words, the good life in solidarity with the collective.

In 1909 Kropotkin formulated the question that anarchism asks in the following way: "What forms of social life assure to a given society, and then to mankind generally, the greatest amount of happiness, and hence also vitality?" (Kropotkin 1909, p. xx) One hundred years later, in 2008, Marshall stated that "If there is no joy, imagination, spontaneity, conviviality and fun, it isn't my free society" (Marshall 2008, p. xx).

Anarchy is far from being a new position in political philosophy. The word itself is of ancient origin. Anarchy is derived from Greek, "anarchos". The pronoun "an" means, in this context, "without", and the following word "archos" denotes ruler or authority. Hence, anarchy means "without ruler", or more precisely, alternatives to and absence of such types of governance based on leaders and followers, i.e., the absence of hierarchy and authority. It is the condition of a people governing themselves without a constituted authority.

Classical anarchism

According to Marshall, it would be difficult to offer an exact definition of anarchism, since by its very nature it is a complex and subtle philosophy, embracing many different ideas and thoughts. At first sight it seems a hopeless task to incorporate anarchist theory into one general ideology. Guérin is more optimistic and argued that "in spite of contradictions and doctrinal disputes which were often centered on false problems, anarchism presents a fairly homogeneous body of ideas" (Guérin 1970, p. 4).

The point is that anarchism is best understood as a pluralistic movement of movements "constantly shifting and transforming as it is prefigured, performed, pursued and practised" (White, Springer and De Souza 2016, p. 8) in response to shifting shadows of domination. "Anarchism is like a river with many currents and eddies, constantly changing and being refreshed by new surges but always moving towards the wide ocean of freedom" (Marshall 2008, p. 3). Reclus uses the term "anarchy" to refer to a future society characterized by a synthesis of liberty and equality "that is free from institutionalized forms of domination" (Clark and Martin 2013, p. 53). Anarchy, because it signifies absence of government, implies "natural order, harmony of everyone's needs and interests, utter freedom in solidarity" (Guérin 2005, p. 355).

According to Judith Suissa, academic texts and public perceptions both often involve "simplifications, distortions or misunderstandings of anarchism", indicating that "it is utopian, impractical or over-optimistic regarding human nature" (Suissa 2010, p. 1). In daily language, "anarchism" and "anarchy" are regularly mistaken for political and social "chaos" or "without order". Anarchists are therefore often perceived as people who prefer chaos, people who want a return to the "jungle law". However, this is an incorrect interpretation of anarchism. It is, therefore, essential to point out that anarchy means "without leader" and not "without order". Anarchy represents a kind of society that is self-organized, one in which people govern themselves, without (or with minimal) hierarchical organization, both political (including administrative) and economic. The challenge is to create a world where everyone rules themselves, where there is no separation between the rulers and the ruled. In other words, anarchism is a way of organizing and coordinating a society without hierarchies:

> No more authority! This means free contract in place of absolutist law; voluntary compromise instead of State arbitration; equitable and reciprocal justice; rational morality, instead of revealed morality; the balance of forces replacing the balance of powers; economic unity instead of political centralization.
>
> (Guérin 2005, p. 96)

Since ancient times various forms of anarchism have existed in philosophy and practice. The Greek philosopher Heraclitus was the first to anticipate the anarchist belief that constant change takes place within a natural order. Anarchist thought also stretches back to the Stoics and Gnostics of ancient times and to Christian mystics in the middle ages. Kropotkin labelled Zeno the best exponent of Anarchist philosophy in ancient Greece since he proclaimed the supremacy of natural law over man-made law. They found in the law of nature a guide which preceded all human-made laws. If human beings lived in conformity with nature, all would be great. The Stoics favoured "cooperation and self-sufficiency as alternatives to the authoritarian state" (Mac Laughlin 2016, p. 4); Zeno "opposed Plato's state communism by offering his own ideal of a free community without government" (Marshall 2008, p. 70). Zeno argued that human beings had two different instincts: one of self-preservation, which leads to egoism, and a social instinct, which leads to cooperation for the common good. Where Plato was for the improvement of the few, the Stoics extended the philosophy to all people.

In the late 17th century, anarchism was put forward to eliminate the negative side effects of the founding principles of capitalism. According to Marshall, Rousseau deserves a prominent place in the anarchist tradition for his stress on

> The close link between property and government, his attack on social inequality, his criticism of elitist culture, his concern with popular democracy and sovereignty, his belief in the natural goodness of humanity and his praise for the simple life close to nature.
>
> (Marshall 2008, p. 128)

Later, anarchists in England and Germany argued that cooperation and individual initiative, rather than competitive struggle and the suppression of individualism, should be the guiding principles of social progress. They claimed that all authority is oppression and that the power of the State had to be eliminated to ensure human freedom. The anarchists saw the State as a big machine made for large-scale modern production of public services, and they wanted people to take over. Not like the selfish liberty of the bourgeois liberalism, but like the liberty that "acknowledges no other restrictions than those laid out for us by the laws of our own natures" (Bakunin in Guérin 2005, p. 147). Some of these ideas came back and took root in the romantic era of the late 18th century.

> Those laws are not foisted upon us by any external law-maker living either alongside or above us, they are, rather, immanent, and inherent within us, representing the very foundations of our being, material, intellectual and moral alike: instead of finding them curtailments, we should look upon them as the actual conditions and effective grounding of our liberty.
>
> (Bakunin in Guérin 2005, p. 147)

To give an extensive interpretation of anarchism, I consider the thoughts and ideas of different contributors to anarchism, from the classic anarchists such as William Godwin (1756–1836), Pierre-Joseph Proudhon (1809–1865), Mikhail Bakunin (1814–1876), Elisée Reclus (1830–1905), Peter Kropotkin (1842–1921), Emma Goldman (1869–1940) and Leo Tolstoy (1828–1910) to modern anarchists such as Jens Bjørneboe (1920–1976), Murray Bookchin (1921–2006) and Noam Chomsky (1928–), and philosophers such as Paul Feyerabend (1924–1994), John Clark, Peter Marshall and Todd May.

Godwin, Proudhon, Bakunin, Kropotkin, Reclus and Tolstoy developed the theoretical fundamentals of anarchism. William Godwin, "the father of philosophical anarchism" (Clark 2013, p. 172), published *An Enquiry Concerning Political Justice* in 1793. It was the first theory of non-governmental socialism, i.e., anarchism. He maintained that individual freedom and autonomy are linked to social freedom and the common good. Bakunin agreed and stressed that "the welfare of society and the self-realization of the individual person are complementary rather than in conflict" (Clark 2013, p. 173).

They were motivated by a sense of abundant vitality of life in their philosophy, which conquered existing values and institutions. Even if Godwin never actually used the concept of anarchism, he was an influential writer, educationalist and, indeed, anarchist philosopher. He articulated the idea of replacing the hierarchical State with a system of localized, participatory, community-based institutions. According to Suissa, Godwin placed

> Great emphasis on the development of individual rationality and independent thinking, believing that the road forward lay not through social revolution but through gradual reform by means of the rational dissemination of ideas at the level of individual consciousness.
>
> (Suissa 2010, p. 10)

He was not a revolutionary and regarded education and convincing arguments as the keys to freedom. In 1793 Godwin pointed out that technological developments would proceed so quickly that it would release people from practical work, so much so that in the near future it would be necessary to work for only half an hour a day. In addition he argued that the society should be organized as free associations and be as inclusive and decentralized as possible. And it is also interesting to note that Godwin, in common with Kropotkin, "refused to outline a blueprint of his stateless society on the grounds that to do so would contradict his most important teachings on process and social justice" (Mac Laughlin 2016, p. 29).

Proudhon was the first, in 1840, to use the concept of anarchy in connection with the no-government state of society, and he was the first to design a comprehensive program of anarchism. According to Guérin, Proudhon was also the father of "scientific socialism, of socialist political economy and of modern sociology, the father of anarchism, of mutualism, of revolutionary syndicalism, of federalism and that particular form of collectivism that has recaptured a fresh relevance today as self-management" (Guérin 2005, p. 39). According to Proudhon, to be ruled is to be continually "noted, registered, inventoried, priced, stamped, rated, appraised, levied, patented, licenced, authorized, annotated, admonished, thwarted, reformed, overhauled and corrected" (Proudhon in Guérin 2005, p. 97).

Proudhon became famous for his shocking quips such as "property is theft" and, to emphasize that anarchism is not chaos, he used the slogan "anarchy or chaos". By anarchism he understood anything but disorder.

Proudhon's teachings spread rapidly in France and Germany, especially among craftsmen and workers in small industries, who felt threatened by the expansion of large industrial companies. For Proudhon, revolution was not just a historical episode; it was a driving force in historical development. Revolution was a force "against which no power, divine or human, can prevail, and whose nature it is to grow by the very resistance it encounters" (Mac Laughlin 2016, p. 43).

In the 1860s Bakunin developed Proudhon's ideas and gave them a more aggressive feel, claiming the need to get rid of the ruling state power through revolt. He argued that freedom without socialism is privilege and injustice, and socialism without freedom is slavery and brutality. And, more strongly, he claimed that all power corrupts, and that absolute power corrupts absolutely. If you take the most radical revolutionary and install him on the throne of Russia or give him unilateral power in one year he will have become worse than the Tsar himself, Bakunin warned.

Communitarian anarchism

In the following chapters, my main sources of inspiration are the communitarian anarchists Peter Kropotkin (1842–1921) and Elisée Reclus (1830–1905), who explored the intersection between nature and society. These early anarchists had an overstated belief that if we only got rid of the authoritarian hierarchies, people would voluntarily cooperate with each other in associations, and what might almost be called "paradise states" would develop based on peace, freedom, and free access to all kinds of commodities. The precondition was their belief that people are naturally good but the authorities have corrupted them. When one gets rid of the authority and lets people live their own lives in freedom, they will do well and behave in solidarity with others. The need for freedom is particularly important, and the anarchists claimed that freedom of others does not limit their own freedom; on the contrary, in fact, they saw freedom of others as a precondition for the individual's freedom. They argued that it is possible to develop a classless and stateless society where everyone contributes to the best of their ability and receives in accordance with their needs. While competition may be the law of the jungle, cooperation is the law of civilization.

Kropotkin and Reclus argued that anarchism originated from the demands of practical life, and they made a powerful contribution to introducing ecological perspectives into anarchist thought. Kropotkin tried to put anarchism into a fresh context and expound his political principles in a language that was understood by people. He argued that the chief aim of anarchism is to awaken those constructive powers of the people, which "at all great moments of history came forward to accomplish the necessary changes, and which, aided by the now accumulated knowledge, will accomplish the change that is called forth by all the best men of our own time" (Kropotkin 2002, p. 170). Or, as Marshall expressed it, Kropotkin and Reclus "offer a critique of the existing order, a vision of a free society, and a way of moving from the one to another" (Marshall 2008, p. 36). Anarchism could be portrayed as seeking to combine the greatest individual development with the greatest communal unity. Kropotkin presents anarchism as something that "historically ebbs and flows in wider tides of social progress and reaction, but even at low water exercises a formidable hidden influence" (Adams 2015, p 80). The idea is that individual and societal tendencies, which are often contradictory, should in fact be mutually reinforcing. According to Guérin,

> The anarchist sets two sources of revolutionary energy against the constraints and hierarchies of authoritarian socialism: the individual, and the spontaneity of the masses. Some anarchists are more individualistic than social, some more social than individualistic.
>
> (Guérin 1970, p. 27)

Kropotkin's main idea is that networks of small cooperative local societies are the precondition for freedom and responsibility, and he emphasizes that freedom is inevitably connected to responsibility, and responsibility is connected to freedom. The centralized power constellations within politics and economics have the opposite effect. Even if Kropotkin was a forerunner of ecological anarchism, Reclus was the one who introduced into anarchist theory themes that "were later developed in social ecology and eco-anarchism" (Clark and Martin 2013, p. 16). Their main ideas are close to process philosophy in that they express that harmony in nature works through a tendency of tension between dissonance and imbalance. To the extent that "there is a balance of nature it is not a simple balance of elements but rather a complex balance of order and disorder" (Clark and Martin 2013, p. 20).

The anarchists criticized both capitalism and communism. Anarchism is necessarily anti-capitalist in that it "opposes the exploitation of man by man". But anarchism also opposes "the domain of man over man" (Chomsky 2013, p. 9). Anarchist theory is also against the distinction between owners and people without property. Therefore, the vast majority of anarchists oppose the classical capitalist system, in which ownership of production and distribution funds require a small minority of property owners and a large majority of people without property. The latter rely on the property-possessing minority to get work and resources to sustain life. They are wage earners, and the added value they create through their work does not come to them but goes to and is controlled by the property owners. According to Chomsky (2013), private ownership of the means of production and the abuse of the weak by the strong, on one hand, and control of production by the State, no matter how benevolent its intentions may be, must be overcome.

Kropotkin argued that anarchists aim to remove the private property right of production and distribution resources, at least to the extent that the owner must buy other people's labour. The same basic idea is found in the cooperative movement. We must, starting now, begin to transfer all that is needed for production: "the soil, the mines, the factories, the means of communication, and the means of existence, too from the hands of the individual capitalist into those of the communities of the producers and consumers" (Kropotkin 2002, p. 170). The means of production would be owned not by the State but by associations or communes of producers. They would be organized on a voluntary basis and connected federally. Proudhon, Bakunin, Kropotkin and Reclus call for the ownership of the land and factories by the producers themselves in village communities. "All should work and education should be universal, combining mental and manual skills" (Marshall 2008, p. 312).

In the economic field, anarchism has come to the conclusion that the root of modern evil lies not in the fact that the capitalist appropriates the profits or the surplus value; rather it lies in the very possibility of these profits, which accrue only because millions of people have literally nothing other than their labour to sell at a price which makes profits and the creation of surplus values possible (Kropotkin 2002, p. 193).

The anarchists introduced a "right of use" instead of "property rights". People can only be free and happy when they share the work and the goods they produce. The characteristic of possession is to "be your own master", on an individual or cooperative basis. At the same time, anarchists accept private property that is not used to exploit others.

Kropotkin argued in *Modern Science and Anarchism* (Kropotkin 1908) that "The economic liberalization of man will have to create new forms for its expression of life, instead of those established by the State" (Ward 2004, p. 29). He argued that there are plenty of examples to show that there is order in many sectors of human activity where the government does not interfere. A consistent anarchist must oppose not only alienated labour but also the ludicrous specialization of labour that takes place when the means for developing production devalue the worker into a fragment of a human being, degrade him to become a mere part of the machine, make his work such a torment that its essential meaning is destroyed, and "estrange from him the intellectual potentialities of the labor process in very proportion to the extent to which science is incorporated into it as an independent power" (Chomsky 2013, p. 10).

Kropotkin opposed capitalism not only because he was critical of the way goods were produced, distributed and consumed, but also because of the ontological assumption of superiority. "These men wanted to change how human beings interrelated with nature and how they perceived their own beings" (Mac Laughlin 2016, p. 231). Hence, when people behave badly, it is due to the institutions that the power forces have built up. The theory of "balancing of powers" and "control of authorities" is a hypocritical formula, invented by those who have power, "to make the 'sovereign people', whom they despise, believe that the people themselves are governing" (Kropotkin 2002, p. 135). Contrary to capitalism's claims that society should be governed by principles where competition and selfishness are ideals, the anarchists claimed that mutual aid and solidarity should be the true ideals in a society.

Freedom depends on the ability to realize humanity within society and then through the collective endeavours of the society as a whole. In other words,

> freedom is not a phenomenon of isolation, but of contemplation, not a factor of exclusion but rather a factor for liaison, the freedom of every individual being nothing more than the mirror image of his humanity or his human rights in the consciousness of all free men, his brothers, his equals.
>
> (Bakunin in Guérin 2005, p. 151)

This is also an important principle of Marxism. But unlike Marxists, anarchists do not want to go through a period of state-directed socialism to create a better society because anarchists deny the very idea that some individuals, classes or parties have the right to decide for other people. When communism takes over the governance of society, only the people in the government are replaced. The existing power structures are thus empowered. Whereas Marxism is based on economics, Read argued that "anarchism is based on biology, in the sense that it insists on the consciousness of an overriding human solidarity" (Marshall 2008, p. 592).

Kropotkin, who took his inspiration from Thomas More's *Utopia* (1516), assumed that the anarchist society was characterized by "sufficiency of goods for each to take what he needed and to work as much as he felt" (Kropotkin 2002, p. 75). Kropotkin sought progress in the fullest emancipation of the individual from the authority of the State; he wanted the greatest development of individual initiative, along with the limitation of all the governmental functions and surely not their extension (Kropotkin 2002, p. 184).

> We want freedom, which is to say, we claim for every human being the right and wherewithal to do whatsoever he may please, and not to do what does not please them: to have all of their needs met in full, with no limit other than natural impracticability and the equally valid needs of his neighbors. We want freedom and we hold its existence to be incompatible with the existence of any power, whatever may be its origins and format, whether it be elected or imposed, monarchist or republican, whether it draws its inspiration from divine right or popular right, from Blessed Blister or universal suffrage.
>
> (Kropotkin in Guérin 2005, p. 299)

Anarchism in the 19th century

The 19th-century American anarchists put theory into practice by creating communes, cooperatives, alternative schools, local currencies, and schemes for mutual banking. They wanted to contribute to the development of smaller centers connected to the surrounding areas. They were busy social inventors exploring the potential of autonomy, including women's liberation and race equality (Ward 2004, p. 69). Anarchism is thus neither chaos nor romanticized idyll, but a realistic view of the good society, ruled without rulers. "Free agreement is becoming a substitute for law. And free cooperation a substitute for governmental guardianship" (Kropotkin 2002, p. 63).

In the beginning of the 19th century, a group of anarchists called the Kristiania Bohemians formed around the Norwegian writer Hans Jæger, in whose book *The Bible of Anarchism* (1906) we have the most detailed presentation of the foundations of anarchism in the Nordic language. These anarchists were different from the anarchists whose backgrounds were in the emerging industrialization in Europe. Bohemian living was a big-city phenomenon and occurred in parallel with the explosive growth in the number of students. Socially, the bohemians were essentially a group of intellectuals from the upper class. They were "better people's children" with a relatively safe societal background, caught up in the new ideas of the time. It was an expression of a youth revolt against the establishment; the central values of the bohemian were personal freedom, individualism and modernity. The bohemian lifestyle disconnected from the norms that characterized bourgeois existence. They were often in conflict with their own family traditions and they broke away from their parents' lifestyle. The Norwegian anarchists indicate that the ideas of Kropotkin and other influential anarchists were spreading to groups other than the working class and craftsmen in the modern society.

Even though anarchism never broke through as widely as many hoped, it has influenced the development of modern Western societies and had an impact on both left and right-wing parties. Describing anarchy as dialogue, creativity and decentralization captures a diversity that makes it relevant for modern societies. Dialogue gives independence a wider scope by encouraging us to seek out new ideas. Since the 1960s, anarchist ideas have played a role in ideological debate and, of special importance, anarchist thinking was also one of the driving forces behind the student revolts we saw in Western Europe and the United States in the 1960s and 1970s.

Experiments in the 1960s with alternative lifestyles and production forms also referred to theories of anarchism. While its practical results were few and short-lived, it has probably had greater indirect significance as the source of inspiration for a number of modernist art directions as well as for intellectual left-wing movements in the '60s in Europe and the United States. The idea of direct action, local self-government and simpler lifestyles, in harmony with human nature, appealed to large groups of people, not least a variety of social and environmental activists. But it was only after the student revolt in Paris in 1968 that the interest in anarchism was revitalized. Anarchists have expounded on the need for a political change towards decentralized, interrelated social units.

Jens Bjørneboe wrote the essay "Anarchism as a Future" in 1969. In 1971 he gave a speech to the Student Society in Oslo on the theme "Anarchism … today?" Bjørneboe was a spokesman for an evolutionary development towards an anarchistic society. Since nothing seems to be perfect in real societies, there are degrees of imperfection and degrees of perfection. A perfect anarchistic society will never exist. Anarchism can only exist as an element, so to speak, as an adjective; there will be more or less strong elements of anarchism. Society is healthier in direct proportion to its more anarchic features. Because Bjørneboe did not believe in the absolute, only in combinations of different tendencies, he argued that the "either or" attitude in politics is unworkable because it is unrealistic. It is as unrealistic as the ancient idea of absolute freedom. There is no absolute, total freedom; there are only degrees of freedom. Bjørneboe greatly influenced the emerging anarchist movement in Norway.

In an international context, Chomsky argues in much the same way as Bjørneboe when he claims that there is no contradiction between holding anarchist ideals and pursuing certain reforms through the State when there is a chance for a more free, more just society in the short term. "Such humility is a necessary antidote to the self-defeating purism of many anarchists today" (Chomsky 2013, p. xi). The new social movements of the 1980s and 1990s, centered on "environmentalism, feminism, municipalism, and pacifism" (Marshall 2008, p. 622).

Concluding remarks

In a historical perspective, anarchism represents a diversity of ideas that have some common characteristics. First of all, anarchism argues that the good society is anchored in freedom for all people. Human beings find the best solutions when they can participate in decision processes on an equal basis without any external pressure.

Anarchism was also a protest against the industrial community that the anarchists perceived as artificial and inhuman because people became slaves of technological development. Technological development is not incompatible with anarchism, but the new technology should facilitate the decentralization of production. In other words, anarchism is hostile to the centralized large-scale industry and agriculture found in modern capitalism and socialism.

Anarchism is not committed to a policy of economic growth and mass production and consumption (Marshall 2008, p. 652). In 1908 Kropotkin argued that "anarchism was born among the people; and it will continue to be full of life and creative power as long as it remains a thing of the people" (Kropotkin 1908, p. 5). The great achievement of anarchism has been the actualization of affinity groups, intentional communities, cooperative projects, and a variety of movements for social transformation.

Referring to the Sustainable Development Goals, anarchism indicates that the solutions should be developed in the local societies and integrated up to the global level. The general principle is that cooperation between all people is the way forward and, from an anarchist perspective, top-down solutions are, to say the least, problematic.

6   Outline of anarchist philosophy

Introduction

In this chapter, I present the main ideas in anarchism concerning scientific understanding, Darwinism, human nature, freedom, pedagogy and education, and pacifism. As a starting point, anarchism has a holistic vision of humanity in nature and society in nature. One of Reclus' most significant legacies is his contribution to "our growing self-knowledge as human beings and as planetary beings" (Clark and Martin 2013, p. 100). He pointed out that the development of an individualized and social self depends on its integration in a cooperative social network which is harmoniously integrated in nature. According to Ward, it seems inevitable that the classical anarchist concepts will be reinvented and rediscovered continually "in fields never envisaged by the propagandists of the past" (Ward 2004, p. 31). The question is, what do people value in their lives and how can they obtain what they want? The explanation is that people search for alternatives to the crudities and injustices of both "free-market capitalism and bureaucratic managerial socialism" (Ward 2004, p. 31).

Today the ultimate ideas in anarchism are relevant not only to realize individual happiness but even more in answering the huge challenges we are facing concerning both the natural and social environments. Anarchism was first and foremost developed to answer the following questions:

- What forms of social life offer a given society, and then to mankind generally, the greatest amount of happiness and, hence, vitality?
- What forms of social life allow this amount of happiness to grow and develop, quantitatively as well as qualitatively – that is, to become more complete and more varied (Kropotkin 1908, p 58)?

Scientific anarchism

Both Kropotkin and Reclus refer to natural science in their theories about economy and society. Kropotkin argued that anarchism should be based on the method of modern science:

These laws are not imposed on us by some outside legislator, beside us or above us; they are immanent in us, inherent, constituting the very basis of our being, material as well as intellectual and moral; instead therefore, of finding them a limit, we must consider them as the real conditions and effective reason for our liberty.

(Marshall 2008, p. 39)

In order to give anarchism intellectual status, as well as a new direction, Kropotkin rooted his political philosophy in a self-consciously scientific epistemology, and he was "the first to formulate a scientific basis for the principle of anarchism" (Kropotkin 1970, p. 2). Anchored in his faith in science and confidence in the power of rational persuasion, Kropotkin claimed that anarchism was scientifically verifiable, and he related the discoveries of the natural and social sciences to anarchist theories of progress and evolutionary and revolutionary social change. According to Kropotkin, an anarchist refuses to recognize inherited, established and conventional facts before a critical examination of their validity. The willingness and ability to think critically is of vital importance, and knowledge should be based on the results of empirical investigation. His attitude is in accordance with the ideas of the scientific community active at his time that a true scientific attitude should be skeptical for sure but, in questioning scientific hypotheses and theories, should never be destructive. He fused the best principles of the Enlightenment with the "new knowledge" of the natural and social sciences (Mac Laughlin 2016, p. 33). His methodology was to adapt generalizations based on natural science to human institutions.

Kropotkin refers to philosophers in the 18th century who tried to embody knowledge about the whole of nature in one general system. The inductive-deductive method helped in framing interesting hypotheses about both natural and social phenomena. The new science made it possible to understand nature and organic life without "resorting to the power of a creator" (Kropotkin 1908, p. 25). Anarchism is a world concept embracing the whole of nature including society, economy, politics and ethics. Its method of investigation is that of the natural sciences in which "every scientific conclusion must be verified" (Kropotkin 1908, p. 53). The aim was to develop a philosophy that integrates all phenomena of nature and society. Kropotkin argued that by using this method it was possible to prove that the liberalist political economy was based on "laws" that were nothing more than unverified guesses.

As an example, Kropotkin argued that theoretical criticism of the existing conditions must be connected to constructive pictures of what one would put in place of the existing state. Consequently, "consciously or unconsciously, the ideal, the conception of something better is forming in the mind of everyone who criticizes the institutions" (Kropotkin 2002, p. 156). And he warns, "to tell people, first let us abolish autocracy or capitalism, and then we will discuss what to put in its place, means simply to deceive oneself and others" (Kropotkin 2002, p. 156).

Hence, the anarchist conception of society consists of two different but closely connected processes: firstly, the criticism of hierarchical organizations and the authoritarian conceptions of society, and secondly, the constructive analysis of the predispositions that are seen in the reformist activities of mankind, both in the past and still more so in the present. Kropotkin was alert to "the immense power of knowledge in achieving revolutionary social change" (Mac Laughlin 2016, p. 155).

Today anarchists are critical of the close connection to logical positivism. Bookchin does not trust modern science and its methods. He refers to Maslow, who observes that "Many sensitive people especially artists are afraid science besmirches and depresses, that it tears things apart rather than integrating them, thereby killing rather than creating" (Bookchin 2004, p. 20). The problem is that modern science has lost its critical edge. Feyerabend provides some very interesting ideas about the methodology in anarchist science. He points out that we need an external standard of criticism and we need a set of alternative assumptions constituting an entire alternative world. He underlines that his intention is not to replace a set of general rules with another such set. Instead he argues that "all methodologies, even the most obvious ones, have their limits" (Feyerabend 1975, p. 32). Thus, anarchism is not only possible, it is necessary for the internal process of science. In other words, critical thinking combined with constructive progress are core concepts in the anarchist philosophy of science.

Ecological thinking was an important part of Reclus' philosophy. He had an integral and holistic vision of the intimate connection between humanity and the natural world. Close to Feyerabend's anarchist philosophy of science, Reclus combined scientific research methods with aesthetic, poetic, and even spiritual aspects in his far-ranging integrative perspectives. According to Clark and Martin, such a fusion of forms of rationality and imagination "is one of the most noteworthy dimensions of Reclus' thought" (Clark and Martin 2013, p. 17).

Moving from an exploitative relationship with nature and society to an ecologically balanced relationship has ideological as well as institutional aspects. Federalism and decentralization are means to transform society, with the municipality and the labour union as key social units. This implies "bottom-up" initiatives rather than "top-down". The positive idea at the root of Kropotkin's teachings is "individual liberty through free cooperation as the basis of all social life" (Baldwin 1970, p. 3). Kropotkin maintains that

> A further advance in social life does not lie in the direction of a further concentration of power and regulative functions in the hands of a governing body, but in the direction of decentralization, both territorial and functional – in a subdivision of public functions with respect both to their sphere of action and to the character of the functions.
>
> (Kropotkin 2002, p. 51)

Reclus combined the concern for justice and rationality with the need for solidarity and care. The individuals were dynamic participants in the organic unity of society. In line with this approach, most anarchists are not followers of political activity in traditional terms, fighting for power neither within the State nor in other areas of society. "Life would be simplified, once the mechanism created for the exploitation of the poor by the rich would have been done away with" (Kropotkin 2002, p. 166).

Darwinism

Today ecology has become the most convincing source of information in eco-politics. To develop sustainable societies we have to live in balance with nature, and our ecological principles give us crucial guidelines as to how sustainable societies should be organized. Ecology deals with the interplay between nature, society and economy. Bookchin argues that the indications of history show freedom to be the basis for ecological societies and "spontaneity in social life converges with spontaneity in nature" (Bookchin 2004, p. xii).

Evolution was the main subject in Darwin's book, *On the Origin of Species* (1859): "the process by which all earth's species have descended from a common ancestor" (Bryson and Msindai 2017, p. 10). The book triggered several important discussions in the natural sciences. One of the most important was the question of natural selection of favoured behaviour based on cooperation or competition. Kropotkin criticized Darwinism's focus on competition and everyone's struggle against everyone and urged, rather, that cooperation was the driving force. For Kropotkin, Darwin had "provided the strongest scientific evidence that an anarchist community was a viable proposition; that humanity, and indeed animal societies, was underpinned by an ethos of mutual aid counterbalancing the propensity to individual competitiveness" (Adams 2015, p. 50). Instead of rejecting Darwinism, he adopted the inductive methodology of the new sciences to challenge the assertions of Darwinism. To launch anarchism as a modern sociological science, Kropotkin used methods from natural science; he saw the translation of scientific concepts from natural to social philosophy as "an unproblematic exercise" (Adams 2015, p. 50). Kropotkin demonstrated how cooperation to overcome different challenges was more representative than competition in evolution:

> I failed to find – although I was eagerly looking for it – that bitter struggle for the means of existence, among animals belonging to the same species, which was considered by most Darwinists (though not always by Darwin himself) as the dominant characteristic of struggle for life, and the main factor of evolution.
>
> (Kropotkin 2014, p. 5)

One of the clearest statements of that position is represented by Kropotkin in his book *Mutual Aid* (1902). Here Kropotkin argued that "cooperation among humans and other animals (as) an effort to further their family, neighbors, and at times species is as much a motive force of action as competition for survival" (May 1994, p. 62). Kropotkin showed how evolution is rooted in collaboration and "mutual aid" more than competition. He confronted what he saw as the increasing trend to read Darwinian evolutionary theory through the lens of an aggressive individualism. He wanted to verify that the

> simplistic notion of the survival of the fittest was a misleading inter-pretation of evolutionary theory, and that Darwin himself had noted man's social qualities as an essential factor in his evolutionary survival.
> (Suissa 2010, p. 26)

The idea of continuous development and evolutionary adaptation to chan-ging environmental conditions was applied to the study of nature as a whole, including the development of human beings and society. The strug-gle to survive is best understood as cooperation among the members of a society, and natural predispositions would ensure harmony in society.

Kropotkin's empirical studies indicated that "mutual assistance" dominated both in the animal world and in social life. He discovered that "mutual help" was dominant everywhere and concluded that cooperation holds the greatest significance for life, conservation of each species and its further development. Mutual aid is the principle which favours the maintenance and development of the species, together with "the greatest amount of welfare and enjoyment of life for the individual, with the least waste of energy" (Suissa 2010, p. 27). Based on his observations, he concluded that "competition within species is far less significant than cooperation as a precondition for survival" (Ward 2004, p. 7). In other words, "in all animal societies solidarity is a natural law of far greater importance than that struggle for existence" (Kropotkin 2002, p. 95). Kropot-kin went on to argue that "without this solidarity of the individual with the species" (Kropotkin 2002, p. 97) the animal kingdom would never have developed or reached its perfection.

> If we turn our minds to a close observation of nature and to an unprejudiced history of human institutions, we soon discover the Mutual Aid really appears, not only as the most powerful weapon in the struggle for existence against the hostile forces of nature and all other enemies, but also as the chief factor of *progressive evolution.*
> (Kropotkin 1908, p. 44)

The idea of a continuous development and a continual adaptation to a changing environment found in evolutionary theory inspired Kropotkin to apply it to the study of men and their social institutions.

Kropotkin transposed his insight in evolutionary theory to further the devel-opment of anarchism. Development, he claims, depends on cooperation, or mutual assistance, in both animal and human societies. Both politics and science were united in the law of mutual assistance, and cooperation is the overall force that contributes to biological and social life. Kropotkin's main contribution was to merge Darwinian evolutionary theory with anarchism. His thesis was that

> The intellectual faculty in animals and humans was eminently social and that it fostered the communication skills and imitative behavior that enabled species to learn from experience.
>
> (Mac Laughlin 2016, p. 165)

Kropotkin believed that the knowledge of cooperation and mutual help in nature shed light on the importance of human cooperation and that the transition from competition to cooperation might help save humanity from destroying itself. Mutual aid and free cooperation between humans were characteristics of the rich communal life in Europe's medieval cities.

Kropotkin designed cooperative anarchism in the 1870s as an attempt to contribute to the greatest possible happiness for all based on freedom, equality and brotherhood within society. "Mutual aid would be considered, not only as an argument in favor of a pre-human origin of moral instincts, but also as a law of Nature and a factor of evolution" (Kropotkin 2014, p. 7). Rejecting the competitive economic image of nature, Kropotkin adopts an ecological image which sees nature as essentially creative, directive and cooperative.

Clark and Martin maintain that the most significant intellectual influences of Reclus are "his contribution to the development of the modern ecological worldview" (Clark and Martin 2013, p. 16), and his role in the creation of radical ecological social thought in anarchist political theory. He argued that humanity was closely related to nature, humanity in nature. He developed a holistic science where he synthesized scientific, aesthetic, poetic and spiritual aspects in his integrative theoretical perspectives.

Reclus links ethics to our relationship with nature and argues that the abuse of animals is morally unacceptable. Our behaviour towards other species reflects our level of sentience of connectedness to the whole of nature. Animals have inherent value and should not be treated in a way that "reduces them to a level at which their lives and experience seem less valuable" (Clark and Martin 2013, p. 32). Our growing knowledge of animals and their behaviour "will help us to delve more deeply into the life sciences, increase our knowledge of the nature of things, and expand our love" (Reclus 2016, p. 136).

Kropotkin published a number of books where he, amongst other things, linked the anarchist collaboration to Adam Smith's concept of sympathy. The most serious mistake of Adam Smith was, according to Kropotkin, that he had not understood that the same "feeling of sympathy in his habitual stage exists among animals as well as among men" (Kropotkin 2002, p. 95). More recently, anarchists have become more and more concerned by man's power over nature. Based on an organic worldview, man is an integral part of nature. From a holistic point of view, nature is not a lump of minerals, but a complex web of life which is charged with ethical meaning. Kropotkin's attempt to deduce a code of ethics from a philosophy of nature is problematic. He could be guilty of the naturalistic fallacy of unjustifiably inferring "ought" from "is" and arriving at "a statement of how things should be from how things actually are" (Mac Laughlin 2016, p. 242).

Based on the works of both Kropotkin and Reclus, ecological thinking became an important source of inspiration in the development of anarchist theory and practice. Since Bookchin's influence in the 1960s, ecology has become the central theme in the anarchist discussion. On the one hand, anarchists argue that human societies have developed in a dialectical interaction between human beings and nature. Human self-realization is closely connected to the flourishing of the global eco-systems. On the other hand, environmental problems will continue as long as the society is organized by a system that dominates nature and has a negative impact on human self-realization. The eco-communitarian perspective is inspired by a vision of human communities achieving their fulfilment as an integrated part of a larger self-realizing society:

> If social ecology is an attempt to understand the dialectical movement of society within the context of the larger dialectic of society and nature, Eco-communitarian anarchism is the project of creating a way of life consonant with that understanding, that is, a world of free, just ecologically responsible communities.
>
> (Clark 2013, p. 248)

The critical message of ecology is that natural and societal variety is of the greatest importance in order to establish balance and harmony. In other words, technical standardization should be exchanged for organic differentiation. This approach assumes a careful exploration of the nature and possibilities of community at the individual level of society, and directs our hopes towards a project of regenerating human society and liberating human creative powers. The precondition is that the society

> Always remains an organic, dynamic, dialectically developing whole, the product of human creative activity, and not least of all, the result of the kind of primary relationships that human beings enter into with one another.
>
> (Clark 2013, p. 156)

Bookchin distinguishes social ecology from environmentalism by stressing that environmentalism reflects instrumentality and a mechanistic nature, while social ecology argues in accordance with deep ecology: Firstly, man is part of nature, therefore, expanding the natural environment enlarges the basis for social development. Secondly, spontaneity is important to releasing potential. Thirdly, an expanding whole is created by growing diversification and enrichment of its parts. Instead of hierarchical power structures, a new ecological sensibility must develop which has "a holistic outlook and celebrates play, fantasy and imagination" (Marshall 2008, p. 611).

Human nature

Stirner rehabilitated the individual at a time when "the philosophical field was dominated by Hegelian anti-individualism. The first tendencies of existentialist philosophy are visible in Stirner's lively reasoning:

> I start from the hypothesis by taking myself as a hypothesis (. . .) I use it solely for my enjoyment and satisfaction (. . .) I exist only because I nourish my Self (. . .) The fact that I am absorbing interest to myself means that I exist.
>
> (Guérin 1970, p. 29)

According to May, the core of the anarchist project is the assumption that "human beings have a nature or essence" and that "that essence is good or benign" (May 1994, p. 63). It enables humans to live justly with others in the society.

> Whether the good-making characteristics go by the name of "sociability", "cooperation" or "competence", the thought remains the same: people naturally tend to their affairs in ways that are helpful to themselves and to others and that are not, or mostly not, harmful or destructive.
>
> (May 1994, p. 63)

People are naturally good; if the obstacles to developing goodness are removed, then people will work together in their activities. The anarchist conception of human nature is the key to understanding much of the anarchist political philosophy and economy. An important part of the anarchist project has been to investigate "the degree to which 'goodness', or grounding for 'goodness', can be found in human nature" (Clark 2013, p. 19). Both Proudhon and Bakunin argued that human nature is twofold, involving both an egoistical potential and a sociable, and altruistic potential. A similar perspective arises from the work of Kropotkin, who "more than any other theorist within this tradition, devoted considerable energy to developing a systematic theory of human nature" (Suissa 2010, p. 26). There is more to Kropotkin's individuality than reasoning, emotions and productive force. It also includes "inventive spirit, the full (. . .) expansion of what is original in man, an infinite variety of capacities, temperaments and individual energies" (Ritter 2010, p. 57). This argumentation is in contrast with the Western intellectual tradition, which ignores our embodied human nature and our "necessary existence in a web of human social relationships" (Levitas 2017, p. 3).

Kropotkin based his reflections on political philosophy on the idea that human beings are integrated parts of society and nature. Implicit in his concept of man was the proposition that "individuation must proceed pari passu with integration" (Adams 2015, p. 176). So, "man did not create society, society existed before Man" (Marshall 2008, p. 322). His constructive conclusion is that we are products of the social environment and we are capable of changing it. To develop personal individuality, the community is recognized as the substantial groundwork. Community both "produces man as man and is produced by him, because individuality and community are reciprocally dependent" (Ritter 2010, p. 4). The social context is essential to make individuality flourish. The community represents the context for understanding phenomena such as confederation, interdependence and freedom. Buber argued that the interrelationship between persons were at the center of the social question. He asks, "how we can recreate ourselves as the kind of persons who can collectively constitute an authentic nondominating co-operative community and, ultimately, an entire society consisting of such communities" (Clark 2013, p. 160).

We cannot revolt against nature so, therefore, it is sound to argue that nature should take priority over the individual. According to anarchism, the individual good is in harmony with the social good. History shows that human beings have the potential for solidarity, and they are capable of living peacefully together. According to Marshall, we may be born into a particular situation, "but we are largely what we make of ourselves" (Marshall 2008, p. 642). Reclus affirmed the close and inseparable connection between personal and social freedom. He offered a deep defense of individual freedom regarding speech, conduct, association and many other areas, but "always in the context of growing communal ties based on mutual aid and social cooperation" (Clark 2013, p. 174).

Reclus carries out ideas that are in accordance with this line of argument when he situates humanity within a larger reality: "humanity's place in nature is dialectical, critically holistic, and developmental" (Clark and Martin 2013, p. 21). This means that humanity is emerging within nature rather than outside nature. Consciousness of our integral place in nature leads us to become more aware of our responsibility for the planet. According to Bookchin, the imbalances humanity has produced in the natural world are caused by the imbalances produced in the social world. "Man has produced imbalances not only in nature, but, more fundamentally, in his relations with his fellow man and in the very structure of his society" (Bookchin 2004, p. 23).

Man is not by nature "good" or "evil" but behaves in ways that have positive or negative consequences for himself and his surroundings. Man has an inherent sense of justice, but authorities have often, to a greater or lesser extent, destroyed it. With the proper development and use of technology, the reduction of man to an appurtenance of the machine, a specialized tool of production, might be overcome, rather than enhanced. "Under the conditions of autocratic control of production man is made an instrument to serve production goals, overlooking his individual purposes" (Chomsky 2013, p. 11).

Far from living in a world of visions where men are imagined as better than they are, Kropotkin argues that it is important to see them as they are. Dominating authorities reduce the freedom of humans and make them passive and indifferent. "Individuals are not to blame, they are driven mad by horrible conditions" (Marshall 2008, p. 316). People like to work and be useful in their societies as long as work gives a feeling of play, but with its emphasis on discipline, the modern factory system has destroyed the instinctive pleasures of work. We are social human beings who need to cooperate to find solutions within a natural context. Even more important, we recognize our own self in that of the other. Reclus maintains that human beings can transform themselves into active, conscious agents by under-standing the determinants of the social world. Understanding how the natural world influences culture is important to individual and collective self-realization.

The ultimate criteria for judging social progress are the advances in human self-realization in harmony with the natural world, and technologi-cal development or economic growth need not apply. Self-realization is a social process in which the individual merges with society. Reclus' view of the individual in society has much in common with Aristotelian philosophy "both in his multifaceted conception of human self-realization and in his belief in the inseparable interconnection between individual attainment of diverse virtues or excellences and the collective realization of the common good" (Clark and Martin 2013, p. 45). Human self-realization is, according to Reclus, the complete development of the individual. In addition to perfecting the character by becoming noble, generous and devoted, it includes "the improvement of the physical being in strength, beauty, grace, longevity, material enrichment, and increase of knowledge" (Clark and Martin 2013, p. 44).

He emphasized the importance of "intimate co-operation among mem-bers of each level of living things as a fundamental factor" (Mac Laughlin 2016, p. 165) in the process of developing harmonic well-being. Even if all living things are related so closely to one another that each impacts all the others, "they lead their own life without being subordinated to a central organ" (Kropotkin 2002, p. 120). Humans are born equal and at the same time each individual is unique. Just as each person expresses his personality according to the scale of values to which he refers, his manner of living is also of great importance. In order to unfold our potential, man must enter into mutually binding relationships with the environment. When we begin to see ourselves as integrated parts of the global eco-system and conceive of ourselves as nature becoming self-conscious, "we realize that the process of attaining freedom through self-realization encompasses not only humanity but also the earth as a whole" (Clark and Martin 2013, p. 47).

This reasoning urges us to strive for the greatest possible development of personal initiative in every individual and group and to secure unity of action, not through discipline but "through the unity of aims and the mutual confidence which never fail to develop when a great number of persons have consciously embraced some common idea" (Kropotkin 2002, p. 185). Reclus stresses the holistic dimension in Aristotle's thoughts. When a being attains its end within a larger whole, "it is an organic part of a larger whole" (Clark and Martin 2013, p. 61). However, Reclus argues that human beings are not simple "structural cells or organs in the body politic but rather dynamic participants in the larger organic unity" (Clark and Martin 2013, p. 61). Bookchin argued that instead of dominating hierarchical modes of thought, "a new 'ecological sensibility' must develop which has a holistic outlook and celebrates 'play, fantasy and celebration'" (Marshall 2008, p. 611). A free and democratic society is an integrated unity in which solidarity and impulsive, voluntary activity are synthesized. Clark, a defender of communitarian anarchism, maintained that the holistic vision does not "espouse any 'totality', aesthetic or otherwise, that is alleged to be full, complete, and 'without remainder'" (Clark 2013, p. 4). And he concludes, "Such closure is anathema to the anarchist communitarian vision" (Clark 2013, p. 4).

Process is more focused on relations than on objects. For anarchists the goal is reflected in the process. In his thinking, which is close to a philosophical understanding of process, Kropotkin argued that the capacities for life are developing all the time, in line with the more and more complex integration of organisms. In short, each individual is a cosmos of organs, each organ is a cosmos of cells, and each cell is a cosmos of infinitely small ones. And in the complex social world, the well-being of the whole depends entirely on the sum of well-being enjoyed by each of the living entities. Since networks of living entities are of vital importance, the relations between them are focused. In other words, well-being depends on the organizational structure. In accordance with process philosophy, Kropotkin describes evolution in nature as governed by necessary laws. Likewise, humans are social beings and their change processes are gradual.

> The life of society itself we understand, not as something complete and rigid, but as something never perfect – something ever striving for new forms, and ever changing these forms in accordance with the needs of the time. This is what life is in Nature.
>
> (Kropotkin 1908, p. 80)

Within a system of nested networks, it is possible to reach full individualization, which is not possible under either the present capitalist system of individualism or any system of State socialism (Kropotkin 2002, p. 285).

Whereas Proudhon tended to fear social revolution because it may lead to chaos, Kropotkin welcomed it because it would liberate the people's suppressed capacity for self-organization. (Mac Laughlin 2016, p. 229). Kropotkin insisted that the anarchist thinker study society and try to discover its tendencies, and his ideal merely points out how dire it is. The potential for social revolution is inherent in the philosophy of life (Kropotkin 2002, p. 119).

Reclus maintains that everything in nature changes as part of an eternal movement and that revolutions do not necessarily constitute progress. Progress and regression are two parts of evolution: "if some evolutions tend toward the growth of life, there are others that incline toward death" (Clark and Martin 2013, p. 139). Despite periods of regression, Reclus argue that there is an overall movement of evolutionary progress in history. Radical dialectic sees the social and natural world as the site of constant change and transformation through "processes of mutual interaction, negation, and contradiction" (Clark 2013, p. 21). The objects of dialectical analysis are seen as always being in motion. In accordance with Alfred North Whitehead's process philosophy, becoming is more real than being (Whitehead 1978, p. 65). Changes in consciousness precede and give rise to fundamental societal changes. As an example, he emphasizes that the modern society is more developed than more primitive societies concerning human self-realization. Thus, "the more 'primitive' society often has the advantage of greater 'coherence' and 'consistency with its ideal', while the 'civilized' one has gained in 'complexity' and 'diversity'" (Clark and Martin 2013, p. 37).

There is a need for periodical revolutions, according to Reclus, who interprets such events as the culmination of gradual changes over a long time span. "Progress is the result of interdependent revolutionary and evolutionary processes" (Clark and Martin 2013, p. 36). The life of society is understood, not as something complete and rigid, but as something never perfect – something ever striving for new forms. The changing processes influence these forms in accordance with the needs of the time, "this is what life is in nature" (Kropotkin 2002, p. 184). The society itself is not something complete and rigid; it is always imperfect. The society is always striving for new forms, and the forms are changing in accordance with the needs of the time. "This is what life is in Nature" (Kropotkin 1909, p. 80). As seen in organic life at large, harmony would result from an ever-changing adjustment and re-adjustment of equilibrium between the multitudes of forces and influences, and "this adjustment would be the easier way to obtain as none of the forces would enjoy a special protection from the State" (Kropotkin 2002, p. 284). The anarchist ideal of unity in diversity indicates a general tendency of things to merge into a dynamic organism in which all parts are in reciprocal interdependence.

Kropotkin argued that a free society would be best achieved by gradual changes in public opinion. Even if all changes always begin with the people, changes need time to incubate, time in which people may begin to free themselves from their former indifference and resignation and find themselves "very slowly becoming imbued with the revolutionary spirit" (Kropotkin 1908, p. 89). Therefore, it was important to encourage any tendency which "checked government power and promoted solidarity and co-operation" (Marshall 2008, p. 316). "It is the continual becoming of human community in mankind, adopted and proportioned to whatever can be willed and done in the conditions given" (Buber 1996, p. 56). The goal is to strive for the greatest possible development of individuals and societies and to secure unity of action, not through discipline "but through the unity of aims and the mutual confidence which never fail to develop when a great number of persons have consciously embraced some common idea" (Kropotkin 1908, p. 81).

Freedom

Godwin maintained that freedom is "the most valuable of all human possessions", while Proudhon acclaims freedom as his "banner and guide", and Bakunin was "a fanatic lover of liberty". Kropotkin "seeks a form of society which will leave to the individual man complete and perfect freedom" (Ritter 2010, p. 9). The individual understands that he will be really free in proportion only to the degree that all others around him become free (Kropotkin 2002, p. 166). "In a society of equals this would be quite sufficient for preventing those unsociable actions that might be harmful to other individuals and to society itself, and for favoring the steady moral growth of that society" (Kropotkin 2002, p. 157). According to Kropotkin the golden rule of ethics is: "Do not to others what you would not have done to yourself" (Kropotkin 2002, p. 176).

In accordance with the evolutionary preconditions in anarchism, Sen presented development as "a process of expanding human freedom (...) he added real substance to his message by developing the idea of capabilities, the capacity of individuals to do the things that make their lives meaningful" (Miletzki and Broten 2017, p. 30). Expansion of freedom is not only a desired end of development, but "the main means of development" (Miletzki and Broten 2017, p. 34). Sen makes a distinction between what he calls the "process aspect of freedom (the capacity to perform certain aspects of freedom within the rules of society) and the opportunity aspect of freedom (the capacity actually to achieve freedoms in society)" (Miletzki and Broten 2017, p. 35).

Berlin distinguishes between negative and positive freedom. On the one hand, negative freedom focuses on the absence of obstacles "in the form of coercive action, to the pursuit of one's goals" (Clark 2013, p. 54). Other people are regarded as resistant forces and hindrances that must be overcome. Because negative freedom defines other people as a force of resistance and hindrance to freedom, negative freedom is in conflict with anarchism's positive image of man. In addition, negative freedom narrows the acceptance of diverse values and contradicts the idea of plurality.

Positive freedom, on the other hand, focuses on the search to be a self-determined subject. "I wish to be the instrument of my own, not of other men's acts or will" (Clark 2013, p. 54). A basic dimension in anarchist philosophy concerning freedom is the free development of the potential of the individual. The anarchist notion of freedom is anchored in the thesis that "the elimination of forms of domination will liberate the potentialities for diversity on the levels of the person, the community, and the natural world" (Clark 2013, p. 88). Anarchists have pointed out that the existing system hinders diversity and inspires the development of monocultures.

In other words, freedom is more than (negative) freedom from control; (positive) freedom is the ability to create, or the freedom to become. Freedom is a process of self-realization and not a static state of rest. To be free is both to do what one likes and to realize one's full potential in an Aristotelian meaning of human flourishing as the actualization of a wide spectrum of human potentialities. Without positive freedom, people might be legally free, but in practice powerless and locked up. Anarchism replies to the need for freedom that is essential for creativity and individual and societal fulfillment. According to Godwin, "A free man must not only act freely; in his prior deliberations he must consult his own reason, draw his own conclusions, exercise the powers of his understanding" (Ritter 2010, p. 11). In other words, it is not enough to act freely; the individual must also have freedom to decide. This means that drawing conclusions about the future restricts what we can do. Communitarian anarchist philosophy synthesizes negative and positive freedom in the realization of the self, and talk about absolute freedom as active participation in the collective self-determination of a free community.

This means that we can only be free to realize ourselves in company with others. Individual freedom is intimately and intrinsically connected with the lives and freedom of others. Bakunin maintained, "Man is truly free only among equally free men" (Marshall 2008, p. 36). It must be emphasized that most anarchists do not take absolute freedom to be possible; it is a question of degree. No association could be established and developed without certain limits being placed upon freedom, as "some limitation upon freedom is inevitable everywhere. For one could not shrug them all off" (Stirner in Guérin 2005, p. 23).

For anarchists, freedom is the vital, concrete possibility for every human being to bring to full development all their powers, capacities, and talents with which nature has endowed them and turn them to the good of society. For Bakunin, this is the only kind of liberty that is worthy of the name:

> In the full development of all the material, intellectual, and moral powers that are latent in each person; liberty that recognizes no restrictions other than those determined by the law of our own individual nature, which cannot properly be regarded as restrictions since these laws are not imposed by any outside legislator beside or above us, but are immanent and inherent, forming the very basis of our material, intellectual and moral being – they do not limit us but are the real and immediate conditions of our freedom.
>
> (Bakunin in Guérin 1970, p. x)

In accordance with Bakunin's assertion that freedom for the individual depends on the freedom of the people around the individual, anarchists argue that each one of us has potential to develop a consciousness that makes it possible to identify with others. To be enabled to express our individual personality with self-control and self-discipline is important. Developing cooperative attitudes forms the basis of trust that is the very glue of the society. The good society is based on social diversity and all associations are voluntary, ever changing and taking new forms. Stirner gives an illustrating example of the process character of freedom when he states that once freedom of thought is acquired, "our time's impulse is to perfect it, in order to exchange it for freedom of the will, the principle of a new epoch" (Stirner in Guérin 2005, p. 17). Bakunin emphasized that all humanity is physically and socially equal, and insisted that since man is truly free among equally free men, "the freedom of each is therefore realizable only in the equality of all" (Marshall 2008, p. 49). Therefore, the realization of freedom through equality, both in principle and in fact, is justice.

The strength of anarchism is that it offers a more comprehensive and inclusive interpretation of freedom than libertarianism's negative concept of freedom and "the one-sidedly positive conception of freedom in welfare statism" (Clark 2013, p. 177). Freedom could also be characterized as a means to the development of the potential in individuality and community. This is to say that freedom combined with solidarity encourages the development of "self-consciousness, to enrich personality, and to direct emotions into channels that are strengthening to the self" (Ritter 2010, p. 31). The absence of any connections to others leads to intellectual, material and moral death.

For anarchists, individual freedom set out in decentralized social networks gives the best opportunities for the development of human potential. Free workers require free organizations anchored in free agreements and free cooperation. In other words, no actions should be imposed upon the individual through fear of punishment, or required of him by society, except for those which receive his free acceptance. This shows and makes clear that the majority has no more right to dictate to the minority, than the minority has to dictate to the majority. To be aware of oneself as an individual, it is of great importance to be reflected by others. A free community is based on the dialectic of social determination and creative self-transformation. The free community is

> A becoming-whole that presupposes that as members of a community the participants always count themselves in, but as members of a free association they always also count themselves out, since they and their community itself are in a process of going beyond any given communal bounds.
>
> (Clark 2013, p. 5)

As long as it is not a threat to its neighbours, each nation, region, and commune must be free to organize itself, politically and economically. Societies organized on these principles would not limit man in the free exercise of his powers in productive work by capitalism or the State. In addition he would not be limited in the exercise of his will through a fear of punishment or "by obedience towards individuals or metaphysical entities, which both lead to depression of initiative and servility of mind" (Kropotkin 2002, p. 285).

> Acknowledging the equal rights of its members to the treasures accumulated in the past, it no longer recognizes a division between exploited and exploiters, governed and governors, dominated and dominators, and it seeks to establish a certain harmonious compatibility in its midst – not by subjecting all its members to an authority that is fictitiously supposed to represent society, but not by trying to establish uniformity, but by urging all men to develop free initiative, free action, free association.
>
> (Kropotkin 2002, p. 123)

Reclus argued that social freedom is a mature expression of moral autonomy. Anarchists from Godwin on have stressed that "moral responsibility is impossible without moral autonomy" (Clark and Martin 2013, p. 52). Bjørneboe argued that freedom is intrinsically connected to responsibility, freedom is not possible without responsibility, and responsibility is not possible without freedom. This connection explains why many people fear freedom because of the responsibility it entails. "In times of economic insecurity and social unrest (people) look to strong leaders to tell them what to do" (Marshall 2008, p. 41).

Kropotkin reasoned that biology provides the ground for morality. By studying human society from the biological point of view, he believed that it was possible and desirable to deduce the laws of moral science from the needs and habits of mankind. Nature is the first ethical teacher of men. The social instinct, innate in men as well as in all the social animals, "is the origin of all ethical conceptions and all the subsequent development of morality" (Marshall 2008, p. 320). In accordance with Kropotkin, Bookchin argued that nature offers the basis for ethics, and that it is possible to learn from the ways of nature.

Kropotkin distinguishes between our innate moral sense and the rigid moral codes imposed by authority (Marshall 2008, p. 321). We are naturally social, cooperative and moral. But while society is a natural phenomenon, the State and its coercive institutions are an artificial and malignant growth (Marshall 2008, p. 323). Reflection on free action and reaction between his own self and ethical conceptions of his surroundings makes man "enabled to obtain the full development of all his faculties, intellectual, artistic, and moral" (Mac Laughlin 2016, p. 167). It is not possible to reach full individualization under either capitalism or any system of State socialism. Tolstoy argued that we need a moral revolution, the regeneration of man. "Since only a person living in accordance with his conscience can have a good influence on others, he urged that one try to achieve inner self-perfection" (Marshall 2008, p. 378).

In order to develop a code of ethics suitable for the new scientific age, it was necessary to ensure that morality was grounded in present-day realities. The purpose of ethics is to set before humans, as a whole, a higher purpose, an ideal which "better than any advice, would make them act instinctively in the proper direction" (Mac Laughlin 2016, p. 173). Anarchism states that freedom means freedom from everything except rational arguments. To be rational, all consequences for all involved individuals must be included in the decision. I act rationally in anarchy "no matter what I do, just as long as systematic, critical, particularized deliberation is the means I use to choose my conduct" (Ritter 2010, p. 148).

A choice is free if it is reasonably based. This means that reasoned arguments impose restrictions on the behaviour through internalized standards of conduct. They "influence us in the same way as our reading, through reasons (...) presented to the understanding, which help us to deliberate more rationally by suggesting arguments and evidence we could overlook, if we decided alone" (Ritter 2010, p. 13). The anarchists argue that values and norms in the society are internalized and become part of the individuals' frame of reference. The point is that the directives being internalized are not imposed by an external legislator. Internalized norms and values are inherent in us and they constitute the very basis of our being; "hence instead of finding limits in them, we should consider them as the real conditions and the necessary foundation of our freedom" (Ritter 2010, p. 15). By leaving action unrestrained, the anarchists argue that internalization is far more liberating than any use of sanctions.

This is very different from government rules of conduct that are imposed by force. Freedom is to act not because of command but due to an understanding of what is good for both the individual and society. For anarchists, "a completely free agent is liberated in both action and choice from every removable hindrance, except for those arising from his rational deliberation" (Ritter 2010, p. 147).

Because there is enough solidarity, love, reason, and good will in humans, anarchists assume that people can act morally and govern themselves. The final aim of ethics is twofold: one, increase the happiness for individuals and, two, contribute to the physical, intellectual and moral development of society as a whole (Mac Laughlin 2016, p. 173).

To sum up, liberty for Proudhon has a generic similarity to quality of life, individually and collectively (Proudhon in Guérin 2005, p. 53):

- Liberty is equality, because liberty exists only in the state of society, and, outside of equality, there is no society.
- Liberty is anarchy, because it countenances no government of the will, only the authority of law, which is to say, of necessity.
- Liberty is of infinite variety, because it respects every will, within the limits of the law.

- Liberty is proportionality, because it affords full scope to merit's ambition and to the emulation of glory.
- Liberty is essentially organizing in order to ensure equality between men, equilibrium between nations, agriculture and industry, and centers of education.

And freedom is (Proudhon in Guérin 2005, p. 79)

- Freedom of association
- Freedom of assembly
- Freedom of religion
- Freedom of the press
- Freedom of thoughts and of speech
- Freedom of labour, trade and industry
- Freedom of education
- In short, absolute freedom

Liberty and freedom are interconnected and dependent on each other, and a precondition for individual freedom is societal liberty. Liberty includes diversity because each individual is respected as an equal and unique at the same time. Since diversity is closely connected to resilience and sustainability, individual freedom is a central prerequisite for a good life in a good society in harmony with nature.

Pedagogy and education

Unsurprisingly the aim of anarchist-inspired education is the individualization of the self. Consequently pedagogy ought to promote the development of the free personality as its starting point and main purpose. According to Ferrer, "the real educator is he who can best protect the child against his (the teacher's) own ideas, his peculiar whims; he who can best appeal to the child's own energies" (Graham 2017, p. 229). Feyerabend maintained that "teaching is to be based on curiosity and not on command, the 'teacher' is called upon to further this curiosity and not to rely on any fixed method" (Feyerabend 1975, p. 187). All teaching should accept that spontaneity reigns supreme, both in thought and in action. The aim of education is to train the students in freedom: that being free is really living. To do that, "knowledge must perish, in order to be resurrected as will and to recreate itself daily as free personality" (Guérin 2005, p. 20).

Ritter points to modern schools that draw on the ideals of anarchist pedagogy by emphasizing the necessity of including questions and problems suggested by the children, "which is of the very greatest aid in developing the children as separate, thinking individuals and as members of the social unit" (Ritter 2010, p. 159). In addition, it is important to inspire the children to organize their games freely in order to develop their individual personalities.

Kropotkin, in common with Feyerabend, rejected the usefulness of "parrot-like repetition in favour of encouraging children to discover (...) proofs by themselves and building their own arguments" (Adams 2015, p. 152).

From the time of Godwin, anarchists have recognized the importance of education – on the one hand as a means of social liberation and on the other hand as an authoritarian means of social control. "It was Bakunin who developed the concept 'integral education' which was meant to help overcome the division between intellectual and manual labour" (Graham 2017, p. 220). The purpose of education is to inspire the child to be interested in finding out how nature is constituted and functions in order to stimulate the desire to understand the dynamics of how everything is interconnected. He encouraged integrated education, combining mental and manual work. The aim is to produce the complete human being, trained to use his brain and his hands, especially as an initiator and an inventor in both science and technology. Learning is best achieved by doing, as children far prefer real work to abstract theory.

Following the same line of argument, Kropotkin maintained that the individual is at his best when "he is in a position to apply his usually-varied capacities to several pursuits in the farm, the workshop, the factory, the study or the studio, instead of being riveted for life to one of these pursuits only" (Mac Laughlin 2016, p. 232). Far from being inferior to the specialized students from the universities, "the complete human being, trained to use his brain and hands, excels them" (Kropotkin 1912, p. 154). To develop, we have to study, work, play and laugh. Education should contribute to the integrated development of our whole personality. "Work is to our higher faculties what food is to the physical body" (Kumarappa 1952, p. 61). Our emphasis in education and work must be on the opportunities to make people grow rather than on the material things we produce. There should no longer be either workers or scholars – only human beings.

Only through integrated education and the equality of conditions will human beings be able to free themselves from their instincts. In the development of civilization, social human beings will not only evolve the full range of their artistic and intellectual abilities but will also become more truly individual. Man is therefore both social and individual, with physical and mental needs. According to Bakunin, "well-rounded living persons must develop muscular and mental activities equally and these activities, far from harming each other (...) will reinforce each other" (Graham 2017, p. 221). The willfulness of children is just as acceptable as their thirst for knowledge. In addition to focusing on the latter, it is of the greatest importance to develop the natural resource of the will. "Unless the child acquires a sense of self, he fails to learn the most important lesson of all" (Guérin 2005, p. 19).

There exists a link between the disordered state of modern civilization and the dominating authoritarian educational system in schools and universities. Reclus attacks the existing system of education as a process of preparing children to fit well into institutions based on egoism, domination and unthinking obedience. If the pedagogical system is focused merely on pumping information into the children's heads, then that is not real education. "Through its hierarchical structure this system teaches competition for personal advantage rather than cooperation in pursuit of the general good" (Clark and Martin 2013, p. 95). From the first day at a university, the students learn (unfortunately) that they are rivals and combatants.

According to anarchist philosophy, the development of integrative pedagogy will open up a far wider comprehension of the phenomena of life. Bakunin was convinced that education in the future will have a natural spontaneity. The system of freedom "is characterized by risk throughout the entire learning period" (Graham 2017, p. 233). In harmony with this understanding, Reclus' conception of education focuses on the ideal of the free self-realization of the child. He argues against the use of any controlling methods.

Anarchist educational theory aims at encouraging people to think and act for themselves and not rely on others simply because they happen to be in authority. Critical judgement and creative imagination are of great importance. Education should focus on the needs of the poorest sectors of society, according to Kropotkin. Education should empower the poor and the uneducated, "thereby providing them with the tools to interpret and reconstruct the world about them in their image, rather than that of their rulers" (Mac Laughlin 2016, p. 156). Reclus argued that the primary goal of education is to inspire the individual to develop in harmony with their own nature. The learning methods should combine intellectual and practical activities. Tolstoy advocated the same education for men and women (Marshall 2008, p. 367).

Kropotkin argued that enlightenment is a combination of theory and practice. This pedagogy initiates society's goal to synthesize intellectual and manual labour. Just as a system of open-minded education is necessary "to create a community of free, compassionate, and co-operative human beings, a system of authoritarian education is essential to the production of a hierarchical society of dominant and submissive individuals" (Clark and Martin 2013, p. 95). The chief aim of education is not to make a specialist from a beginner, but

> To teach him the elements of knowledge and the good methods of work, and above all, to give him the general inspiration which will induce him, later on, to put in whatever he does a sincere longing for truth, to like what is beautiful, both as form and contents, to feel the necessity of being a useful unit amidst other human units, and thus to feel his heart at unison with the rest of humanity.
>
> (Marshall 2008, p. 331)

The vast majority of human individuals are not identical, but they are equivalent and hence equal. In communitarian anarchist pedagogy, the development of uniqueness and social consciousness of the individual are both involved. Thanks to the fact that humans are different, they will complement each other in humanity as a whole. As a result, Bakunin asserts, "This infinite diversity of human individuals is the fundamental cause and the very basis of their solidarity" (Graham 2017, p. 222). For Kropotkin, the strength of anarchy lies precisely in that "it understands all human faculties and all passions, and ignores none" (Marshall 2008, p. 323).

Human individuals are guided in their actions by their own understanding. This would bear the impression of free action and reaction between themselves and the ethical conceptions of their surroundings. Man would then be enabled to obtain "the full development of all his faculties, intellectual, artistic and moral, without being hampered by overwork for the monopolists, or by the servility and inertia of mind of the great number" (Kropotkin 2002, p. 285).

Pedagogy and education, according to Freire, should inspire and drive collective transformative practice. Transformation depends on our ability to no longer see the current society as normal and natural, but "instead understand the world as emerging from historical and cultural processes that are open-ended" (Westoby and Dowling 2013, p. 27), open to questioning and able to be transformed. In order to move people into a new understanding of their world, they maintain that education should respect people and honour their knowledge.

Pacifism

According to Ritter, it is unlikely that individuals living in societies characterized by anarchist philosophy will cause harm because their close interdependence and the equality of power, prestige and wealth discourage them from doing harm. "The sincerity, respect, or benevolence that is anarchy's dominant social attitude" (Ritter 2010, p. 150) provide a context in which exercise of freedom based on procedural rationality is rather safe. Kropotkin's study of the evolution of human societies shows that

> The habits and customs of mutual aid, common defence, and the preservation of peace, which were established since the very first stages of human pre-historic times – and which alone made it possible for man, under very trying natural conditions, to survive in the struggle for existence.
>
> (Kropotkin 1908, p. 48)

Kropotkin was a spokesman for pacifism and cooperation, and he wanted to implement the ideas of anarchism through the establishment of voluntary associations, self-governing collectives, decentralized structures and local self-government. People will regulate their relationships by a combination of custom and free agreements. From this, a spontaneous natural community, one that is not dictated to by rulers, will develop. Anarchism is therefore referred to as social individualism. The anarchists claimed that the condition to ensure that people trust the laws and follow them was that the laws were developed by the people themselves. Kropotkin rejected the individual use of violence and wanted to build communities as free federations of small producer and consumer groups where both production funds and consumables were commonplace. The key in anarchism is the greatest possible freedom for the individual in responsible interaction within collaborative networks. Anarchism is based on, and appeals to, people's potential for independent thinking, co-determination, and co-responsibility. Kropotkin claims that cooperation is rooted in

> One instinct that has been slowly developed among animals and men in the course of an extremely long evolution, and which taught animals and men alike the force they can borrow from the practice of mutual aid and support, and the joys they can find in social life.
>
> (Kropotkin 2014, p. 8)

Most anarchists argue in the following way:

> You cannot use violence against individuals as the principal means to bring about a peaceful society (...) you cannot use coercion to bring about a free society. You cannot force others to be free.
>
> (Marshall 2008, p. 696)

To realize a free society, anarchists agree that pacifism anchored in decentralized processes that promote peace is a necessary precondition. Pacifism is in accordance with anarchist philosophy because violence is authoritarian and coercive. As a logical consequence, Tolstoy maintained that anarchy could not be instituted by revolution because violence is used to force people against their own will to do the will of others. Therefore, "as long as any violence, designed to compel people to do the will of others, exists, there will be slavery" (Tolstoy, in Graham 2017, p. 157). One needs a strong anarchic consciousness in the population, but it is not always enough. In many ways, anarchism is a strong moral ideology, which implies self-discipline and solidarity because of the rejection of external authorities. According to Bookchin, peace and order are great ideals and deserve to be realized, but under one condition: "that this peace is not that of the grave" (Clark and Martin 2013, p. 143).

Violence is used to protect the privileged position against the exploited masses. In other words violence is connected to the hierarchical structure of society. Use of non-violent action could be necessary to make fundamental changes in society. Ward maintains that pacifist anarchism follows from the anti-militarism that accompanies rejection of the State and from "the conviction that any morally viable human society depends upon the uncoerced goodwill of its members" (Ward 2004, p. 3).

Anarchist pacifism is connected to both religious and philosophical positions, such as Taoism, Christian pacifism (Tolstoy), and Buddhist pacifism (Gandhi). In addition, Rudolf Steiner's anthroposophical philosophy is often mentioned as a source of inspiration in anarchist pacifism.

Taoism

Like most anarchists, the Taoists in China argued that all people could live in natural and spontaneous harmony with nature without interference from a dominant government. The Taoist perception of nature is based on the ancient Chinese principles of Yin and Yang, "two opposite but complementary forces of the cosmos which constitute ch'i of which all beings and matter are formed" (Marshall 2008, p. 54). Yin is the feminine power; Yang is the masculine power. Energy flows between Yin and Yang all the time. Both forces are at work within men and women as well as in all things. The tension between them leads to a dialectical process where everything changes and nothing is constant. The spontaneous order of society involves a dynamic interplay of opposite forces. The course in which things happen cannot be ruled by interference from outside, as human beings and society flourish best when allowed to follow their own nature. Taoists reject all forms of imposed authority, government and state, and argue that disorder will follow if "a ruler interferes with his people rather than letting them follow their own devices" (Marshall 2008, p. 56). The ideal is a free and cooperative society in harmony with nature, without a dominant state.

Christianity

In order to bring about a free and just society, Tolstoy completely opposed the use of physical force. He clearly understood that "it is impossible to use violent means to bring about peaceful ends" (Marshall 2008, p. 377). Tolstoy is of special interest when it comes to spirituality and anarchism, as he combined Christianity, pacifism and anarchism. He suggests anarchism as the only rational solution to "the poverty, the hunger, the political repression and the ecological degradation that constitutes the present world order" (Morris 1999). Tolstoy was a major influence on Gandhi's philosophy of non-violence and pacifism. "Gandhi developed Tolstoy's doctrine of non-resistance into a highly effective weapon in the campaign to oust the British imperial presence (in India)" (Marshall 2008, p. 382).

Buddhism

Reclus was inspired by the Buddhist appeal to direct experience and the teachings of non-attachment and compassion. Reclus refers to the message in Buddhism arguing against the hierarchical structure of society and proclaiming that society should be constituted by "brothers comrades, and companions who work together!" (Clark and Martin 2013, p. 41). Buddhist philosophy shares the idea of a free, international, and classless world with Taoism and anarchism.

Important presuppositions for movement in that direction include cultural and economic development. This includes the use of means such as civil disobedience, criticism, peaceful protest, pacifism, and frugality. Though Gandhi was a Hindu, he proclaimed himself a Buddhist, saying that Buddhism was rooted in Hinduism and represented its essence. "He saw Buddhism as cleansed Hinduism" (Bala-chandran 2006). In the following reflections I connect Gandhi to Buddhist philosophy, well aware that he was a Hindu.

According to Dr. Dhawan, "Gandhi was a philosophical anarchist because he believed that the greatest good for all can be realized only in the classless, stateless democracy" (Fatal 2006). Everyone rules themselves in such a manner that they are never a hindrance to their neighbours. Gandhi argued that the principle of swaraj ultimately leads to a grassroots, bottom-up, oceanic circle of self-ruling communities (Fatal 2006). Change is based on progressively replacing the hierarchical state with a growing sphere of decentralized organizations and villages. The common focus in anarchism and Gandhism is "on replacing the centralized nation-state with a decentra-lized society consisting of free, self-managed communities working together through voluntary cooperation" (Clark 2013, p. 222). He aimed to create self-disciplined freedom without hierarchical domination. Gandhi's non-vio-lent ideology was inspired by a variety of anarchist sources.

> From Tolstoy he evolved his policy of non-violent resistance, from Thoreau he took his philosophy of civil disobedience, and from a close reading of Kropotkin his programme of decentralized and autonomous village communes linking agriculture with local industry.
>
> (Ward 2004, p. 12)

Gandhi was inspired by Kropotkin and Tolstoy when he designed his strategy of non-violence as the ideal for decentralized communities built by self-governing society. Buddhism, (...) has, in common with Taoism, a strong libertarian spirit. "Both reject hierarchy and domination" (Marshall 2008, p. 65). Clark points out that Gandhi put into practice such anarchist values as "radical decentralism, antistatism, local participatory democracy, economic self-management" (Clark 2013, p. 25), and focus on the central position of individual transformation and "base organization in the process of social revolution" (Clark 2013, p. 25). Based on these principles Gandhi argued that economy should initiate local forms of production anchored in participatory cooperation. Changes were to be brought about by passive resistance and civil disobedience.

Anthroposophy

The core of anthroposophy is thoroughly anarchistic. The essence of anthro-posophy has anarchistic elements. Steiner provides the basis for a spiritual-philosophical anarchism in his 1894 work, *The Philosophy of Freedom*. In addition to anarchism, anthroposophy is connected to esoteric Christianity and to Buddhism. It is worth noting that Steiner's anarchistic tendencies articulate through his clear pointing out that he himself would not be considered an authority, just a supervisor. He maintained that in our day the tendency to surrender to authorities of all kinds represents a serious obstacle to the development of freedom. Together with anarchists, Steiner pointed out liberty, equality and fraternity as the dominant values in his theory of the threefold society. In addition he talked about cooperative decentralized associations as the basic part of the economy. Steiner claimed that everyone could develop their inherent abilities if the prerequisites for free action were present. To develop the "free spirit", Steiner argued that each had to free himself from both inner and outer tyranny. So, along with Bakunin, Proudhon, Kropotkin and Tolstoy, Steiner is also very relevant to anarchistic thinking. Both Steiner and Kropotkin argued that the aim is to organize society through voluntary associations of individuals. Steiner maintained, just as the anarchists, that modern competition-based societal development leads to chaos and that a human society can only be built on decentralized voluntary associations and autonomous entities, following the basic principle of anarchism that nobody may decide for others.

Change

According to Reclus, a free, cooperative society can only emerge out of a social revolution, but "this revolution will itself depend on a long history of liberatory thought and practice" (Clark and Martin 2013, p. 54). There are many spheres of thought and action where anarchist philosophy can contribute to social progress. No matter what, the long journey towards an anarchist society requires a first step in the right direction. In a communitarian anarchist perspective, the process of change is self-transformative.

On the one hand, the best way to bring about change is to convince people of the benefits of a decentralized society operating without hierarchical power structures. We will have a free society when there are enough people who want to be free. To impose anarchism on a society by force is against the idea of anarchism. Reclus discussed the idea that social emancipation requires forms of communication that are free from domination, and it is necessary to destroy "the boundaries between castes, as well as between peoples, so that humanity will finally be able to draw on the experience of all cultures and all individuals in formulating its goals and values" (Clark and Martin 2013, p. 47).

On the other hand, it is often said that the best incitement for radical change is a massive social or ecological catastrophe that will create the conditions for extraordinary action anchored in mutual aid, solidarity and communal cooperation. Such an accident brings about an acceptance of drastic solutions that will change the course of development. Clark demonstrates that "a moment of crisis and catastrophe can help give rise new forms of liberatory struggle and grassroots community organization" (Clark 2013, p. 25).

Reclus had a balanced view of the relationship between evolution and revolution. All phenomena have "positive and negative moments and both progressive and regressive purposes" (Clark and Martin 2013, p. 55). The first step should be the creation of small communities based on solidarity and freedom. A successful break with the system can only be achieved through "diligent collective work of self-transformation and at times the development of special skills that can contribute to that transformation" (Clark 2013, p. 230).

Kropotkin himself would have claimed that his major contribution to anarchism was the application of scientific principles to practical problems. "But his real contribution was the humanization of anarchism, the constant relating of theory to details of actual living, which gave the doctrine a concreteness and a relevance to everyday living" (Mac Laughlin 2016, p. 241). Kropotkin argued that the organic worldview was the context for interpreting everything from pedagogy to economy. Another important contribution to anarchist philosophy was his endeavour to demonstrate that "anarchism represents existing tendencies in society towards political liberty and economic equality" (Mac Laughlin 2016, p. 242), e.g., freedom, equality, solidarity, social justice, free contract, free initiative, antimilitarism, internationalism, decentralization and self-management. There will be no real anarchism without sufficiently integrating ecology and no real ecology without anarchism in a social perspective. Anarchists want to increase intrinsic functioning and diminish extrinsic power. The challenge is to develop a decentralized society based on humanistic technology and face-to-face democracy.

Concluding remarks

Anarchism differs from liberalism and Marxism by explicitly connecting to evolutionary theory. Kropotkin and Reclus argue that the whole of nature is characterized by cooperation in decentralized networks. They transfer this principle to human societies and, specifically, to economy. Nature functions as self-organizing systems without any dictates from outside. According to anarchism, local societies will function optimally if all people are empowered to participate in the development of communities. Freedom in solidarity is the foundation of communitarian anarchism. Human beings are a product of the society and are, at the same time, capable of changing it. Freedom is a prerequisite for harmony between people and between humans and nature. Anarchist pedagogy gives priority to the development of individuality and self-realization of the pupil or student. Critical judgement and creativity are abilities that should be stimulated. Freire (2001) argued that education is an important factor in social change processes. In the transforming process of society, violence is prohibited. One reason is that violence means use of power, which is against the principle of freedom. To establish living communities, Gandhi recommended one specific action – to be the change you want to see, "in other words an emphasis on personal life and self-transformation" (Clark 2013, p. 163).

7 Anarchism and the good society

Introduction

According to Levitas, the problem of the future is political: "we need to imagine sustainable prosperity, in a way that re-imagines what it means to prosper and thrive and which enables us to envisage a society in which that will become possible" (Levitas 2017, p. 13). The fundamental challenge for society is, according to Reclus, "to discover and develop fully every area in which humanity has progressed, while at the same time uncovering and negating every tendency toward regression" (Clark and Martin 2013, p. 39). Modern society is superior in complexity but it also leads to a global monoculture that is established by the global capitalist economic order.

In the following paragraphs I describe and discuss how society and economy could be organized based on anarchist principles such as associations, communes and mutualism. Anarchism's worldview is organic and assumes wholeness and interconnectedness. In today's society, where the mechanistic worldview dominates, atomistic competition is more prominent. Referring to anarchist philosophy, the roots of the ecological crisis are situated in an economic system anchored in mechanism and a political platform based on centralized hierarchic structures. The case for anarchism rests on the assumption that the right kind of society is like a self-regulating organic being. In keeping with his holistic view of nature, Kropotkin demonstrated that "the organic world of plants and animals, and the 'inorganic' physical universe, were all subject to the same organizing principles" (Mac Laughlin 2016, p. 169).

By referring to his own empirical findings that a feeling of solidarity characterizes all animals living in societies, Kropotkin argued that well-being in harmonic societies depends on our ability to establish systems based on cooperative, decentralized, nested networks. He described anarchy as organized living societies where the society thinks, talks and behaves "like an organism". Social anarchism was developed by Proudhon and Bakunin. They called their interpretation of anarchism collectivist. Proudhon defined the society (or commune) as a sovereign being. Because of that it has the right to "govern and administer itself". In the future society, there will be a dual structure: "economic in the form of a federation of self-managing workers' associations; administrative, in the form of a federation of the communes" (Guérin 1970, p. 63). The conception of community advanced by anarchists is every bit as varied as their conceptions of individuality. For Godwin, the model of community is dialogic relations; for Proudhon and Bakunin it is productive enterprise.

Kropotkin "bent the doctrine in a more rigidly utopian and optimistic direction" (Guérin 1970, p. 4). His model of a community includes more than productive enterprises and embraces every kind of cooperative association. By bringing more activities and emotions into anarchism, Kropotkin enlarged the anarchist conception of community. Every human being is aware of the others; awareness is reciprocal because everybody understands their fellow beings as they understand themselves. Even if it is impossible to claim that anarchists seek a particular form of community, they share a common belief that "community involves reciprocal awareness" (Ritter 2010, p. 27) and that such awareness can be their common goal. Development of the self as a combination of individuality, community and freedom is the goal of anarchism.

A new form of economic organization will necessarily require a different form of political structure. And, whether the change be accomplished "suddenly, by a revolution, or slowly by the way of gradual evolution, the two changes, political and economic, must go on abreast, hand in hand" (Kropotkin 2002, s. 181). Kropotkin argued that since these changes lead to a more decentralized structure and are closer to daily life, it is self-evident that they will be more popular than "a system based on hierarchical power structures" (Kropotkin 2002, s. 184). No wonder that anarchism has always been regarded as the ultimate evil by people with power (Chomsky 2013, p. 29).

Snyder supported any cultural and economic revolution that moves clearly towards a free, international, classless world by using means such as "civil obedience, outspoken criticism, protest, pacifism, voluntary poverty and even gentle violence if it comes to a matter of restraining some impetuous redneck" (Snyder 1961). It indicates a deep change concerning different aspects including schooling, religion, crime and punishment, technology, political organization, ownership, money, patriarchy and environmental concerns.

According to Feyerabend, the hallmark of political anarchism is its opposition to the established order of things: "to the state, its institutions, the ideologies that support and glorify these institutions" (Feyerabend 1975, p. 187). The discrepancy between actuality (ideology) and potentiality (utopia) generates energy and direction in change processes.

Communes and associations

Proudhon maintained that society should be organized through decentralized networks of associations. A precondition and consequence of introducing associations based on self-management is education for all. Associative organization is a guarantee for equality and fairness, diversity and dialogue. According to Guérin, the most vital task for free associations is to educate the members. "It is more important to create a 'fund of men' than to form a 'mass of capital'" (Guérin 1970, p. 48). The argument goes both ways, as associations depend on education and associations are learning arenas. Reconciliation and community are impossible within a society characterized by great inequality. If structural inequalities exist in a society, the application of the law is likely to be unequal: "one law for the rich, and another for the poor" (Marshall 2008, p. 48).

Without real equality, the sense of justice can never be universally developed, because justice implies the recognition of equality; while in a society in which the principles of justice would not be contradicted at every step by the existing inequalities of rights and possibilities of development, they would be bound to spread and become a way of life. In such a case the individual would be free, in the sense that his freedom would not be limited any more "by the fear of a social or a mystical punishment, or by obedience" (Kropotkin 2002, s. 167). Kropotkin argued that associations should be "free, temporary, and convoked to address a specific need, intended to prevent the sedimentation of particular interests" (Adams 2015, p. 147). Stirner argued that "the human association is only fruitful if it does not crush the individual but, on the contrary, develops initiative and creative energy" (Guérin 1970, p. 30).

From his natural science perspective, Kropotkin believed he could show that cooperation is more natural than competition. "The fittest in the organic world are those who grow accustomed to life in society; and life in society necessarily implies moral habits" (Kropotkin 2002, p. 74). He draws a distinction between "first nature", which is nature as the result of biological evolution, and "second nature", which is society as a result of social evolution. "We must recover the continuum between our 'first nature' and our 'second nature', our natural world and our social world, our biological being and our rationality" (Marshall 2008, p. 612). The idea is that we have to transcend the two natures into a new domain of "free nature".

Organization without compulsion, based on free agreement and voluntary cooperation, is the only cure for authority. Cooperative communities and self-managed worker organizations could well foster such relationships. Buber argued that the communitarian movement would achieve its goals by establishing "a large number of diverse, fully co-operative communities based on the land, and which would federate with one another to create a new organic whole" (Clark 2013, p. 158). A free society can only be an organic community of communities regulated through a participatory, decentralized form of communitarian anarchism. The forms of self-organization change with time and place.

He found that cooperation between farmers in villages was linked to good production results. The most important finding was that cooperation was more developed the further away from the central authorities the villages were located. Kropotkin drew the conclusion that "small-scale human societies based on the ecology of the regions" (Ward 2004, p. 87) were better than bigger units. Kropotkin also discussed the role of scientific innovations and modern technology in the decentralization of industrial and agricultural production at a whole variety of levels. He examined the possibility of "using scientific techniques and new technologies to recreate the traditional organic links between town and country and between intellectual and manual labour" (Mac Laughlin 2016, p. 223).

So, in the anarchist society the existing contradictions between town and country, work and play, industrial work and rural work, mind and body, individual and society, humanity and nature are eliminated. This has the potential to reduce the disparities between the metropolis and the periphery, "thereby fostering the development of small units responsible for their own development, and responsive to local needs and traditions" (Mac Laughlin 2016, p. 233). Consequently, cooperative organization is only a step towards "the co-operative building of life as a whole" (Buber 1996, p. 64). This process would realize the ideal of a complete person while social life would fall into a well-balanced, harmonious whole. A mixed economy based on cooperation and mutual aid, decentralization of agriculture and industry, were considered favourable to production efficiency, to personal development and to environmental and social effects. The cooperation between different groups and institutions is a prerequisite for the society to be called a community. If the communes expand freely, their frontiers would soon interweave, "criss-cross and overlap, thereby forming a compact one and indivisible network" (Guérin 2005, p. 309).

The picture of power and struggle that emerges in the anarchist perspective is one of the intersecting networks of power rather than of a hierarchy. Anarchist struggle is conceived not in terms of substituting new and better hierarchies for the old ones but "in terms of getting rid of hierarchic thinking and action altogether" (May 1994, p. 51). May refers to the contemporary anarchist Colin Ward, who maintains that

> We have built networks of pyramids. All authoritarian institutions are organized as pyramids: the state, the private or public corporations, the army, the police, the church, the university, the hospital: they are all pyramidal structures with a small group of decision-makers at the top and a broad base of people whose decisions are *made for them* at the bottom. Anarchism does not demand the changing of labels on the layers, it does not want different people on top, it wants us to clamber out from underneath.
>
> (May 1994, p. 51)

Kropotkin maintains that society is a natural phenomenon existing prior to the appearance of man, and "man is naturally adapted to live in societies without artificial regulations" (Marshall 2008, p. 319). Therefore, man must enter into relationships with other individuals, but a characteristic of these relationships is that there is no authority between the individuals. No one may or may not decide for others. It is possible to distinguish four principles which characterize the anarchist theory of organizations: they should be voluntary, functional, temporary and small (Ward 2004). The free contract replaces law and "if there are disputes, these are judged by arbitration panels within the groups where the dispute originate" (Guérin 2005, p. 235).

In an association, individuals are free and live as individualists because the association does not "own" the individual; on the contrary the individual owns it. "Society makes use of you, but it is you that makes use of association" (Guérin 2005, p. 26). These associations should be models for agriculture, industry and trade. This sort of association becomes a factor of decentralization, "for no longer is it a matter of founding within each country a center common to all industries, but each one of them will be centered upon the loyalty where it is most developed" (Guérin 2005, p. 218). Associations imply a sacrifice of freedom for the common good. The associations band together primarily to assure one another

> Of the use of instruments of labor in the possession of each property of the corporative federation as a whole; furthermore, by federating one with another, the groups are empowered to exercise a constant watching brief of production, and, as a result, to add to or subtract from the intensity thereof, in reflection of the needs manifested by society as a whole.
>
> (Guérin 2005, p. 264)

An anarchist society would be composed of networks of voluntary associations of equal individuals which include both consumers and producers. When all branches of production are organized along such lines, they represent interwoven networks "composed of an infinite variety of groups and federations of all sizes and degrees, local, regional, national and international, temporary or more or less permanent for all possible purposes" (Marshall 2008, p 326). Such associations make it possible to determine, in a rational way, "the number of hours in the normal working day, the cost price of products and their exchange value, as well as how many of these products have to be made in order to meet consumer demands" (Guérin 2005, p. 265).

Voluntary associations, which are already beginning to cover all fields of human activity, would hold a still greater role so as to substitute themselves for the State and all its functions. They would represent interwoven networks, composed of infinite varieties of groups and federations of all sizes and degrees, local, regional, national and international, temporary or more or less permanent, for all possible purposes: "production, consumption and exchange, communications, sanitary arrangements, education, mutual protection, defense of the territory, and so on; and on the other side, for the satisfaction of an ever-increasing number of scientific, artistic, literary and social needs" (Kropotkin 2002, p. 284).

For Proudhon, federalism had to be achieved by building a new society from the ground up instead of destroying the existing social arrangements. Federalism was for Proudhon connected to mutualism, "the common project of forming a society without private property" (May 1994, p. 58). Bakunin thought the first step to undermine private property was the elimination of the right of inheritance.

The anarchist society should be a federative society built by small, self-governing entities, the management of which is chosen by the members. Everyone is obliged to take part in education and to take responsibility. The small entities are characterized by short distances between the leaders and people and thus have the advantage that the individuals easily see the consequences of their actions. The ideal community should be highly decentralized, with the self-governing small village as the main unit. True progress lies in the direction of decentralization, both territorial and functional, in the development of the spirit of local and personal initiatives, and of free federation from the simple to the compound, in lieu of the present hierarchy from the center to the periphery (Kropotkin 2002, p. 286). Kropotkin had confidence in the creativity and virtue of people living in simple societies. Indeed, he inferred from his study of nature and human history the permanent presence of a double tendency: on the one side, towards a greater development of sociality and, on the other side, a consequent increase in the intensity of life, which results in progress – physically, intellectually, and morally.

Anarchism describes society as a living organism based on voluntary agreements between different groups to ensure that economics and society work in a harmonious interaction without external authorities. The State is thus perceived as an obstacle to human organization. A modern global company does not distinguish itself from a state in any way worth mentioning, either in terms of its structure, its essence, its goals, or its working methods. A decentralized leaderless network of self-governing and autonomous communes is essential to counter the dominating hierarchical power structures in modern society. The more we decentralize, the more we use methods on a higher moral level. Decentralization is good for both individuals and the cultural life of the society. With their principles of decentralization, anarchists encourage an organic grouping of people, based on cultural and natural criteria. They accept "the validity of bioregions, living areas shaped by natural boundaries like watersheds rather than by the bureaucrat's ruler on a map" (Marshall 2008, p. 646).

The village commune, as the nucleus of the evolving society, has to exert a powerful pull on the people dedicated to this evolution and to exercise a formative structural effect on social periphery. "The dynamics of history determined the dynamic character of the relations between Village Commune and society" (Buber 1996, p. 143). A real community need not consist of people who are perpetually together, but it must consist of people who have a readiness for one another. The internal questions of a community are thus, in reality, questions relating to its own genuineness, "hence to its inner strength and stability" (Buber 1996, p. 145).

Economy

Because communes and associations are self-organizing systems, it is impossible in principle to predict what the economy in an anarchist society would look like – it is up to free people to decide, so we can only indicate some possible broad outlines. But, given some common aims, an anarchist economy will be based on free voluntary participation of people who create solutions within networks with limited hierarchical structures. The main goal is to ensure production in accordance with what people want to consume, i.e., commodities of utility and beauty. There will be different forms of cooperative economics existing side by side. It requires that producers agree to exchange products and services on terms that are not merely "equitable or fair but supportive of each other" (Clark 2013, p. 280).

For the economic era that is coming, we must seek a new form of political organization closer to self-government. According to Kropotkin, anarchism has come to the conclusion that the root of the problems with the existing economy is not that the capitalist takes the profits or the surplus value, but in the possibility of taking these profits, which accrue "because millions of people have literally nothing to subsist upon without selling their labor-power at a price which makes profits and the creation of 'surplus value' possible" (Kropotkin 1908, p. 93). Kropotkin imagined a community allowing free use of products on the condition that "you consecrate four of five hours a day to some work recognized as necessary" (Adams 2015, p. 159). For Kropotkin, the anarchist society was the next step in the natural progression towards increased freedom and equality. Anarchism understands that providing food, clothing and shelter for all is the most vital concern of political economy. Each member of the community should receive a sufficient and equal supply of life's necessities. The goal is to give the necessities of life freely.

Proudhon had an ambivalent idea of property. On the one hand, he argued that property is a source of injustice and exploitation, and, on the other hand, he pointed out that property was a guarantee of the independence of the individual. Only those things that are for personal use should be private property. The solution was a combination of property and community. The means of production and exchange must be controlled by the associations of workers, and not by either the capitalists or the State. Proudhon distinguished between possession and ownership. "Ownership is absolute, aristocratic, feudal; possession is democratic, republican, egalitarian: it consists of the enjoyment of an usufruct which can nether be alienated, nor given away, nor sold" (Guérin 1970, p. 48).

> Self-management contains the seeds of the full economic emancipation of the working masses, but these seeds can only germinate and grow when capital itself, industrial establishments, raw materials, and capital equipment (...) become the collective property of workers associations for both agricultural and industrial production, and these are freely organized and federated among themselves.
>
> (Guérin 1970, p. 56)

In such organizations the workers become their own employers. Only by "producing and consuming without counting each individual's contribution and by proclaiming the right of all to wealth – whatever share they may have taken in producing it" (Ritter 2010, p. 81) – can the anarchist society become a reality. Because anarchists choose need over productive contribution, people with extraordinary talents will receive less material advantage than in other societies. It is interesting to notice that luxury is not prohibited in anarchism. According to Kropotkin, a person wanting luxury products has to cooperate with others in producing the commodities themselves. This cooperative method of producing luxuries is seen by Kropotkin "as fostering individuality by enabling each producer to acquire diverse tastes and skills and as fostering community by enabling those who share these tastes and skills to cultivate them in concert" (Ritter 2010, p. 85).

Proudhon argued for what is understood as an inversion of human ideas: property is theft, meaning it results from the exploitation of the weak by the strong. "Proprietor and thief were forever contradictory terms, just as the entities they describe are antipathetic; every language has articulated this contradiction in terms" (Proudhon in Guérin 2005, p. 48). His idea was to register a protest to highlight the immaturity of our institutions. "Property is theft" and "property is freedom" are two propositions that are equally demonstrable and co-exist, one alongside the other; "within the *System of Economic Contradictions*" (Proudhon in Guérin 2005, p. 55). Concerning all economic factors, including property, harm and cruelty cannot be disconnected from the good, any more than debit can be detached from asset in bookkeeping. They do necessarily depend on each other.

> I adopt the same approach with regard to each of the economic categories, the division of labor, competition, the State, credit, Community, etc.: demonstrating, turn and turnabout, how these concepts, and consequently, how the institutions deriving from them have a positive and a negative aspect, how they give rise to a double series of diametrically different outcomes: and in every case I concluded that what was required was agreement, conciliation or synthesis.
>
> (Proudhon in Guérin 2005, p. 55)

Mutualism

Mutualism is an anarchist school of economy, originally based on the ideas of Proudhon, where each person (individually or collectively) possesses the means of production. Mutualism is an economic system based on the idea that the value of a product should be equivalent to the amount of labour necessary to produce a similar article. Proudhon imagined a utopian society where each person possesses a means of production, individually or collectively. Mutualism supports labour-owned cooperative firms and associations. It is possible to imagine a broad spectrum of "self-managed enterprises, individual producers, and small partnerships that would enter into a growing co-operative economic sector that would incorporate social ecological values" (Clark 2013, p. 281).

According to Proudhon, "the working brotherhood is pledged to supply society with the goods and the services asked from it at prices as near as possible to the cost of production" (Proudhon in Guérin 1970, p. 52). Even if the anarchists are against laissez-faire competition, they are open to a higher principle of competition in the spirit of solidarity. Competition should protect individual initiative and bring wealth back to the society.

Buber is referring to Proudhon when he argues that in mutuality, reciprocity exists when all workers in an industry work for one another and thus collaborate in the making of a common product whose profits they share amongst themselves instead of working for an entrepreneur who pays them and keeps their products.

> Extend the principle of reciprocity as uniting the work of every group, to the Workers' societies as units, and you have created a form of civilization which from all points of view – political, economic and aesthetic – is radically different from all earlier civilizations.
>
> (Buber 1996, pp. 29–30)

The mutual understanding among participants in anarchy is their desire

> To develop their native talents, the satisfaction they find in their voluntary, varied work, and their ability, owing to polytechnical education and occupational mobility, to understand the productive process as a whole are some of the reasons why it is unnecessary in an anarchy to distribute economic benefits according to claims of contribution, ability or effort.
>
> (Ritter 2010, p. 144)

Anarchist economy aims at satisfying the basic needs of all people, where the individuals have freedom to make decisions concerning both production and consumption. Mutualism results in a higher level of well-being than that brought about by struggle between competitors. When the distribution of wealth is based on self-determined needs, people are free to engage in whatever activities they wish. On the one hand, in contrast to a competitive market economy, in an anarchist economy the horizontal connections between the economic actors are based on cooperation instead of competition. On the other hand, in contrast to socialist economy, the vertical connections are based on bottom-up initiatives instead of top-down orders.

The ideal is an economic system in which land is common at the local level, and "the production is organized through direct democratic decision-making by all the members of the local community and administered by their elected delegates" (Clark 2013, p. 232). According to Suissa,

> *Mutualism* represents the basic anarchist insight that society should be organized not on the basis of a hierarchical, centralist, top-down structure such as the state, but on the basis of reciprocal voluntary agreements between individuals.
>
> (Suissa 2010, p. 11)

Anarchist economics is characterized by being "small-scale". According to Ward, this is not surprising, as industrial psychologists repeatedly report that satisfaction at work is directly related to the degree to which the workers are "free to make their own decisions" (Ward 2004, p. 49). Under the conditions of freedom, Humbolt argued,

> All peasants and craftsmen might be elevated into artists; that is, men who love their own labor for its own sake, improve it by their own plastic genius and inventive skill, and thereby cultivate their intellect, ennoble their character, and exalt and refine their pleasures.
>
> (Humbolt in Guérin 1970, p. xi)

Even if an anarchist economy rejects accounting in the individualist sense – that of reducing every exchange to a quantifiable number on a monetary scale – it may well be desirable in an anarchist economy to take account of exchanges in terms of their social and ecological values.

Kropotkin advocated a fundamental reorganization of production: each country should become as self-sufficient as possible. As a reaction against industrial agriculture, which is becoming more and more poisoned by the profit motive, anarchists recommend that we each grow some of our own food (Schneider in Chomsky 2013, p. xiii). Rather than concentrating large factories in cities, he called for economic as well as political decentralization, believing that diversity is the surest way to fully achieve development of production by mutual cooperation. Decentralizing industry, and combining industrial with agricultural work, would not only give people more choice in their work, but give them greater control of production and distribution. Another element of this idea is that "earnings, spending, savings and investments remain primarily in the local community" (Westoby and Dowling 2013, p. 104).

Reclus foresaw the global culture dominated by economic values. He remarked that the essential motive in that culture would be "the goal of commanding others by the means of the omnipotence of money" (Clark and Martin 2013, p. 84). But living in accordance with nature indicates that the basic unit of social life must itself become an eco-system or a diversified and balanced eco-community. The lifestyle is cultivated by a wide range of stimuli, by diverse activities and by a social scale that "always remains within the comprehension of a single human being" (Bookchin 2004, p. 9).

Kropotkin further advocates industrial decentralization, regional self-sufficiency, integration of town and country, and more intensive methods of food production (Marshall 2008, p. 327). The aim is to produce the greatest amount of goods necessary for the well-being of all and with the least possible waste of human energy. As man does not live in a solitary state, habits and feelings develop within him that are useful for the pre-servation of society and the propagation of the race. "Without social feelings and usages, life in common would have been absolutely impossible" (Kropotkin 2002, p. 203).

Anarchists are not negative to technology. It is only the "untrammelled technology that they deem virulent; appropriately controlled technology is for them a growing source of hope" (Ritter 2010, p. 84). Decentralization is important to ensure use of appropriate technology which people can iden-tify, understand and control. Appropriate technology should be accepted as suitable by the workers in a given situation. The possibility to use and develop individual capacities is essential for individual self-realization. Bookchin is an advocate of small-scale technology anchored in regional economic networks. The question is whether a future society is organized around technology or whether technology is organized around society.

If the local community is organized as a face-to-face democracy, it will take primacy over the State. On a general level, Reclus argues that capital-ism is based on a principle which allows one single person to allocate the product of the work of thousands of workers: "such a monstrous accumu-lation of wealth is always the result of defective social conditions" (Clark and Martin 2013, p. 126).

In reality each person is both a producer and a consumer observed from two different viewpoints. Proudhon asks, why should not the same be true of capitalist and labourer? And of labourer and artist? When we separate these qualities in the organization of the society, we inevitably create "castes, inequality and misery; amalgamate them (...) and in every indivi-dual you have equality" (Proudhon in Guérin 2005, p. 73). Liberty depends on equality, hence, there can be no liberty in a society where a minority operates a monopoly of the capital.

Many anarchists advocate a system based on horizontal relations between economic actors which effectively communicate information to help balance and connect production, distribution and consumption to the actual needs of individuals and society. In a utopian perspective, anarchists talk about free access to all kinds of commodities. In a society characterized by freedom, people will not take more than they need. There are many examples which clearly demonstrate that free access does not lead to abuse – amongst others, libraries and water. According to Eric Fromm (2013), consumption for the sake of consumption will take place in a capitalist society where people define themselves by what they have and not by who they are.

Trade is based on values anchored in equivalent amounts of labour. Proudhon reasoned that the exchange value of all merchandise could be measured by the amount of labour necessary to produce it. When a product is sold, it ought to receive a commodity that represents exactly the same amount of labour. Workers should be paid in work vouchers: "trading agencies or social shops were to be set up where they could buy commodities at retail prices calculated in hours work" (Guérin 1970, p. 49). Products should be exchanged at cost-value, by means of labour checks representing the hours of labour required to produce each given commodity. Under such a system, all exchanges of services would be strictly equivalent. Besides, such a bank would be able to lend money without interest, levying only something like one percent, or even less, to cover the cost of administration (Kropotkin 2002, p. 291).

Labour notes based on time used in production combined with banking based on free credit were implemented in the USA as early as 1827. Robert Owen's colony, New Harmony, turned against communism and in 1827 founded, in Cincinnati, a "store" in which goods were exchanged on the principle of time-value and labour checks. Such institutions remained in existence up until 1865 under the names of "equity stores", "equity village" and "house of equity" (Kropotkin 2002, s. 161).

The notes indicate how many hours of work they did, and the notes could be exchanged for commodities which took the same time to produce. Alternative currencies are limited to local societies or regions. They represent a solution to situations where there is a lot of work to be done but no (official) money available. Free banking is anchored in the idea that credit has a social function; it is not a means for private speculation.

Individuals, corporations and organizations can create alternative or local currency as an alternative to the dominant currency systems. Complementary currencies are used in combination with a dominating currency. In the new society, there will be no more commerce, at least not in the sense attached to that term today. Every commune will establish an exchange agency, the workings of which we are about to explain as clearly as possible. The exchange agency will issue producers with exchange vouchers to the value of their products: these exchange vouchers will be acceptable currency throughout the whole territory of the federation of communes (Guillaume in Guérin 2005, p. 255).

> Today, the bakery, butchery, wine trade and colonial produce trade are at the mercy of private industry and speculators, who, through all sorts of frauds, seek to enrich themselves at the consumer's expense. The new society will have to remedy this state of affairs immediately, and that remedy will consist of elevating to the status of communal public service anything having to do with distribution of essential foodstuffs.
> (Guillaume in Guérin 2005, p. 258)

Mutualism forbids individuals to receive income through loans, investments and rent, quite simply because this income is not based on work. Proudhon supports worker-owned cooperative firms and associations based on the workers' self-management. Cooperatives are associations run by the workers. According to Westoby and Dowling, cooperatives are one way of building local economies because they ensure both "member and/or worker control of the organization, and link business imperatives into the kind of broader ethic of co-operation and community-oriented values" (Westoby and Dowling 2013, p. 104). The idea of association is a new one in the world of economics. Associations are anchored in the principle of collective ownership as the economic basis of the organization of society, and "the principle of autonomy and federation, as the basis upon which human individuals and collectivities are banded together" (Proudhon in Guérin 2005, p. 233).

Bakunin agrees with Proudhon and points out that he was "convinced that cooperation in every branch of labor and science is going to be the prevailing form of social organization in the future" (Bakunin in Guérin 2005, p. 214). No society can prosper and develop freely unless its foundation is equality, "when all capital, all the instruments of labor, including the land, will have been handled back to labor as collective property" (Bakunin in Guérin 2005, p. 48).

Later, Steiner argued in the same way when he, in his anthroposophy, contended that an economy should be based on associative principles. Workers should organize themselves into free associations with equal conditions for all members. The people who work in different enterprises, either in production or distribution, should take part in all the processes in a democratic manner. In the associations, the workers are partners, all on an equal basis.

In an organic economy, everybody depends on each other, therefore, everybody has the same value, and in associations they are not "wage-slaves", as they are in hierarchical structures. Wage-slavery as a concept is used to criticize unbalanced bargaining power, where the workers are paid low wages and have no influence on their own working conditions. Wage-slaves have no control of their own activities, so wage-slavery should be abolished. Work, in the sense of doing necessary things in freedom, is of great importance, and it helps to increase the individual's self-esteem and well-being. Operations requiring cooperation between different specialties should be organized in associations that stimulate creativity and help people to express themselves. Production that could be performed by a single worker does not require associations.

A participatory economy (parecon) uses participatory decision-making to guide the production, consumption and allocation of resources in a society. In accordance with mutualism, the workers own the means of production and take part in all decisions in the associations. Self-management is essential as a means to empower people and develop their abilities. The challenge is to develop organizations that help people express individuality through self-management. The nature of the work has great influence on the societal character of the individual. Parecon is inspired by values such as equality, solidarity, diversity, and worker self-management.

According to Suissa,

> Federalism is basically a logical development from mutualism, referring as it does to social and economic organization between communities, as opposed to within communities. The idea is that the society of voluntarily organized communities should be coordinated by a network of councils.
>
> (Suissa 2010, p. 12)

There are no fixed roles, as the workers organize themselves, and income is distributed equally among all workers in the productive unit. The values of all the commodities are measured by the amount of labour necessary to produce them; all exchanges between the producers are carried out through a national bank which accepts payment in labour checks; a clearing house would handle the daily balance of exchanges between the thousands of branches of this bank. The services exchanged by different people would thus be equivalent; the bank would be able to lend the labour checks' money without interest, and every association would be able to borrow it at a cost of only one percent to cover administration costs; capital would lose its pernicious power and could no longer be used as an instrument of exploitation (Kropotkin 2002, s. 160). Feyerabend argued that free associations, where everyone does what suits their talents best, would replace the petrified institutions of the day so that no function can be allowed to become fixed, and, he continues, referring to Bakunin, "the commander of yesterday can become a subordinate of tomorrow" (Feyerabend 1975, p. 187).

Russel argued that anarchism had an advantage concerning liberty and freedom. Technological developments have made it possible to work less and enjoy more leisure time. He reasoned that a "certain small income, sufficient for necessaries, should be secured to all, whether they work or not" (van Parijs and Vanderborght 2017, p. 78). This kind of basic income secures the freedom artists need to keep creativity alive, that same creativity which our sober, serious modern society tends to kill. Another possibility, according to anarchism, is that all the necessities of life are free, regardless of whether the recipient works or not.

The living community

Kropotkin saw history as a fluid process in which achievements could be lost at any time. "The organic commune spontaneously flowered to meet various social needs" (Adams 2015, p. 88), and at the same time the State developed, which embodied control, centralization and exploitation. To prevent the development of destructive tendencies, anarchist philosophy suggests the commune as a local decision unit consisting of autonomous institutions. The goal is to show that anarchism is able to create a society that gives the vital energy to meet both individual and collective needs. Kropotkin stressed that "anarchist communalism would not demand the dissolution of individuality in the sea of social conformity, but rather that such a society would provide the base for freethinking actors to emerge" (Adams 2015, p. 175).

Guérin points out that we no longer live in the age of small autonomous societies; we live in an era of federations. The federal system is the opposite of state centralization. All people should be united in federations of federations. The communes should be autonomous and characterized by solidarity among the people. Solidarity is inseparable from freedom. Buber argued that a free society is made up of a network of smaller communities in which freedom and solidarity are practiced in all aspects of life. An isolated commune could not survive a week without being "compelled by circumstance to establish consistent relations with industrial, commercial and artistic centers" (Guérin 2005, p. 308). The living community is always an open universality in which the contrast between the whole and its parts drives the development. The society is a society of societies created bottom-up. The classical anarchists fully acknowledged that the contradiction between town and country must be removed. The urban milieu consists of a complex whole integrating urban and rural entities. The culture of cities thus exemplifies "the concept of dialectical interrelationship between unity and diversity" (Clark and Martin 2013, p. 65). The commune is a generic term, symbolizing free combinations of equals with no borders.

> All the inhabited areas of western Europe are so intimately bound up one with another that isolation has become an impossibility for any of them: there is no village perched so high upon a mountain crest that it does not have its industrial and commercial center, toward which it gravitates, and with which it can no longer sever its connections.
>
> (Guérin 2005, p. 308)

There will be millions of communes that unite individuals locally, regionally and globally. Each city was "federated" with other small communities and sub-towns that were arranged around the mother city, each maintaining its own way of living and working, and resolutely defending its social and cultural independence (Mac Laughlin 2016, p. 230). Every village is a center of itself and the "center" has only a small authority over it. Each urban village within the city had its popular assembly, forum, tribunal, militia and the symbols of independent local authority. It is on the local level we find the locus of real democratic power. According to Bookchin, new integrated politics could be developed "in the village, town, city, or neighborhood" (Bookchin 2004, p. xxviii).

Reclus maintained that each city has its "unique individuality, its own life, its own countenance, tragic and sorrowful in some cases, joyful and lively in others" (Clark and Martin 2013, p. 65). Cities can be healthy organisms if they are expressions of the collective self-realization of all citizens. In the words of

Bookchin, "a community in which that social environment is decentralized into rounded, ecologically balanced communes" (Bookchin 2004, p. 7).

Decentralization and radically altered urban communities, not only rural villages, would effect social change. Because independence begins at the bottom, it follows that every village has to be self-sustained and capable of managing its own affairs. In such a structure composed of innumerable villages, there will be a free and voluntary play of mutual forces, ever-widening, ever-ascending circles.

It is a society based on voluntary work, on moral rather than material incentives (Marshall 2008, p. 329). Voluntary work has always been more productive than work stimulated by wages. Well-being, meaning the satisfaction of physical, artistic and moral needs, "has always been the most powerful stimulant to work" (Marshall 2008, p. 329).

Our society seems no longer able to understand that "it is possible to exist otherwise than under the reign of law, elaborated by a representative government and administered by a handful of rulers" (Kropotkin 2002, p. 197). Relatively speaking, law is a product of modern times. For ages and ages, mankind lived without any written law, even that graven in symbols upon the entrance stones of a temple. During that period, human relations were simply regulated by customs, habits and usages, made sacred by constant repetition, and acquired by each person in childhood, exactly as he learned how to obtain his food by hunting, cattle-rearing, and agriculture (Kropotkin 2002, p. 201).

Anarchists conceive a society in which all mutual relations of its members are regulated, not by laws, nor by authorities, whether self-imposed or elected, but

> By mutual agreements between the members of that society and by a sum of social customs and habits – not petrified by law, routine, or superstition, but continually developing and continually readjusted in accordance with the ever growing requirements of a free life stimulated by the progress of science, invention and the steady growth of higher ideals, in a continual evolution.
>
> (Kropotkin 2002, s. 157)

In these formulations, there is an echo of the overarching ontology that development is a product of multiple individual and communal actions. Harmony is obtained, not by submission to law, or by obedience to any authority, but by "free agreements concluded between the various groups, territorial and professional, freely constituted for the sake of production and consumption, as also for the satisfaction of the infinite variety of needs and aspirations of a civilized being" (Kropotkin 2002, p. 284). If people are given the opportunity to have experiences without interference from magistrates or theoretically profound leaders, they are by nature good and reasonable enough to organize societies without inequality, oppression and war.

Local public services would go to the communes to be run under the direction of the local administrative body itself, nominated by the trade unions. Public services on a larger scale would be managed by regional administration consisting of nominees of the federation of communes (...) while those on a national scale would come under the (...) combination of free workers communes.

(Guérin 1970, p. 62)

The anarchist society was to be built within the existing system, as the collective associations gradually tore the bottom from under the old power structures. If that will happen, it remains to be seen. An anarchist community is based on a synthesis of cooperative production, cooperative consumption and cooperative living. Cooperation weaves the commune into a pattern, which builds unity. This kind of organic unity counteracts tendencies to disintegration, splitting up and conflict. The anarchist goal is "a society of strongly separate persons who are strongly bound together in a group" (Ritter 2010, p. 3).

Concluding remarks

The anarchists asked the following question: "What forms of social life assure to a given society, and then to mankind generally, the greatest amount of happiness, and hence also vitality?" (Kropotkin 1909, p. 58). The answer they suggest is to organize society and economy in order to facilitate freedom and solidarity. To be free in this perspective is to realize individual freedom in company with others. The problem in the existing system is that the hierarchical system could eliminate the potential for solidarity and develop egoistic and selfish individuals. Bakunin argued that freedom without solidarity is just as negative as solidarity without freedom. A society anchored in individual freedom must give priority to associative diversity. Moral responsibility is impossible without moral autonomy.

Kropotkin and Reclus based their anarchist philosophy on evolutionary ecology, where human beings are integrated parts of nature. Their image of man indicates that the whole person – not only as a consumer or producer, but the unique individual – is integrated in the eco-systems and social systems. One of the most fundamental principles in nature is cooperation in decentralized networks. Learning from nature, anarchists describe society and economy as decentralized cooperative networks. Instead of authoritarian hierarchies, the society and the economy should be organized as self-organizing systems, anchored in knowledge of local culture and nature.

Godwin was the first to articulate the idea of replacing the hierarchical state with local, participatory institutions. The workers ought to be the real managers of industries. Organic networks of small communes should replace the dominating state as political principle. Agriculture and industry would co-exist together in free communities. Instead of an atomistic competitive economy based on growth, anarchists talk about small-scale economy integrated in local networks.

Mutualism is the anarchist school of economy, saying that the value of a product is identical to the amount of labour necessary to produce a similar article. The participative anarchist economy is characterized by labour-owned cooperative businesses, and participative associations. A fundamental value is that all humans have a right to satisfy all their basic needs: food, clothing and shelter for everybody. This includes construction of new homes containing healthy, spacious and comfortable lodgings. This is one of the prime tasks of the liberated society. In addition, accommodations should be free of charge.

In summary, an anarchist society and economy is characterized by the following: Anarchism is based on an organic worldview and describes evolutionary development as a dialectic process where evolution and revolution follow one another. Societies develop within nature and have to be in harmony with ecological principles. Since we cannot revolt against nature, we have to learn from nature. Communitarian anarchists discuss "the good life in the good society". Eco-communitarianism goes one step further and adds "... in a sustainable nature".

The living society could be briefly described as a web of integrated parts. Local societies are interconnected through different kinds of associations and other arenas for communicative dialogues. Figure 7.1 indicates how communes and associations are integrated in societies with high resilience.

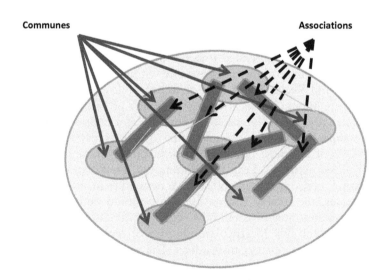

Figure 7.1 The living society – communes and associations

Inspired by nature's eco-systems, the societies should be organized as decentralized networks of smaller communes where hierarchies are minimized. Equity in diversity is a prerequisite for freedom. Political organization anchored in freedom, solidarity, and direct participation in democratic decision-making is a prerequisite for self-realization, individually and collectively. Self-realization includes positive freedom and satisfaction of scientific, artistic and moral needs. Human flourishing is also more dependent on the development of solidarity from inherent values and self-discipline than on regulations from outside.

The economy is organized as voluntary cooperative networks (associations) of small-scale businesses. The anarchists describe an integrated economy as a synthesis of cooperative production, consumption and living. Mutual aid and decentralized small entities, both in agriculture and industry, are central elements in anarchist economy. Local currency could encourage the development of local and regional economy.

In one sense, anarchism is utopian in that it imagines the world as it could be. But it is also realistic in that it conserves and develops ancient traditions of self-help and mutual aid, and profound libertarian tendencies within society. Above all, anarchism addresses itself to homo ludens (playful humanity), along with homo faber or homo sapiens (working or thinking humanity). If there is no joy, imagination, spontaneity, conviviality and fun, it is not a free society (Marshall 2008, p. 705). Utopia is no longer a dream but an actual possibility (Marshall 2008, p. 609). "The desire to promote evolution in this direction determines the scientific as well as social and artistic activity of the anarchists" (Kropotkin 1909, p. 59).

8 Principles in ecological economics

Introduction

In this chapter I demonstrate the breadth of ecological economics, which spans such a wide variety of subfields and perspectives that it is a very demanding challenge to synthesize all the interconnecting characteristics of its many divergent positions. Even if the different positions deal in various ways with economy as embedded in society and nature, it is still hard to agree on a common definition of ecological economics. What we can hope to achieve, however, is the identification of some fundamental principles which represent the quintessential nature of ecological economics as a transdisciplinary field of science.

Most contributors to the development of ecological economics would agree on the following broad, strongly interwoven criteria: Firstly, on an ontological level, ecological economics is based on an organic worldview, and ecological economics refers to an economic system that is consistent with and respects the basic principles of ecology. In accordance with organic reasoning, the general normative principle in ecological economics is to enrich nature's life-processes. Secondly, on an epistemological level, ecological economics learns from nature, not just in order to maximize the extraction of resources, but to concentrate on developing an economy that is life-enhancing at both the individual and social levels within sustainable eco-systems. On a societal level, the great challenge of our time is to build and nurture resilient communities within a healthy economy in harmony with the living nature. Following this line of argument, the overriding goal of ecological economics is to encourage peace between humans and nature, between humans, and within the individual human being.

In accordance with these principles, ecological economics can be traced back to Aristotle in classical Greek philosophy. However, as an academic field of science, the history of ecological economics is comparatively short: ecological economics was first introduced as a university course in Maryland, USA, in the late 1980s. At about this time, an international society of ecological economists was established, which held annual international conferences. Research in this new field of transdisciplinary science is published in the academic journal *Ecological Economics*. It is worth noting that ecological economics was founded almost at the same time as the publication, in 1987, of the UN report *Our Common Future*. Ecological economics asked the same kinds of questions and discussed solutions on how to develop an economy that could initiate sustainable solutions to the environmental and social challenges mentioned in the UN report. Spash explained the establishment of ecological economics by criticizing mainstream economics for failing to address, or even notice, its environmental impacts:

> Ecological economics was founded upon the importance of placing the economy within its biophysical limits, while recognizing the need for the conduct of human society to respect others both present and future, human and non-human. Key concerns included the failures of economic policy to address environmental impacts and the existing economic structure and its institutions to meet minimal standards of ethical conduct.
>
> (Spash 2017, p. 3)

Herman Daly, the founding father of ecological economics, argued that ecological economics provides "a bridge to unite economics and ecology in the furtherance of sustainable development" (Daly 1996, p. 73). Robert Costanza, another pioneer, pointed out that ecological economics addresses the relationship between ecosystems and economic systems in the broadest sense (Costanza 1989). Transdisciplinarity demands that economists and ecologists study processes as part of "the web of life". As it is a transdisciplinary field of science, ecological economics is neither a sub-discipline of economics nor a sub-discipline of ecology.

Transdisciplinarity means bridging a number of different studies, such as ecology, economics, psychology, anthropology, archaeology, history and philosophy. Transdisciplinarity also includes practice and art. Transdisciplinarity is a prerequisite if we are to get an integrated picture of how to develop an economic system that interacts with the natural and cultural environments in a sustainable manner. It's an attempt to look at economics as embedded in the societal and ecological systems. Figure 8.1 illustrates how ecological economics integrates and depends on the interplay between the natural world, the physical world and the social world.

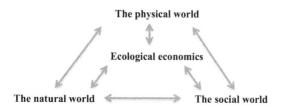

Figure 8.1 Ecological economics in the world

The integration of the physical, natural and social worlds

Many global challenges are illustrated by conflicts that arise from the combination of biological necessity, limited access to low-entropy materials, and man's essential nature. According to Georgescu-Roegen, human beings are the only factor that can be changed. "Man can change, but it was pure fantasy, in Georgescu-Roegen's view, to imagine that technological means would be found to rescue humans from their worst impulses" (Beard and Lozada 1999, p. 123). The purpose of Georgescu-Roegen's environmental advocacy was to change people's minds.

> For example his constant criticisms of mechanical analogies in economic theory, and the neo-classical treatments of environmental inputs, were made precisely because he believed such patterns of thought were a substantial barrier to accurate thinking about the future of mankind.
>
> (Beard and Lozada 1999, p. 129)

An important premise in Georgescu-Roegens' reasoning is that economic actors always act within an interconnected physical, natural and social world. Economic processes change all three dimensions in the environments, and at the same time these changes affect the economy. Economic practice should therefore be adapted to regional conditions because it then becomes easier to discover and experience how economic processes directly and indirectly affect, and are affected by, individuals, communities and the environment. Serious negative and unintended consequences may come about if economic theory and practice neglect this (see the challenges discussed in the UN reports in Chapter 3).

Three interdependent goals of ecological economics

Ecological economics assumes that economic activities are in constructive interplay with the cultural and natural effects that originate from them. The pioneers in ecological economics focus on three key goals: sustainable scale, fair distribution and efficient allocation.

Sustainable scale

Scale refers to "the physical volume of the throughput, the flow of matter-energy from the environment (. . .) and back to the environment" (Costanza et al. 1997, p. 80). Production and consumption must be sustainable both in the long and short term. Economic growth, as an end in itself, is based upon the highly questionable assumption that "there are no limits to the planet's ability to sustain it" (Pearce 2001, p. 7). In contrast, sustainability implies an underlying recognition of the fact that natural and social capital are not infinitely substitutable by technology and human capital, and that "there are real biophysical limits to the expansion of the market economy" (Costanza 2008, p. 33). So we can see that a sustainable economy should, at some point, stop growing, but that doesn't mean it needs to stop developing, as there is absolutely no necessary connection whatever between development and growth, and, quite conceivably, development could occur without growth (Georgescu-Roegen 1975). In contrast to quantitative growth, connected as it is to physical entities, qualitative development is connected to increasing numbers of relations and connections. According to Costanza et al., respecting ecological limits is a requirement for sustainable scale (Costanza et al. 2012, p. vii):

- Establishment of systems for effective and equitable governance and management of the natural commons, including the atmosphere, oceans, and biodiversity
- Creation of cap-and-auction systems for basic resources, including quotas on depletion, pollution, and greenhouse gas emissions, based on basic planetary boundaries and resource limits
- Consuming essential non-renewables, such as fossil fuels, no faster than we develop renewable substitutes
- Investments in sustainable infrastructure, such as renewable energy, energy efficiency, public transit, watershed protection measures, green public spaces, and clean technology
- Dismantling incentives towards materialistic consumption, including banning advertising to children and regulating the commercial media
- Linked policies to address population and consumption

A sustainable scale is one that, over time, does not erode the environment's capacity to carry it. Daly maintains that if "we keep the throughput within the natural capacity of the ecosystem to absorb wastes and regenerate depleted resources, then the scale of the economy is ecologically sustainable" (Daly 2007, p. 86).

Fair distribution

Distribution refers to the division of resources among people. Distribution of resources, as embodied in final goods and services, must be fair. Fairness implies recognition that the distribution of wealth is an important determinant of social capital and quality of life (Costanza 2008, p. 33). We must move from an economy oriented far too much towards the satisfaction of the wants of the rich and turn instead to an economy committed to satisfying the basic needs of all human beings. Everybody should have access to the basic necessities required to make human life possible, such as "a good diet, shelter, clothing, health care, education, and sanitation" (Albritton 2012, p. 148). Instead of focusing on economic growth and increasing profits, the global economy must include and take into account (possibly for the first time) moral considerations and equity. Modern systems biologists have discovered that the healthy functioning of any living system depends on collaboration. "Most all living organisms exist, thrive, and co-evolve only within living communities engaged in a continuous synergic sharing and exchange that from a big-picture perspective is fundamentally co-operative" (Korten 2015, p. 70). Costanza et al. maintain that a fair distribution contains many protective capabilities which allow a society to flourish (Costanza et al. 2012, p. vii):

- Sharing the work to create more fulfilling employment and more balanced leisure-income trade-offs
- Reducing systemic inequalities, both internationally and within nations, by improving the living standards of the poor, limiting excess and unearned income and consumption, and preventing private capture of common wealth
- Establishment of a system for effective and equitable governance and management of the social commons, including cultural inheritance, financial systems, and information systems like the Internet and airwaves

A fair distribution is one where the degree of inequality is limited to or is within an acceptable range. The point is that everybody should have access to the goods and services necessary for a good life. Daly and Farley also point to the fact that "a less unequal distribution of resources may generate public goods such as economic stability, lower crime rates, stronger communities, and better health" (Daly and Farley 2011, p. 442).

Efficient allocation

Allocation refers to "the relative division of the resource flow among alternative product uses" (Costanza et al. 1997, p. 80). True economic efficiency implies the inclusion of all resources that affect sustainable human well-being in the system of allocation, not just putting goods and services on the market. "Our current market allocation system excludes most non-marketed natural and social capital assets and services, which are huge contributors to human well-being" (Costanza 2008, p. 34).

At the business level, ecological economics indicates the introduction of production systems designed to lead to decreased extraction of raw material and reduced amounts of waste. Currently we find ourselves at the beginning of the search for an assertive and integrated theory and practice of environmental management that includes efficient systems for recycling. Costanza et al. suggest the following means to build sustainable and efficient allocation (Costanza et al. 2012, p. viii):

- Use of market prizes as a tool to internalize externalities, set a monetary value on non-market assets and services, reform national accounting systems, and ensure that prices reflect actual social and environmental costs of production

- Fiscal reforms that reward sustainable and well-being-enhancing actions and penalize unsustainable behaviours that diminish collective well-being, including ecological tax reforms with compensating mechanisms that prevent additional burdens on low-income groups
- Systems of cooperative investment in stewardship (CIS) and payment for eco-system services (PES)
- Increased financial and fiscal prudence, including greater control of the money supply and its benefits and other financial instruments and practices that contribute to the public good
- Ensuring availability of all information required to move to a sustainable economy that enhances well-being through public investment in research and development and reform of the ownership structure of copyrights and patents

An efficient allocation is one that "allocates resources among product end-uses in conformity with individual preferences" (Costanza et al. 1997, p. 80). If we are to reach the goals concerning efficient allocation and fair distribution, the market simply does not work because it cannot solve the conflict between efficiency and justice. On scale, the market has no mechanism whatever to stop growth whereas the eco-systems do set a limit. Daly and Farley sum up the three goals of ecological economics in the following way: "a good allocation of resources is efficient, a good distribution of income and wealth is just, a good scale is at least ecologically sustainable" (Daly and Farley 2011, p. 477).

Examples of misplaced concreteness in mainstream economy

If economic knowledge is expressed in terms of mathematical models of general validity, which are entirely removed from the physical, natural and social contexts, then economic knowledge becomes a mere abstraction and economics diverges from life. On a general level, Daly based his criticism of mainstream economy on Whitehead's definition of "the fallacy of misplaced concreteness". "This fallacy consists in taking our abstractions as more real than the concrete experiences that our abstractions seek to explain" (Daly 2007, p. 235). According to Whitehead (1978), the problem is that we tend to forget that theories and models are abstract representations of reality. Even more illusory is our insistence on equating abstract knowledge and reality and then drawing conclusions about reality which lose sight of the high degree of abstraction involved. In their book *For the Common Good* (1994), Daly and Cobb Jr. argued that concepts and theories in mainstream economics are not connected to reality and are, instead, pure abstractions.

> Recognizing the fallacy of misplaced concreteness is particularly important to establishing economics for community, because community is

precisely the feature of reality that has been most consistently abstracted from modern economics.

(Daly and Cobb Jr. 1994, p. 43)

Abstractions in science are both powerful and necessary – we cannot think without them – but it is of great importance to be aware of their limits. To solve the problems connected to mainstream economics, Daly and Cobb Jr's intention was to bring ecological economics down to earth. To reach this goal, a paradigmatic shift in economic theory and practice is required. In *For the Common Good*, they gave several examples of misplaced concreteness in mainstream economy.

The trouble with monetarization

According to Daly and Cobb Jr., the classic instance of the fallacy of misplaced concreteness is money fetishism. "It consists in taking the characteristics of the abstract symbol and measure of exchange value, money, and applying them to the concrete use value, the commodity itself" (Daly and Cobb Jr. 1994, p. 37). To be included in market economic calculations, all kinds of values have to be transformed into a monetary scale. One important consequence of economization is that inherent values are substituted with instrumental value. Land is reduced to a factor of production and has lost its inherent value for life in general.

> Land was abstracted from the totality of the natural world and treated as an exchangeable commodity. Work time or labour was abstracted out of life and treated as a commodity to be valued and exchanged according to supply and demand. Capital was abstracted out of the social inheritance, no longer to be treated as a collective patrimony of heirloom, but as an exchangeable source of unearned income to individuals.
>
> (Daly and Cobb Jr. 1994, p. 61)

There are massive consequences if we only value the parts of nature which have economic significance and ignore the inherent value of land.

> It is evident that (...) Cartesian worldview has provided the context and assumptional matrix for economic thought. For economic theory, value is found solely in the satisfaction of human desires. The subjective theory of value has totally replaced earlier "real" theories of value that took land (...) as the locus of value.
>
> (Daly and Cobb Jr. 1994, p. 107)

The most important consequence of putting price tags on every living and non-living entity in nature is that the relationships between them disappear and, as those relationships vanish, nature dies because true life has connections in nature, society and economics. An entity bereft of connections has no future.

The trouble with GDP

GDP is a mere measure of economic activity, not of well-being or consumption. Mainstream economics argues that any growth in GDP has to be a sign of a healthy market economy. Daly and Cobb Jr. remind us that there is a tendency to forget that GDP only measures some aspects of well-being. GDP also includes many costs, such as activities linked to individual, societal or natural accidents. However, in practice mainstream economics treats GDP as a general index of well-being. Daly and Cobb Jr. point out that this mistake is a typical instance of "fallacy of misplaced concreteness".

Growth should refer to quantitative expansion in the scale of the physical dimensions of the economic system, while development should refer to the qualitative change of a physically non-growing economic system in dynamic equilibrium with the environment (Daly and Cobb Jr. 1994, p. 71).

The definition states that the Earth is constantly developing; it is not growing. According to Costanza et al., "the entire concept of economic growth (defined as increasing material consumption) must be rethought, especially as a solution to the growing host of interrelated social, economic and environmental problems" (Costanza et al. 1997, p. 4). Daly argues that growth in GDP could be uneconomic because growth in economic activity might cost more "in terms of environmental and social sacrifices than it is worth in production benefits" (Daly 2007, p. 26). Because there are social and ecological indicators that correlate negatively with growth in GDP, it represents an inadequate measure of well-being. Increased consumption of tobacco, alcohol and unhealthy food are counted positively in GDP but count negatively in terms of the state of the public's health.

The trouble with the economic man

Costanza et al. maintain that "homo economicus as the self-contained atom of methodological individualism, or as a pure social being of collectivist theory, is a severe abstraction" (Costanza et al. 1997, p. 81). Daly and Cobb Jr. argue that the extreme individualism of *homo economicus* is far from being a real person. Other people's satisfaction or sufferings are not included in the definition:

> We have argued that *Homo economicus* abstracts from human feelings about what happens to others and about one's relative standing in the community. It abstracts from the kind of fairness and from judgments of relative value. We have shown that this abstraction leads to differences between behavior posited of *Homo economicus* and that of real people.
> (Daly and Cobb Jr. 1994, p. 95)

Mainstream economics is anchored more in mathematical theorems than in characteristics of reality. The consequence is that humans are looked upon as maximizing calculators, "on the basis of a pre-ordinated set of preferences" (Spash 2017, p. 5). The economic man has no freedom because he is solely executing a mathematical formula. Similarly, business firms are expected to maximize profits. Daly and Cobb Jr. point out three more crucial problems:

> The tendency for competition to be self-eliminating, the corrosiveness of self-interest on the moral context of community that is presupposed by the market and the existence of public goods and externalities.
>
> (Daly and Cobb Jr. 1994, p. 49).

In opposition to the abstract economic man, our concrete experience says that "we are individual persons, but our very individual identity is defined by the quality of our social relations" (Costanza et al. 2012, p. 82). We are also related to future generations and other species.

Four theoretical foundations of ecological economics

Contemporary ecological economics is inspired by knowledge derived over the last few decades from philosophy and natural and social sciences. In the 1970s, scholars from different scientific backgrounds published interesting thoughts and ideas which were highly relevant for ecological economics. Firstly, the Romanian economist Georgescu-Roegen (1975) argued that thermodynamics is the most fundamental law in economics – thermodynamics connects economics to the physical world. He used the concept of entropy to refer to the amount of unavailable energy in a thermodynamic setting. It is interesting to note that Georgescu-Roegen argued that the second law of thermodynamics is very special and quite unlike other physical laws. He states that the law is evolutionary and that it is as valid as it is relevant and clearly illustrates the total inadequacy of the mechanical worldview dominant in mainstream economics. If economists could bring themselves to accept thermodynamics, they would be free to escape from the mechanical "prison" of their worldview. To be consistent with this line of argument, he called his position *bio-economics*.

Secondly, Boulding (1981), the English economist and peace researcher, maintained that Darwinist evolutionary theory is essential to economic theory and practice because it explains development by referring to systemic processes in nature. He argued that the principles found in nature are essential for understanding the economics of an organic world. His question was "How is economy connected to natural evolution?" Boulding reasoned that evolutionary theory is suitable as a basis for developing the new economic theory, namely *evolutionary economics*.

Thirdly, inspired by anthroposophy, the Norwegian economist Holbæk-Hanssen developed an economic position which he called *collaborative economics*. To understand the most serious challenges that characterize the economy of modern society, he argued that there was a need for a complete shift in our conception of reality, in our methods of seeking knowledge, and in our way of acting. He claimed, for example, that problems related to the overuse of resources, problems of pollution and poverty, are difficult, if not impossible, to solve within the framework of established economic theory. Speaking from the point of view of anthroposophy, he argued that the economy was a part of the social organism.

Fourthly, the German economist Schumacher began to ask critical questions about the Western economy's one-sided emphasis on, if not obsession with, efficiency and profitability. Schumacher was particularly concerned about the rising conflict between economic growth and the natural constraints of eco-systems. He believed that the unilateral emphasis on knowledge that gives humankind power over nature has resulted in over-consumption of the Earth's resources at an ever-increasing speed. According to Schumacher, any new economic theory and practice must be filled with spirituality and values rooted in wisdom inspired by Buddhism. He termed his position *Buddhist economics*.

Bio-economics

There are many consequences of taking thermodynamics seriously. First and foremost, it is essential to develop an economy that is as resource-effective as possible. Mass media has a tendency to dramatize global environmental problems linked to CO_2 and changes in climate, but in fact humanity faces a host of other environmental problems which are seldom mentioned, and it is important to shed light on those issues, including the gradual degradation occurring in several different eco-systems, such as the depletion of the soil, desertification, the reduction of the water table, life forms becoming extinct, and many more. In the long run, such changes will not only influence conditions for the sustenance of life (including human beings) in the affected eco-systems, they may have an effect on the development of life on Earth in a wider sense.

Even though Georgescu-Roegen's economic vision is inspired by thermo-dynamics, it does include some important biological elements. Evolution is described as an organic process: "Evolution – true change – was, for Georgescu-Roegen, the starting and ending point for the vast majority of his work" (Beard and Lozada 1999, p. 134). He clearly believed that evolutionary laws, especially the law of entropy, substantially and materially affect social evolution. Ecological economics combines knowledge about biological and social systems with thermodynamics.

From these arguments it becomes clear that the productivity of eco-systems does not only presuppose that the input side of the economy is kept within sustainable limits; it is also necessary to ensure that the output side does not damage nature's own capacity for decomposition and recycling. This means that extraction of natural resources only becomes a problem the moment the level exceeds the eco-system's source and sink capacity.

In the article "Energy and Economic Myths" (1975), Georgescu-Roegen mentions a number of measures that are appropriate to perform within an economic programme based on minimal resource consumption. Firstly, all production of armaments should cease, and the resources transferred towards the enhancement of standards of living in poor countries. Secondly, each waste of energy from "overheating, overcooling, over speeding, over lighting" should be drastically reduced or, better, eliminated. Finally, the lifespan of products should be extended, and repairing them must be made easier than buying new products at an ever-rapidly increasing speed.

Evolutionary economics

Boulding believed that evolutionary theory is suitable as a basis for developing a new theory of economy. "The principle of ecological interaction is the first foundation of the evolutionary perspective" (Boulding 1981, p. 11). In an eco-system, everything depends on everything else. Boulding rejected the atomized mechanical models favoured in dominant economic thinking. He maintained, in reference to Darwin, that the Earth's species have changed and diversified through time under the influence of natural selection – a theory that can be summarized as follows: populations of animals and plants exhibit variations, and some variations provide the organism with an advantage over the rest of the population in the struggle for life. Favourable variants transmit their advantageous characters to their offspring. Since populations tend to produce more offspring, the proportion of favourable variants will be larger than the proportion of unfavourable variants.

Boulding brought evolutionary theory together with environmental challenges, social development and economics into a new field of science that he called evolutionary economics. He pointed out that the basic problem was overconsumption of natural resources combined with increasing amounts of waste. To solve these problems, he argued that the economy must be brought into harmony with the evolutionary principles in nature and society. Boulding was primarily concerned about a long-term problem to be faced by future generations – that of biophysical limits. His efforts in the development of evolutionary economics have had a great influence on the movement of ecological economics.

According to Boulding, the mechanical linear economy,

> which extracts fossil fuels and ores at one end and transforms them into commodities and ultimately into waste products which are spewed out the other end into pollutable reservoirs is a process which is inherently suicidal and must eventually come to an end.
>
> (Boulding 1970, p. 147)

Boulding's argument is based on the fundamental recognition that the Earth is regarded as a living organism in constant development. Its eco-systems consist of interaction between different kinds of species. Nature is a system with limited natural resources and limited capacity to absorb waste. In such a system, the goal to minimize resource consumption is fundamental. By integrating the social, biological and physical dimensions of the economy, Boulding concluded that a reduction in production and consumption is consistent with increased well-being (quality of life).

Although Boulding was most concerned by the deeper underlying problems in economics, he clarified that attention to the negative symptoms of current economics is important if we are to induce change. He pointed out that "there may have been times in the evolutionary process when biological change was very slow and something like a genetic equilibrium seems to have been reached" (Boulding 1981, p. 15). An interesting question is the extent to which catastrophes have influenced the process of evolution. In his essay "The Economics of the Coming Spaceship Earth" (1966), Boulding argued that the environmental crisis would lead to an increased understanding of the necessity, and an increased willingness, to implement measures to change the underlying structures which cause the imbalance between economy and nature.

The development of human consciousness changed the process of evolution. Biological evolution proceeds by non-conscious interaction, while human development is based on conscious interaction. Bio-evolution is characterized by constant ecological interaction, "which is selection, under conditions of constant change of parameters, which is mutation" (Boulding 1981, p. 18). Boulding argues that the evolutionary perspective is extremely relevant if we are to explain the ongoing processes of economic life within the political and social environment. "Economics has rested too long in an essentially Newtonian paradigm of mechanical equilibrium and mechanical dynamics" (Boulding 1981, p. 17).

Collaborative economics

Basing his ideas on anthroposophy, the Norwegian economist Holbæk-Hanssen (2009) argued that all actors in the economy, connected to production, distribution and consumption of commodities, should be working within integrated collaborative networks. In an interesting insight, Holbæk-Hanssen says that everyone working in an economy based on the division of labour earns his income through the work of all the other participants; he never earns it by himself. "One can only work for others, and let others work for oneself. One can no more work for oneself than one can devour oneself" (Steiner 1977, p. 121). Economic activity depends on integration between nature, human labour and legal regulations.

Important conditions for business practice are, on the one hand, the conditions of the eco-systems, climate, regional geography, natural resources, etc., and, on the other hand, the judicial conditions that regulate the interaction between the actors in the market and between economy and nature. In this way, the economy depends on two conditions: the natural base, which we must take as given, and the legal regulations, which should be rooted in a political state independent of economic interests. Seen from this perspective, an economic value "is a nature-product transformed by human labour" (Steiner 1972, p. 29). An important common feature between organisms and businesses is that the resilience of organizations and businesses is weakened over time in the same manner as in all biological organisms. The ability to be constantly evolving is essential to maintain a high level of energy in a society.

According to Holbæk-Hanssen (2009), we are only going part of the way when we use mechanistic concepts and explanatory models such as "market forces" and "price mechanisms" to find solutions to such issues as the environmental and poverty crises. Inflation, currency crises, resource depletion, pollution and centralization are symptoms showing that neo-classical economic theory fails completely to capture the complexity of today's globalized world. In our breathless rush to increase production and consumption, we have overlooked the consequences to the eco-system caused by the extraction of natural resources and energy and the disturbance caused by increasing amounts of waste.

Problems can be explained by pointing to structural weaknesses in the current economic system. Holbæk-Hanssen argued that economic theory and practice have to change from a competitive to a collaborative understanding of reality. A transition to an organic-based economy would have major consequences for the understanding of scientific methods and research in general. According to Holbæk-Hanssen, the harmful consequence of unilaterally using analytical methods to identify and describe the smallest parts in various cause-effect chains, is that we are left with a fragmented and "lifeless" view of reality, where we only have large amounts of bits and pieces about the least human part of economy and society. It is the essence of a living organism that it is continually being formed and unformed. In any organism, there must be continuous production and consumption. In the economic organism, "there must be a constant producing and a using-up of what is produced" (Steiner 1972, p. 62).

Human beings are interdependent and formed within an organic whole. Every human being's personality and character affect others, and therefore every human action is both self-regarding and other-regarding. A further consequence of the fundamental interconnectedness is that human beings cannot hurt other living beings without hurting themselves.

Buddhist economics

Schumacher, taking inspiration from Buddhism, argued that we have to develop a peaceful society based on organic agriculture in harmony with the eco-systems, small-scale, non-violent technology and wisdom. We have to learn how to live peacefully in society and with nature, and, above all, "with those Higher Powers which have made nature and have made us" (Schumacher 1973/1993, p. 9).

Human beings have a four-dimensional nature. Firstly, the body is able to maintain its integrity because it is distinct and clearly separated from others. Wants and desires are situated in the body. The body is the force of physical energy. Secondly, the mind (manos) includes the stream of consciousness from birth until death. Intelligence, intuition and passions are also part of the mind. Even if the mind is distinct from the body, it is still an integrated part of it. The mind is also the center of the ego. Thirdly, the soul (atman) infuses all living beings. The soul is the source of spiritual force or energy. This indicates that the whole living universe has one soul, of which everyone is a part. The world soul/spirit is eternal and indestructible; "it is not an entity, a thing or a being, but as force, and active principle, a source of intelligent energy" (Parekh 2001, p. 55). Fourthly, human beings have a psychological and moral constitution (swabhava).

Schumacher's ideas for increased utilization of local resources through small-scale production are currently being implemented in many poor countries (micro-credit). In recent years, small-scale economics has been put into practice in Europe and the USA. Besides the fact that the environmental benefits of reducing the need for transportation are of great importance, the boom in local jobs has helped to enhance the cultural vitality of many regions. The Schumacher Society has been, and is, an important driver in the work of transforming "small is beautiful" into practical action.

Figure 8.2 illustrates how ecological economics takes inspiration from many different sources, amongst others bio-economics, evolutionary economics, collaborative economics and Buddhist economics.

Topics of relevance in ecological economics

In the following paragraphs, I give my reflections on some topics connecting the theoretical foundations of ecological economics and the holistic (utopian) description of a future society based on ecological economics outlined in

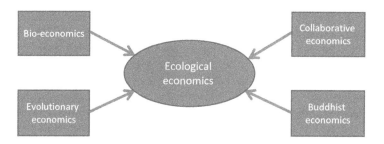

Figure 8.2 Ecological economics – a mosaic of influences

Chapter 9. The topics are all integrated in a holistic mosaic, which means that every topic is present in all the others and the whole illuminates the details.

Human being

I start from the evolutionary position, where the development of human consciousness is connected to social and biological evolution. Biological evolution proceeds on the whole through unconscious interaction and non-dialectical processes, while social development is anchored in conscious interaction between human beings and nature. In 1968, Boulding published "Economics as a Moral Science" in which he pointed out that all cultures (including economics) are based on a set of common values. All human beings are guided by values. "No one could live, move, or act without one" (Boulding 1968, p. 227). According to Boulding, the history of value systems can be regarded as an evolutionary process. In all societies, different groups proclaim new ethical standards all the time. Each new ethical "mutation" "encounters the selective process, (...) some may have survival value in the short run and some in the long run" (Boulding 1968, p. 229). He doesn't claim that selection is the only test of validity, but that it does narrow the field of possibilities. Boulding argued that ethical relativism must be rejected, just as cultural relativism is also unacceptable. Not all ethical answers are equally valid and it is always possible to criticize the values of any culture. So before applying ethical principles to business and economics, we must take a brief look at systemic preconditions. As well as criticizing economic theory as one-dimensionally focused on market-based exchange relations, motivated by egocentric utility maximization (the economic man), Boulding argued that the values of self-sacrifice, love and loyalty must be re-appraised and elevated to a far more influential role within the economy.

Communication and interaction, which bring actors together in organic networks, are fundamental to Boulding's evolutionary economy. He empha-sizes, therefore, that organization through decentralized, collaborative net-works provides better results than those achieved through giant globalized organizations with hierarchical power structures. Large-scale organizations based on hierarchical power structures focus exclusively on economic returns and ignore human values and economic environmental responsibility.

From a Buddhist perspective, Schumacher maintains that wisdom demands a new orientation of science and technology towards "the organic, the gentle, the non-violent, the elegant and beautiful" (Schumacher 1973/1993, p 20). The problem with economics is that something is defined as uneconomic when "it fails to earn an adequate profit in terms of money" (Schumacher 1973/1993, p 28). Mainstream economics cannot produce any other meaning. This means that an activity can be economic even if it has disastrous consequences for nature or society. The market is an institutio-nalization of egoism and non-responsibility, and the entire outlook and methodology of economics has to be called into question.

Right livelihood is one of the requirements of Buddhism. Buddhist economics sees the essence of civilization in the purification of human character, not in the multiplication of wants. "But Buddhism is 'the middle way' and therefore in no way antagonistic to physical well-being" (Schumacher 1973/ 1993, p. 41). The ideals of simplicity and non-violence have fundamental consequences for the economy. Instead of maximizing the use of natural resources, Schumacher argued that we should explore opportunities to minimize consumption as we pave the way to a society based on improved quality of life. In his book *A Guide for the Perplexed* (1978), Schumacher elaborates on the assertion that one consequence of modern economics, based on a materialistic worldview, is that we have lost contact with basic human needs and values. The quest for profit and technological development has led to both environmental degradation and cultural dissolution.

Freedom, creativity and thinking

Daly points to an interesting issue when he asks, "what does free market environmentalism have to say about free trade and the environment? Nothing" (Daly 1999, p. 43), he answers. In articles and books concerning ecological economics, the distinction between negative freedom and positive freedom is discussed almost solely in connection to free trade. Mainstream economics is anchored in a restriction of external constraint (negative freedom), not in positive freedom. In the perspective of ecological economics, positive freedom contributes to improving economic freedom and economic justice; in a mainstream economic perspective positive freedom harms the efficiency of the market mechanisms.

Holbæk-Hanssen (2009), referring to anthroposophy, argued that if we are to capture the life-processes in nature and society, it is necessary to be aware that our thinking is the element through which we participate in society because "our thinking reunites us with the world" (Steiner 1995, p. 101). In other words, to develop a healthy society it is of great importance to facilitate a balanced interaction between a free self-organizing culture, a democratic constitutional system, and an associative cooperative economic sector. Holbæk-Hanssen (2009) argued that freedom, thinking and individuality interweave and enable cultural diversity. Thinking must never be regarded as a merely subjective activity; thinking connects and is a prerequisite for the development of individuality. Freedom depends on the individual's ability to will what they themselves hold to be right.

Holbæk-Hanssen (2009) explains creativity as a phenomenon that occurs in the field of tension between "actuality" and "potentiality". To give direction to creativity, it is necessary that we are free to think continually about the values we want to prioritize. One consequence of this reasoning points ecological economics towards organic structures which initiate constructive cooperation to achieve common goals. We have to establish new arenas, new forums, for dialogue and cooperation between free human beings.

Well-being

Georgescu-Roegen strongly believed that enjoyment of life, experienced by every living being, should be the primary aim and outcome of economic activity. "Anything that contributes to such a 'lux of enjoyment' has value" (Beard and Lozada 1999, p. 126). Every activity leading to enjoyment of life and which helps to create the good life has economic value. Moreover, this value cannot be quantified in GDP and is not equal to the market price. A necessary condition for achieving enjoyment of life is that the basic needs are met through consumption of goods and services. Georgescu-Roegen also clarified that non-market activity, such as leisure, is an important factor in creating quality of life.

The basis for increased interest in the social dimensions of an economy is the intensified awareness that social utility cannot be measured exclusively in terms of money, and it is, therefore, difficult to argue that we should always choose alternatives with the highest monetary value. An economic operation, which is resource intensive and causes pollution, or contributes to an unfair distribution of wealth, can, in many cases, be economically profitable even if it results in negative consequences for nature, society and individuals. Value is not a quality inherent in objects or a static thing produced in measurable quantity, but "a process in which valuation is always occurring in time and is changeable over time" (Kerman 1974, p. 37). Following this line of argument, Boulding rejects the traditional notion of consumption as a measure of wealth and argues instead that "consumption is a bad thing, (...) enjoyment of resources is the good thing" (Kerman 1974, p. 36).

Although Gandhi (Parekh 2001) certainly accepted that there are many positive achievements in modern society, he put forward the view that modern society has undermined man's inherent unity with the natural and social environment. Modern society is characterized by features such as rationalism, secularization, industrialization, the scientific culture, individualism, supposed technological mastery of nature, the drive towards globalization, and liberal democracy. Because modern society is driven by self-interest and self-indulgence, it is dominated by materialistic desires and the goal of the unrestrained satisfaction of wants. Positive freedom is under attack because consumers are manipulated by and through intensive marketing techniques to increase their desire for commodities they don't need and which are not, in any sense, in their long-term interests. Unsurprisingly, based on this, both nature and culture are conquered by an economy based on profits.

Gandhi (Parekh 2001) points out some fundamental principles of the new economics. First of all, nature cannot possibly be privately owned because nature is common property. Secondly, all products are a result of collaboration and nobody has an exclusive claim on them. Thirdly, market interaction should be based on cooperation and dialogue instead of competition and egoism. Fourthly, all reductions in materialism and consumerism are to the benefit of spiritualism and frugality.

Schumacher (1973/1993) argued that work has a great influence on people's well-being. Work gives people opportunities to develop and make use of their abilities and skills. Further, working together with others helps to develop a social understanding, which reduces selfish tendencies. Another major feature of work is that the individual helps to produce goods and services to meet the community's needs for goods and services.

According to Schumacher (1973/1993), all jobs should contribute to the development of each individual's creativity and moral character. In line with this reasoning, Schumacher argued that all (or any) boring, meaningless, and hazardous workplaces are very much to be shunned. Customized technology means that solutions must be rooted in an organic, decentralized, non-violent (to both humans and nature) and aesthetic basic attitude which puts the focus on human development. Potential reductions in our productivity are compensated by and through our having jobs with greater meaning.

Integration

Boulding (1968) drew distinctions between the threat system, the exchange system and the integrative system. Most societies today are dominated by the threat system and the exchange system. The former is based on the use of power – simply put: if you don´t do something nice for me I will do something nasty to you. The exchange system is slightly more human and is characterized by this idea: if you do something nice for me I will do something nice for you. The integrative system is based on a network perspective that says, "what you want, I want". According to Boulding (1968), we can find a mixture of all three systems in every organization and society. For long-term survival, it will be necessary to develop integrative institutions in both the society and the economy. The exchange system in the economy is atomistic and based on instrumentality.

As far as interdependence and cooperation towards common goals are concerned, a healthy society depends on a balanced interplay between different actors in the economy. Integrated networks represent a combination of constructive and destructive processes that take place in parallel, e.g., while production creates values, consumption breaks them down. The task for the future is, through implementing integrated networks, to handle all the tasks necessary for sustainable development.

Associations are economic organizations that allow people to unite in cooperative networks based on reciprocal activities. Sustainable social development requires an autonomous economy within a political context where it is possible to affect economic organizations in such a way that "the individual does not feel that his integration in the social organism is in conflict with his rights-awareness" (Steiner 1977, p. 71).

Through associative cooperation between people with different experiences and perspectives, it is possible to develop a comprehensive insight that helps everyone to understand economic realities from within. From the perspective of associations, it is possible to discover the true meaning of economic life. Exchange processes connected to supply and demand are economic realities. Associations are independent, self-governing cooperative bodies in economic life. Associations can be regional and either horizontally or vertically oriented. Within an association, it is more readily possible to clarify conflicts of interest before they develop into a battle of interests. Mutual trust between the members of an association is necessary for cooperation to work. The task of the future is to find, through associations, "the kind of production which most accords with the needs of consumption, and the most appropriate channels from the producers to the consumers" (Steiner 1977, p. 112).

It is no surprise that mainstream economists raise strong objections to the implementation of collaborative economics. According to Steiner, this is a natural consequence of accepting that real life-processes are characterized by contradictions. Important aspects of collaborative economics are about to be integrated in contemporary ecological economics. These include the importance of embedding the economy into an organic worldview, that is, having an economy integrated into nature and culture, a focus on the real economy, decentralization, coordination through collaborative networking, and far more concentration on bottom-up initiatives.

An important purpose of establishing integrated networks is to contribute to the reduction of tendencies to economic egoism. The idea behind networks is that they put together people with opposing views and let them come up with agreements on difficult or controversial tasks. The networks create better coordination between needs and production, more appropriate utilization of labour, and more efficient use of natural resources and technology. By these means we can get rid of several of the most urgent anomalies in contemporary economics.

In accordance with this mindset, Holbæk-Hanssen argued that global challenges could be addressed through integrated local and regional networks where creative thinking is combined with practical experimentation. Dialogues in cooperative networks make it possible to implement pluralistic values that go far beyond the economy's traditional one-dimensional monetary scale. Everything in economics depends on an open-minded consideration of life as a whole. We must gain a clear vision of the whole of life. In associations, the sense of community (community-spirit) must be a major and dominant force.

Small is beautiful

In trying to set out clearly his ideas about economic matters, Schumacher describes a small, decentralized economy anchored on the personal character of the members organized in local societies. Beyond the relatively self-sufficient villages, society at large would be organized in terms of expanding circles. Central authorities should have enough power to organize the nation but not enough to dominate the local societies. Work is both a right and a duty, as it is through work that individuals develop self-respect and initiative and are empowered to counteract the tendency to egocentric behaviour. Participation in local production gives an added bonus effect of developing the workers' pride and self-discipline.

Although large-scale industries are of great importance, they should be restricted to a minimum. Competition between large-scale centralized industry and local production is problematic because it could eliminate the fundamentals required for small-scale activities. Small-scale technology is necessary to support local production. Patnaik reasons that "productivity combined with creativity preserves and promotes human identity and dignity which are subdued to the point of elimination by the use of large-scale technology" (Patnaik 1991, p. 118).

An important point in Schumacher's description of Buddhist economics is that local and regional small-scale networks are better than giant globalized businesses. The challenges consist in finding an appropriate size for the communities and developing a customized small-scale technology. According to Schumacher, we need both freedom and order. "We need freedom of lots and lots of small, autonomous units, and at the same time, the orderliness of large-scale, possibly global, unity and co-ordination" (Schumacher 1973/1993, p. 48).

Local communities, in this context, could be small villages or neighbourhoods in big cities. For the economy to function, it has to be organized through networks of smaller units. We must learn to think in terms of a network-based structure that can cope with the multiplicity of many interrelated small-scale units. Schumacher suggests some ways to establish healthy economic activity.

The cosmos is a well-coordinated whole where all parts are linked in a mutual supportive system by the deepest relations (bonds). Schumacher also argued, in accordance with Buddhism, that the universe is not just material but is infused with a cosmic spirit. This interconnectedness is expressed in Gandhi's favourite metaphor that "the cosmos was not a pyramid of which the material world was the base and human beings the apex, but a series of ever-widening circles encompassing humankind, the sentient world, the material world, and all including cosmos" (Parekh 2001, p. 50).

Networks

It is fascinating to note that Darwinist evolutionary theory can be interpreted as a rationale for Smith's doctrine of the invisible hand. Smith pointed out that if every economic actor maximizes his or her own profit, the result is the common good. Darwin argued that the net result of each organism engaging in a struggle for its own survival was the continuous evolution of the species as a whole in the direction of better adaption to its environment. "The political implications of this viewpoint are clear" (EP, p. 305). While the social Darwinists of the 19th century saw only competition in nature, we are now beginning to see continual cooperation and mutual dependence among all life forms as central aspects of evolution.

The French philosopher Bergson (Jones 1975) pointed out and discussed some of the major weaknesses in Darwinism. In Bergson's opinion, one of the most important difficulties was the lack of any satisfactory explanation for the source of new genetic information from which natural selection could select. Bergson's theory proposed a non-Darwinian mechanism to produce new genetic information that, in turn, allowed well-documented mechanisms, including natural selection, to function. Bergson maintained that evolution of life results from a vital impulse, not from mechanical forces as Darwinism taught. Following the same line of argument, Whitehead (1978) argued that the driving force in evolution was to be found in the power of creativity, not in a mechanical elimination of the unfit. According to Darwin, nature creates many possibilities through blind "trial and error" and then lets the process of natural selection decide which species survive. From this point of view, the creative process is the unity of three stages: variation, selection and retention of the best combinations.

"The survival of the fittest" principle is, according to Boulding, often interpreted to mean the survival of "an aggressive, macho-type mentality at the expense of the co-operative and accommodating patterns of behavior" (Boulding 1981, p. 18). A much better phrase would be "the survival of the fitting", i.e., the species that fits into a niche in the ecosystem. In biological evolution, cooperative behaviour very often gives a better result than competition. As an example of cooperation in nature, the term "symbiosis" is illuminating. Symbiosis refers to the tendency of different organisms to live in close association with one another to their mutual benefit. It is interesting to note that Darwin himself never used the expression "survival of the fittest", but talked instead of "the struggle for existence". "Survival of the fittest" actually came from Spencer's interpretation of Darwinism.

Boulding also criticizes the metaphor "struggle for existence". In fact, "ecological interaction involves little struggle in the sense of organized and conscious fighting" (Boulding 1981, p. 18). Cooperation is a better strategy for adaption to the environment. According to Capra and Luisi, "co-operation is clearly visible (...) at many levels of living organisms" (Capra and Luisi 2014, p. 202). The evolutionary perspective on society and economics does not deny the existence of dialectical processes, "the view that sees the long processes of the history of the universe as essentially conflicts between mutually hostile and opposing systems, each of which arises out of the contradictions of the other" (Boulding 1981, p. 21).

This process keeps adding useful, improbable, sometimes beautiful things to our world, while entropy keeps tearing down this improbable organization to its eventual end as a thin brown soup. Production and organization are similar building processes, while consumption and death tear things down. But knowledge is a kind of magic that does not obey the laws of entropy but keeps on increasing irrepressibly (Kerman 1974, p. 14).

Knowledge

Ecological economics is defined as a transdisciplinary field of science. Trans-disciplinarity attacks the dominating scientific paradigm in mainstream economics as being too narrow to understand the integrated challenges that the global society faces today, such as the challenges in terms of access to clean water, the increasing movement of refugees, rising poverty, terrorism, climate change, financial crisis and debt crisis. The list goes on. Max-Neef (2005) argues that to deal with these problems we need a new economy based on transdisciplinarity, a holistic science that captures the contexts and relationships of a complex reality. Most universities and business schools have a tradition of specialization and the cultivation of scientific monocultures; for that reason it is obvious that accepting transdisciplinarity involves a substantial, if not revolutionary, change in both research and teaching.

Max-Neef (2005) draws a demarcation line between weak and strong transdisciplinarity. On the one hand, weak transdisciplinarity means that representatives of different disciplines work together to solve complex problems. In other words, weak transdisciplinarity is a practical way of dealing with complex issues that do not require any fundamental change in the perception of reality by the universities. The need for dialogue across disciplines is becoming accepted.

On the other hand, strong transdisciplinarity presupposes a change from a mechanical to an organic worldview. Within an organic worldview, reality can only be understood through holistic science where disciplines are unclear. Strong transdisciplinarity is based on a holistic approach to reality, which includes a spiritual dimension consisting of, among other things, emotion, imagination and intuition. In this context, Max-Neef (2005) refers to Goethe's philosophy of science, where observation consists of both rational and relational aspects of reality. Max-Neef argues that the universities must take a leading position in the change process towards strong trans-disciplinarity, and he pointed out that this very change is indeed underway at several academic institutions.

Holbæk-Hanssen argued that many of the ideas underlying economic theory and practice are based on inherited thought patterns that we use more or less unconsciously, often without considering either their validity or their relevance. An important point in his argument is that the social organism is forever evolving, always unfinished, so it's impossible to prepare ready-made final solutions. What is important is to facilitate processes that help to develop a course for long-term change. An important prerequisite for change is that we become aware of disease symptoms in the community. To do that, we need a holistic or transdisciplinary research model.

Holbæk-Hanssen (2009) argued that hermeneutics and phenomenology represent inspiring alternatives to the empirical-analytical research tradition. Hermeneutics is based on a worldview where everything hangs together in a whole and where knowledge and meaning occur in the interaction between part and whole. Knowledge is validated by eliminating all forms of embedded inconsistencies and shortcomings of logical relationships. The aim is to understand, or find meaning, in different phenomena with reference to a larger context. The meaningful relationship between part and whole represents the basis of hermeneutics.

Switching between part and whole is fundamental in the hermeneutical method. By interpreting the part in the context of the whole and the whole as a totality of integrated parts, we achieve a deeper understanding of how it all fits together in a greater whole. Holbæk-Hanssen (2009) used the phrase "spiritual bend and stretch program" as a designation for research processes where one alternates between concentration down to details and a stretching upward towards larger wholes. He argued that researchers should make more use of methods that are geared towards interpretation of how phenomena relate to each other. The main task is to find concepts, or rather stories, that help us to understand economic life from the inside.

Phenomenology emphasizes the importance of observations and intuitive experience in the concrete reality. Key concepts in the phenomenological research tradition are imagination, inspiration and intuition. Holbæk-Hanssen (2009) defined imagination as the ability suddenly "to see the entire pattern". It is, in other words, a creative process that consists of finding a pattern or creating a pattern where the individual elements, joined together, are synthesized as a whole. This represents more than the sum of its elements, and the patterns are essential. Inspiration is connected to the experience of being in conformity with reality. This experience is part of the living reality and will therefore help to create the direction of development. New knowledge is tested in a confrontation between ideas and reality. Intuition is defined as "the conviction that it is right or good to implement new ideas in practical contexts" (Jakobsen 2017, p. 90).

This approach to knowledge states, specifically, that issues related to economic activities take on a far deeper meaning if they are illustrated by long-term social and ecological contexts. If, for example, we introduce technologies that damage the natural world but increase short-term profitability, then our long-term environmental and social interests could well be harmed. A comprehensive understanding of how things hang together lets our creative abilities develop and we can implement new and better solutions. Holbæk-Hanssen's view on science and scientific methodology is close to Max-Neef's interpretation of transdisciplinarity.

Sustainable development

Daly, Costanza and many other distinguished contributors to ecological economics argue that quantitative growth must be transformed into qualitative development. On the one hand, to grow means to increase in size, therefore, "growth (...) means a quantitative increase in the scale of the physical dimension of the economy" (Daly 1999, p. 6). On the other hand, "development (...) means to expand or realize the potentialities of: to bring gradually a fuller, greater or better state" (Daly 1999, p. 6). Daly concludes, a growing economy is getting bigger; a developing economy is getting better. Sustainable development means that some values should be sustained. Daly argues that both social utility and nature should be sustained: "The future should be at least as well off as the present in terms of its utility or happiness as experienced by itself" (Daly 2007, p. 37), and the physical flow from nature through the economy and back again should not be in decline. More precisely, "the capacity of the ecosystem to sustain those flows is not to be run down" (Daly 2007, p. 37).

One obvious consequence of sustainable development is that the priority given to "efficiency" and "frugality" must change. "A policy of 'frugality first' (...) induces efficiency as a secondary consequence: 'efficiency first' does not induce frugality – it makes frugality less necessary" (Daly 2007, p. 47). Sustainable development, therefore, refers to the qualitative change of a non-growing economy in dynamic equilibrium with the (social and natural) environment. Since growth is impossible, the concept of sustainable growth is both self-contradictory and meaningless. Daly and Farley expect "human society to continue developing, and indeed argue that only by ending growth will we be able to continue developing for the indefinite future" (Daly and Farley 2011, p. 6).

From this brief reflection, it is reasonable to conclude that sustainable development is development (qualitative improvement) without growth (increase in throughput beyond carrying capacity) in order to increase the ability to satisfy human (and non-human) needs in the short and long-term perspectives. The implications for the economy include a reduction in the use of natural resources by introducing a simpler lifestyle where the emphasis is removed from material consumption. Schumacher (1973/1993) refers to Gandhi's well known statement saying that "Earth provides enough to satisfy every man's need, but not for every man's greed". The aim is to obtain maximum well-being with minimum consumption.

Concluding remarks

What distinguishes ecological economics from green economics is, first and foremost, its close connection to nature and the eco-systems. Ecological economics connects to the physical, natural and social worlds. However, ecological economics has many different sources of inspiration, and there are many different interpretations of ecological economics, each focusing on different topics. In this chapter we discussed bio-economics, evolutionary economics, collaborative economics and Buddhist economics. On the one side, research anchored in bio-economics (Georgescu-Roegen) gives priority to questioning economic growth, while on the other side, Buddhist economics (Schumacher) focuses on individual frugality. Both agree that the good life in the good society cannot be reduced to the mere consumption of goods exchanged on the market. Human well-being depends on our integration into social networks and our connection to nature. Freedom is a topic of concern among contributors inspired by collaborative economics (anthroposophy). Holbæk-Hanssen argued that creativity depends on cooperation between free actors and that intuition and inspiration are important ingredients in all scientific work.

Even though it is clearly observable that ecological economics has many traits in common with anarchist philosophy, anarchism has not been discussed explicitly by contributors to ecological economics. Not even those who refer to Buddhism and anthroposophy mention any anarchist inspiration.

9 Utopia inspired by ecological economics

Introduction

We live in a world of uncertainty. The potential for disaster is massive, and at the same time our world is rich in potential for positive possibilities. Eisenstein expressed this powerful contrast by stating that the present convergence of crises "in money, energy, education, health, water, soil, climate, politics, the environment, and more – is a birth crisis, expelling us from the old world into a new" (Eisenstein 2011, p. xx). We can either choose to fire up the engine of capitalism and wealth creation by prioritizing selfishness, individualism and narcissism, or stimulate the ability to say yes to love, kindness, generosity, sympathy and empathy and alleviate the birth woes for a new world. Lindner's (2012) explanation of why destructive competition must not be chosen at the expense of life-enhancing cooperation is much the same as that of Eisenstein. She points out the importance of establishing venues for constructive dialogue that gives impetus to developing an economy based on equality and dignity. "The goal is to create societies with high quality of life rooted in an economy based on equality and dignity" (Jakobsen 2017, p. 189).

A reasonable conclusion is that our current environmental and social dilemmas are due, at least in part, to our much-distorted perception of reality. According to Rees, "Modern economic society operates from an outdated mechanistic perception of the natural dynamics of the Earth" (Fabel and St. John 2007, p. 104). Pearce goes a step further and argues that the failure to address metaphysical questions has led to many of the central errors of conventional economics. Therefore, economics needs an internal metaphysical critique. Daly and Cobb Jr. maintain that

> With each passing year, the positive accomplishments of the economy have become less evident and the destructive consequences larger. There is a growing sense that it is time for a change. The change may well take the form of a paradigm shift.
>
> (Daly and Cobb Jr. 1994, p. 6)

Instead of focusing on physics, quantitative measures and products, economists should discuss metaphysics, qualitative values, and processes (Pearce 2001). Pearce's critique is both valid and relevant to our understanding of the negative symptoms which follow from mainstream economics, and his critique is also an argument in favour of ecological economics. We have to realize, finally and forever, that we will never find solutions to our current bewilderment by using the same old maps. To do more than merely reduce negative symptoms, we have to make deep changes in economic theory and practice. The only valid purpose of the economy is to serve the life-processes in all kinds of social and ecological systems. Every activity and every process within the economy should be a servant of life.

In the report *Building a Sustainable and Desirable Economy-in-Society-in-Nature*, a number of the most influential contributors to ecological economics – Robert Costanza, Gar Alperovitz, Herman Daly, Joshua Farley, Carol Franco, Tim Jackson, Ida Kubiszewski, Juliet Schor and Peter Victor – offer "A new model of the economy based on the worldview and principles in ecological economics" (Costanza et al. 2012, p. v). These principles include

- Economics has to be embedded in society and ecological life-support systems
- We cannot understand or manage the economy without understanding the whole interconnected system
- Development is defined as improvement of sustainable well-being, not growth in consumption
- A healthy balance between nature, human beings, society and culture

Costanza et al. (2012) argue that if we are to solve the most serious challenges of our time, we have to change the dominating economic paradigm. A society based on ecological economics differs from the current society by being ecologically sustainable, fair, efficient and secure. In other words, and this is very clear, ecological economics provides exciting answers to the challenges set out in the UN's 17 Sustainable Development Goals.

It is generally accepted that to break established habits we must see the benefits of the change and the cost of following the old track. What we see, and how we evaluate what we see, depends on our choice of perspective and time horizon. If we try to solve these serious challenges by no more than a one-dimensional treatment of the most visible symptoms, a number of paradoxes could well occur. For example, initiatives to stimulate economic growth have been put forward to solve the financial crisis when we know very well that continued growth in the economy would only serve to worsen the environmental problems. When the rich countries spend billions of dollars on marketing to stimulate growth in production and consumption, the result widens the gap between rich and poor, in both the national and global perspectives. Growth in production and consumption in the rich countries often leads to reduced resource efficiency; the life cycle of products becomes shorter, the distance between production and consumption increases, and the amount of waste grows dramatically. Our tendency to overexploit resources is currently reinforced not only by powerful technologies, but also by cultural norms, particularly those associated with the paradigm of economic growth which is, currently, globally dominant.

Solutions based on quantitative consequences in a short-term perspective are dramatically different from solutions based on qualitative evaluation in a long-term perspective. Ecological economics focuses on the interplay between economy, nature and society in a long-term perspective. Instead of focusing on quantitative growth in GDP, ecological economics gives priority to "enjoyment of life" (Georgescu-Roegen). The goal of ecological economics is to improve human well-being within sustainable societies and eco-systems.

The ideas that fill our mind represent the context of how we interpret the world. At present, there can be little doubt that the whole of mankind is in mortal danger, "not because we are short of scientific and technological know-how, but because we tend to use it destructively, without wisdom" (Schumacher 1973/1993, p. 63). One way of looking at the world as a whole is by means of a map, said Schumacher. He was one of the first holistic thinkers in economics and a great synthesizer, who brought many different perspectives into the economic context. He was well aware of one of the most fundamental explanations behind the challenges in the modern society: that modern man does not see himself as a part of nature but as an outside force destined to dominate and conquer it. "He even talks about a battle with nature, forgetting that, if he won the battle, he would find himself on the losing side" (Schumacher 1973/1993, p. 3). To handle the problems in the modern society, we have to be creative and start getting to terms with alternative futures (utopia). Even just talking about the future can be the start of concrete action.

Utopia – An ecological economic narrative

In order to develop a coherent vision of a future society, it is necessary to create energy and direction in the transformation process to get us from here to there. The search for a single model for a future society is both incoherent and dangerous because different societies have dissimilar histories and traditions. Therefore, some general criteria have to be identified by which a good society could be established and describe processes relevant for further development. However, how to implement ecological economics in practice is up to the people and societies involved.

The reflections in the former chapter, together with the ideas presented by Costanza et al. in "What Would a Sustainable and Desirable Economy-in-Society-in-Nature Look Like?" (Costanza et al. 2012, pp. 18–28), represent the basis for the skeleton of a utopian narrative outlined in the following paragraphs. Costanza et al. (2012) reflect on how to develop a good and simple life that does not disturb the integrity, diversity, rhythm and inner balance in society and nature. On a general level, a sustainable society should institutionalize and stimulate social service, cooperation, and solidarity and discourage all forms of exploitation, domination, injustice and inequality. To reach this goal, it is of great importance to initiate and stimulate dialogue and creative interplay between human beings. Moreover, a sustainable society depends on mutual responsibility, characterized by a high level of self-discipline and self-restraint. Within this framework, a sustainable society should and has to provide the maximum space for personal autonomy. In order to cope with the complexities in the society, a sustainable society has to accept scientific pluralism, i.e., it must appreciate that reason, intuition, faith, traditions, emotions, and accumulated collective wisdom are relevant sources of knowledge. A community's resilience and creative potential rise in direct proportion to the complexity, diversity and coherence of its connections.

The utopian narrative presupposes that we have the opportunity to create a future consistent with "our true nature and possibility as living beings born of a Living Earth" (Korten 2015, p. 1). Scarcity can be overcome, conflict reconciled, and moral dilemmas and psychological frustrations resolved (Davis 2012, p. 129). The question is how to develop a society and an economy that adapt to social and ecological limits and potentials. The main challenge is to create technologies, businesses, physical structures and technologies that strengthen nature's inherent evolutionary ability to sustain life. I have organized the portrayal of the utopian narrative as follows: worldview, networks and open systems, creativity and dialogue, community and politics, economic system and practice, individual level, pedagogy and knowledge. Because the different topics are integrated into the holistic vision of a sustainable society, it is easy to recognize elements of every topic in all the parts.

Worldview

In the future society, "an ecological worldview of complexity and indeterminacy, inspired by nature as mentor, holistic, integrated, and flexible" (Costanza et al. 2012, p. 19) has replaced the mechanistic worldview. In the organic worldview, the material world is defined as a network of inseparable patterns of relationships and "the planet as a whole is a living, self-regulating system" (Capra and Henderson 2009, p. 7). People "recognize that humans are part of nature, one species among many, and must obey the laws and constraints imposed on all of nature" (Costanza et al. 2012, p. 19). Every organism develops as an integrated part of numerous different processes interwoven with one another. Natural growth is characterized by growth and decay, regeneration and development, and human beings and organizations, as the living organisms they are, exist inseparably linked to metabolic and dynamic processes.

In accordance with Whitehead's organic philosophy, these processes are understood from both an individual and a systemic perspective, where the formation of the system is influenced by the characterization of the individuals, "or we can characterize the individuals and conceive them as formative of the relevant process" (Whitehead 1966, p. 98). This means that every organism is constituted of its connections to other organisms. From this ontological position, it is accepted that all living entities derive their character from the social and ecological networks of which they are integrated parts. The principle of relativity says that all living entities are constituted of their relations to other entities and each living entity arises out of its relations and is internally constituted by these relations. Therefore, systems thinking is always contextual thinking, as all systems are part of larger systems (context).

Thus, systems thinking includes both contextual thinking and process thinking. The transformation from mechanism to organism has important methodological consequences. Instead of measuring quantities, the focus in the utopian society is adjusted to mapping patterns of relationships. When we map relationships, we find certain configurations that occur repeatedly. Consequently, focusing on relationships and processes instead of objects indicates a shift away from quantity to quality. Multileveled structures of systems nested within systems characterize both society and the economy (Capra and Henderson 2009). Each individual system is an integrated whole and, at the same time, is a part of the larger systems. In this sustainable society, the needs of the people are in harmony with the rhythms of the ecosystems. Human beings are integrated parts of nature, not nature's masters. Interdependence is the source of the shared humanity, and prosperity is not solely based on income and wealth but more on self-reliance and self-dignity. Costanza et al. maintain that

> We recognize that nature is not something to be subjugated, but instead is something we depend upon absolutely to meet physical, psychological, cultural and spiritual needs (...) and our goal is to create conditions conductive to life in the broadest sense.
>
> (Costanza et al. 2012, p. 19)

People in utopia find their place in a unified, dynamic web of living organisms, disturbing the web as little as possible.

Nested networks and open systems

Networks are particular patterns of connections and relationships. Patterns and relationships are the very essence of systems thinking. Eco-systems are understood in terms of webs of energy, i.e., networks of organisms, organisms are networks of cells, and cells are networks of molecules. According to systems thinking, networks are self-generating within a boundary of their own making. Each component of the network helps to transform and replace other components, and thus the entire network is continually creating, or recreating, itself as living systems undergo continual structural changes while preserving their web-like patterns of organization.

In the sustainable society, relationships include not only the connections among the people but also the relationships between the society as a whole and its environment. This means that the economy is nested in other systems: society, culture, politics, nature, and ultimately Gaia, the living Earth. The essential properties of such a living society arise from the interactions and relationships among its parts and from the relationships in the whole eco-system. The interconnectedness between individuals, organizations and their natural and societal environments means that every human being, business firm and local community is constituted of, and derives much of its character from, connections to other social actors and the eco-systems. For economics on a general level, this implies that nature and society are superior to the economy, and that the economy is the servant of nature, and not, by any means, the master of nature.

Such a systemic and "organismic" view of reality clearly demonstrates the importance of how the relations between the actors are organized. Neither the economy nor society is a mere collection of objects, but both are based on relationships between subjects. They function as integrated wholes and cannot survive atomized any more than any organism can survive in fragments. This means that economists and other social scientists in the future society will study all processes as part of the web of life. Ecological economists accept that if the economy is studied separately from its social and ecological contexts, and knowledge is expressed through narrowly defined mathematical models, it becomes abstract and remote from life. To understand the dynamic interconnectedness in the real world, holistic research models are based on transdisciplinarity.

When it is accepted that both the social system and the eco-system can be described as integrated networks, then the concrete challenge is to create and implement a social system where the focus is on dialogue-based inter-relations between the actors. One of the best ways to build such an economic system is to start by establishing networks of interconnected decentralized communities. The old cities are transformed into networks of mini-cities. These small communities form the basic units of the economy, and the scale of industrialization would be planned accordingly.

The systemic principles of "self-generating networks" and "nested systems," taken together, lead to the vision of a sustainable economy in which economic activities are interrelated and connected to self-organizing and mutually supportive entities. All living systems are materially and energetically open and always operate far from equilibrium. They need an input of energy and material resources to sustain themselves, and all living systems produce "waste" as output. Flows are essential in all aspects of metabolism, the central characteristic of life. Metabolism is defined as the ceaseless flow of energy and matter through a network of chemical reactions, which enables an organism to continually generate, repair, and perpetuate itself. In nature, however, organisms form eco-systems, in which the waste of one species is food for the next so that matter cycles continually through the eco-system, while energy is dissipated at each stage. The only waste generated by the eco-system as a whole is the heat energy of respiration, which is radiated into the atmosphere and is replenished continually by the sun through photosynthesis.

In the economy, materials that are not biodegradable are regarded as "technical nutrients", and these circulate continually within the industrial cycles that make up the technical metabolism. In order for these two metabolisms to remain healthy, great care must be taken to keep them distinct and separate, so that they do not contaminate each another. Things that are part of the biological metabolism, such as agricultural products, clothing, cosmetics and so on, should not contain persistent toxic substances. Things that go into the technical metabolism, such as machines, physical structures and so on, should be kept well apart from the biological metabolism.

The dynamics of open systems are nonlinear and involve multiple interconnected feedback loops which allow the systems to regulate and balance themselves. There is always a potential for the spontaneous emergence of new order at critical points of instability. Actuality and potentiality are organically integrated so as to allow for a genuinely creative cosmos where, even if the past is settled, the future remains widely open.

Creativity and communication

In the society of the future, it will be more important to discover new questions than to find new answers to the old questions, so creative, divergent and original thinking will be essential. Also a strong sense of global citizenship will be necessary to "generate both thought and action that really engage with the problems of human and environmental flourishing at a global level" (Albritton 2012, p. 154).

In accordance with the systems view of life and the philosophy of organism, creativity is seen as the force driving development. Creativity depends on individual freedom to actualize the potential in local societies. Ecological economics presupposes the existence of arenas for free exchange of ideas, knowledge and information. Open information systems lead to democratic decision-making. Dialogue stimulates everyone to contribute according to their ability and to recognize the right of each to meet their reasonable needs with due consideration for the needs of others. Every street will have a house for dialogue and cooperative activities.

The systems view of life has important applications in almost every field of study and every human endeavour because most phenomena we deal with in our professional and personal lives have to do with living systems. Whether we talk about economics, the environment, education, health care, law or management, we are dealing with living organisms, social systems or eco-systems, and so it follows that the fundamental shift in perception from the mechanistic to the organic view is relevant to all these areas.

From this starting point it is possible to draw several implications. Instead of talking about (exponential) growth in the extraction and use of natural resources – which is of course impossible on a finite earth – the focus has to shift to qualitative development. Because of entropy, it is impossible to recycle resources infinitely, so the new question arises of how to use resources in such a way that they contribute to life in nature as well as in society. To stimulate creativity, decentralized bottom-up initiatives are vital, and cooperation is more significant than competition. Instead of maximizing utility (or profits), the challenge is to find solutions that lead to a fairer sharing of natural goods.

Learning from nature, where all living systems interact cognitively with their environment in ways that are determined by their own internal organization, the economy is organized as a network of integrated self-organizing systems. In the human realm, these cognitive interactions involve consciousness and culture and, in particular and essentially, a sense of ethics. It is therefore most urgent to reintroduce an ethical framework within the context of communicative cooperation on all levels between mutually responsible economic actors. The global economy will no longer be characterized by financial flows that have been designed mechanically in the absence of any ethical framework. The old, and current, economic system, based as it is on social inequality and social exclusion, leads to, in line with its design, an ever-widening gap between rich and poor and an increase in world poverty. Because the traditional mechanical and linear way of thinking is limited by its own structure, our problem-solving often brought about unintended and undesirable effects – financial and climatic disasters are but two prime and fine examples of such unintended consequences.

In the utopian society based on ecological economics, all human beings are members of social and natural systems, which means that they all belong to the social community of the global biosphere. As members of humanity, everybody respects human dignity and human rights. And, as members of the Earth Household, we respect nature's inherent ability to sustain life, so our ethical behaviour is based on the two fundamental values of human rights and ecological sustainability. To succeed in this, it is of the greatest importance that people grasp the need to incorporate these ethical values into their personal lives, businesses, politics, and economic life, or, surely, natural selection will see to it that humanity does not survive. People with dialogue-based communication skills are able to elaborate on problems and to contribute to utopian thinking.

Holistic thinking, including adaptability, flexibility, learning, self-organization and cooperation, are central to a society inspired by ecological economics. Ecological internalization implies that environmental and social responsibility are integral and integrated parts of business management. The focus is on measures that stimulate the process of developing an economy and a society that bring to the individual, to society at large, and to the economy, more life and stronger resilience.

Community and politics

The new society is a strong participatory democracy, one in which people have an influence on decisions that affect them personally or their local societies. Participatory democracy is a privilege in smaller communities where people are engaged and active. According to Costanza et al.,

> As citizens come together in regular meetings to discuss the issues and work together to resolve them (even when substantial conflict exists), it creates strong bonds of social capital and plays an essential role in forging a sense of community.
>
> (Costanza et al. 2012, p. 26)

Furthermore, direct democracy, with its increased social interaction, is of great importance in encouraging community members to participate in making decisions about matters that affect their lives and livelihoods. Nurturing social interaction has a positive impact on both physical and mental health.

Societies anchored in ecological economics are dramatically redesigned in order to "integrate living space, community space, and workspace with recreational needs and nature" (Costanza et al. 2012, p. 20). Contributors to ecological economics are united in the description of decentralized cooperative networks as a prerequisite to the development of sustainable societies. The big cities are still there, but they are reorganized into networks of smaller units. Cities are now aggregations of smaller communities that meet the inhabitants' needs for housing, work, social activities and shopping. Costanza et al. maintain that "the 20-minute neighborhood idea – that all basic services should be no more than a 20-minute walk away" (Costanza et al. 2012, p. 20) – is given priority in urban development. Public transport is widely available along with bicycling and, of course, walking. Private homes will be smaller, better designed and energy efficient.

While the social Darwinists of the 19th century saw only competition in nature, ecologists today agree that cooperation and mutual dependence among all life forms are central aspects of evolution. Evolution is no longer seen as a competitive struggle for existence, but rather as "a co-operative dance in which creativity and the constant emergence of novelty are the driving forces" (Capra and Henderson 2009, p. 7). To illuminate this very important point, Capra refers to Margulis and Sagan, who assert that "Life did not take over the globe by combat, but by networking" (Capra 1997, p. 226). Based on the fundamental ideas of complexity, networks, and patterns of organization, a new holistic society will slowly emerge. Vital eco-systems and spaces for social interaction, where everyone participates in civil society, provide a stimulating environment for all humans. Living in decentralized communities "where social goals are actively discussed, people now better understand the importance of their work and feel greater obligation to contribute to the common good" (Costanza et al. 2012, p. 24).

On a political level, "mindfulness can help in our work against consumerism, sexism, militarism, and the many other isms that undermine the integrity of life" (Sivaraska 2009, p. 83). People act in accordance with the Buddhist idea that the universe is both material and spiritual, and ecological economic thinking takes both dimensions into account. One consequence is that material consumption should be minimized to the benefit of spiritualism. People are at the center of Gandhi's economic framework. "Human welfare and social progress cannot afford to ignore the moral and spiritual dimensions" (Patnaik 1991, p. 118).

Economic system and practice

The utopian society is based on acceptance of the organic worldview of forming an economy where people collaborate to find the best solutions for individuals, society and nature. In accordance with the processes in nature, the economy does not grow quantitatively but rather it develops qualitatively. Costanza et al. argue that

> A steady-state economy does not mean an end to development; it simply means that we limit the input of raw materials into our economic system and their inevitable return to the ecosystem as waste to a level compatible with ecological constraints imposed by a finite planet with finite resources.
>
> (Costanza et al. 2012, p. 19)

The sustainable economy is anchored in circular economic processes in three dimensions. In harmony with the Gaia theory, ecological economics recognizes that economy, nature and culture are integrated parts within a "living" organism (Lovelock 1988). The interplay between economy, nature and culture possesses properties such as dynamism, evolution, integrity and change. Accepting that the economy has the ability, through human action, to restructure and reform processes in the eco-systems and societies of which they are a part, economic activities are now in constructive interplay with the cultural and natural effects that originate from them. By their very nature, circular processes are interrelated and interactive (Ingebrigtsen and Jakobsen 2007).

The three dimensions are integrated into a triple helix, and the economy exists as an integrated ingredient in society's and nature's dynamic evolving web of life. In accordance with Whitehead's philosophy of organism, every economic actor is a factor in a larger whole and has significance for the process of the whole. The isolation of an actor in thought has no counterpart in any corresponding part of reality. Economics, simply interpreted within a mechanic perspective that sees the product as an isolated item bereft of all ethical dimensions, has no validity in utopia.

Redistribution is established as a function in the economy that influences the whole circular system. Redistribution connects consumption and production (the ends of the linear value chain). Redistribution consists of several sub-functions, including collecting, sorting, and reprocessing of various materials. Companies in the field of redistribution are representatives of one of the fastest-expanding sectors in the economy, and here we find positive signals which indicate solutions that are in harmony with the organic worldview. Based upon the philosophy of organism, the "product" concept is understood holistically. In the sustainable society where the economy has an extended view, which encompasses the space and time dimensions, all functions, including extraction of natural raw materials, processes of production, means of transportation and distribution, consumption and reprocessing, are seen as an organic whole. In redistribution, a number of questions are addressed concerning what happens to the product when the basic product in some sense is used by the customer. How the used product influences the ecology depends on the total life cycle of the product. To reach the goals of sustainability, it is essential that products are designed for efficient reprocessing and that these processes are combined with the establishment of collective systems for coordinating the companies dealing with redistribution.

The product, from the perspective of ecological economics, is interpreted as an integrated part of social and environmental systems. In the organic economy, where values are inherent in the processes, consumers are more conscious of the prominent role they play in the economic network (Ims, Jakobsen and Zsolnai 2015). In the sustainable society, consumer behaviour is less individualistic and more concerned with the common good, so consumers ask the fundamental question, what processes and which values am I supporting when I buy these commodities?

In this perspective, CO_2 is not a cause; it is a symptom of a carbon-based economy. In other words, to handle climate change, all actors are aware of the patterns of interconnectedness between the input and the output side of the economy. Knowledge and values are essential to develop a life-enhancing economy. "On the one hand, knowledge exerts influence on the innovative processes in the economy and on the other hand changes in the economic sector influence cultural development" (Ingebrigtsen and Jakobsen 2007, p. 289).

To build such a circular economy, technologies and industrial systems are fundamentally redesigned, mimicking the natural ecological cycles. According to Costanza et al., industry has changed dramatically: "Industrial design is now based on closed-loop systems in imitation of nature" (Costanza et al. 2012, p. 21). This is one of the main tasks of ecodesign. Indeed, ecodesigners are promoting the idea of a "service-and-flow" economy, involving two kinds of metabolism: a biological metabolism and a "technical metabolism" (McDonough and Braungart 2002).

When possible, industrial production uses local materials to meet local needs. Circular value chains make it possible to reduce both the consumption of virgin natural resources and the amount of waste that goes back to nature. To establish efficient material cycles in practice, collaboration between governments, manufactures, distributors and consumers is required. Sustainability depends on our ability to discover the connections between input and output of natural resources in the economic value chains.

Culture represents intrinsic value as a context for developing individual and collective identity and life-quality. The output of cultural activities, knowledge and creativity has instrumental value as input to economic processes. Cultural values are integrated into economic behaviour; all actors are conscious of the fact that partnership approaches "require adherence to sets of values held in common between people and with the organization" (Welford and Gouldson 1995, p. 116). In a sustainable society, where cultural and environmental values have fundamental influence on all processes in the economy, the debate over what values reside in culture and nature has highlighted the fact that the core concept is complex and multidimensional. Economic activity does not take place in a vacuum and is always situated in an environmental and a social context. Therefore, business organizations are involved in the development of new social and environmental standards of a more substantial nature. To handle these challenges, we need holistic thinking, including adaptability, flexibility and learning, as important parts of the education system. Workplaces involve variety, and the work itself is "a pleasurable part of our days that engages both mental and physical skills" (Costanza et al. 2012, p. 24).

The sustainable economy depends on an harmonious balance between the eco-systems, social systems and economic systems. To prohibit commercialization of politics, culture (including science) and nature, all dimensions develop in harmony. Self-organization and cooperation are also important characteristics in a society described as a living, self-regulating community. Ecological internalization implies that environmental and social responsibilities are integral and integrated parts of business management. At the level of micro-economics, it is inappropriate to talk about a single business as being sustainable. All businesses are embedded in social and ecological networks, and sustainability presupposes building and rebuilding relations between the different systems. Production, inspired by systems thinking, is based on decentralized closed-loop systems where the feedstock in one industry comes from waste products in another. Local needs are met by local production based on local resources. Just as eco-systems are different depending on environmental conditions, economic practices differ depending on cultural and natural conditions, but the underlying principles are universal systemic principles of life.

An economy in harmony with nature and culture has a structure that copes with a multiplicity of small-scale units. Schumacher argues that there will always be a choice between private ownership of the means of production and various types of public or collectivized ownership. Closely connected to a choice between market economy and various arrangements based on freedom or totalitarianism, respectively, he concludes that there will always be some degree of combination of the alternatives. They are complementary more than opposites. Costanza et al. agree with Schumacher and maintain that, as well as being decentralized and connected to the local community, "most smaller-scale industries consist of a mix of locally owned proprietary firms and smaller corporations (...) and co-operatives and new community-based commons institutions on the other" (Costanza et al. 2012, p. 22). Such businesses pay more attention to the well-being of the workers and the community and stimulate creativity, and feelings of participation and identity.

Economics aims to create viable communities through small-scale production and customized technology. These ideas are in accordance with Costanza et al., who uphold that "most smaller-scale industries consist of a mix of locally owned proprietary firms and smaller corporations" (Costanza et al. 2012, p. 21). Small-scale economies have influenced economic development in many poor countries (micro-credit). In the shadows of the environmental and financial crises, Schumacher's ideas become more relevant even in rich countries. Local initiatives and local currency favour the use of local energy, nutrients, water, and material resources. Local currencies contribute significantly to stimulate the integrity of the community, support fair and balanced trade surplus with neighbours, secure the community's resources against theft by intruding predators (multinational companies), and maintain boundaries around local societies.

The concrete results of this reasoning are societies made up of integrated networks of local communities based on small-scale production units "mostly using local resources in a decentralizing system of economic management" (Patnaik 1991, p. 117). The benefits of small-scale decentralized economy are manifold (Costanza et al. 2012, p. 22):

1. Local production dramatically reduces transportation costs, helping to compensate for sometimes-higher production costs.
2. It makes communities directly aware of the environmental impacts of production and consumption. Cost of disposal are not shifted elsewhere.
3. Industries are more a part of their communities. Most of them are locally owned by the workers they employ, by new cooperative and municipal institutions, and by the people whose needs they meet.
4. The decentralization of the economy means that the economy as a whole is much less susceptible to business cycles, increasing job and community stability – a central requirement of local sustainability planning in general.
5. An emphasis on local ownership and production for local markets has reduced the importance of trade secrets and patents; competition has been replaced to some extent by cooperation.
6. A significant number of larger firms are structured as public and quasi-public enterprises, jointly owned with the workers involved. Thereby less dependent on very short-term profit considerations necessary to meet stock market expectations that foster excessive growth.
7. Decreased competition has led to a dramatic decrease in the size of the advertising industry.

Gandhi was an advocate for small-scale farming and micro-sized industry for local markets, and he supported the idea that local societies should be self-sufficient as far as basic needs are concerned. Buddhism's essence is "to overcome selfishness and transform greed into generosity, hatred into loving kindness, and ignorance into wisdom" (Sivaraska 2009, p. 92). Simplicity and non-violence are closely related in the framework of economics.

Individual level

In a sustainable society based on ecological economics, individualism and freedom are important as long as "individual actions do not have a negative impact on the community" (Costanza et al. 2012, p. 19). Individualism is combined with concern for the common good. People accept that they are integrated parts in society and nature and that it is unfair to impose on the society costs connected to private gain. With the recognition that consumption beyond limit is not only physically unsustainable but "also does little to improve our quality of life, the people understand and accept that a 'steady-state' economy – prosperous but within planetary boundaries – is our goal" (Costanza et al. 2012, p. 19).

In accordance with this reasoning, Schumacher maintains that the essence of civilization is not multiplication of wants, but rather "the purification of human character" (Schumacher 1973/1993, p. 40). Hence, "ever increasing consumption is no longer considered an integral component of human needs" (Costanza et al. 2012, p. 19). Instead people pay attention to other needs such as joy, beauty, affection, participation, creativity, freedom and understanding. With diminished individual needs, the society is able to provide a satisfactory wage to meet everybody's basic needs. Most people contribute through different kinds of work, but it is not forced. Participation in social dialogues creates moral values and common social practices that represent the glue that holds society together.

Knowledge and pedagogy

Education in the sustainable society is integrated into everyday life and not just in classrooms. Nature represents a wonderful research laboratory. According to Costanza et al., education about civic responsibilities and roles is heavily stressed and is characterized as "an interactive balance between online tools and content acquisition, and the on-the-ground problem solving" (Costanza et al. 2012, p. 23). Creative expression and curiosity are important to cultivate wisdom and emotional maturity, which in turn facilitate responsible decision-making.

In the sustainable society, the education system gives priority to developing the student's ability to understand the basic principles of ecology. Such knowledge and understanding are critical for the survival of humanity in the coming decades. This means that ecoliteracy is established as "a critical skill for politicians, business leaders, and professionals in all spheres, and should be the most important part of education at all levels, from primary and secondary schools to colleges, universities, and the continuing education and training of professionals" (Capra 2012). The goal is that every young learner understands that it is impossible to produce something from nothing and, vice versa, it is impossible to make nothing from something. In other words, resources and waste are necessary consequences of all production processes. Therefore, the precautionary principle plays an important role in deciding what to do "when there is doubt over the potential impact of resource extraction or waste emissions on ecosystem goods and services" (Costanza et al. 2012, p. 28).

The idea that research should come up with knowledge that gives human beings power over nature is replaced by a new approach to science, where the aim is to develop knowledge that is relevant to adapting to the principles found in nature. Capra and Luisi (2014) call this new science "the systems view of life" because it is grounded in "systems thinking", or systemic thinking – thinking in terms of relationships, patterns, and context.

Communication and dialogue are extremely important in transdisciplinary research, and a prerequisite in the development of resilient communities. Communication is the glue that contributes to developing connection lines between different parts of society. Instead of developing knowledge concentrated on specialized fields of science, where each specialty and each subject is increasingly isolated, partly as a result of its own specialized vocabulary, education is directed towards developing relations between individuals, organizations, business firms and local authorities. The verbal electric fences (often designed to keep outsiders out) dividing the different sciences are eliminated in order to communicate across disciplinary (and cultural) boundaries.

Transition

The only way to build a sustainable society is to cultivate such drives in human nature as intelligence, happiness, serenity, and thereby the peacefulness of man. According to Schumacher, "there are no final solutions (…) there is only a living solution achieved day by day on a basis of a clear recognition" (Schumacher 1973/1993, p. 218). In the following paragraphs, I set out how the transformation towards a sustainable society based on ecological economics can be inspired and stimulated. We accept an organic worldview as the context for development; all economic activity should encourage viable societies within resilient eco-systems. In other words, the economy should give priority to activities that are in harmony with the overarching goal of maximizing the well-being of human beings, non-humans, and the whole eco-system. The economy's one and only valid purpose is to serve the life-processes of all kinds of social and ecological systems.

In her book *Owning Our Future*, Marjorie Kelly (2012) illustrates this fundamental change with dozens of inspiring examples of organizations that are not publicly traded corporations but embody "private ownership for the common good". They include worker-owned businesses, wind farms operated by "wind guilds", marine fisheries with catch shares, cooperatives and non-profit organizations forming a solidarity economy, customer-owned banks, and so on. What all these ownership designs have in common is that they create and maintain conditions which allow human and ecological communities to flourish. Kelly calls this new kind of ownership generative ownership, because it generates well-being and real, living wealth. She contrasts it with extractive ownership, or the conventional corporate ownership model, whose central feature is maximum financial extraction, and she claims that the family of generative ownership models forms a nascent generative economy.

In principle, it is possible to implement the change to ecological economics on all levels – micro, meso and macro. Firstly, economic systems depend on human beings, so to change the system we, as individuals, must change first. Secondly, it is possible, at least in principle, to change business practice directly. Thirdly, if the systems are bad, people will behave badly, so the transition depends on changes on all three levels simultaneously. On a deeper level, these changes depend on a shift in the worldview or paradigm.

Alongside the UN's Sustainable Development Goals, the Earth Charter also gives us valuable inspiration to understand just what behaviour for the common good could actually mean in practice. The Earth Charter makes it evident that the principles of sustainability, justice and peace are all interconnected. Ethical reflection is of great importance if we are to understand the practical implications of the Earth Charter's 16 goals, because truly sustainable development demands more than merely reducing our negative impact on nature. Equally important measures are contributions to fairness and to reducing the gap between rich and poor. Justice is a necessary condition for peaceful development.

Based on systems thinking, it is easy to be aware of the market as a network of integrated actors, where customers, suppliers, competitors, communities and other stakeholder groups all depend on each other. Trust and responsibility are essential values in such a situation. Cooperation, based on dynamic dialogue, brings about far more integrated solutions than is possible through the mechanics of an atomistic and competitive economy. Equality and mutuality among the involved actors are necessary conditions for constructive cooperation. "When competition is replaced by co-operation as the main principle for interaction in the market, the development of solutions based upon the common good will gradually take place" (Ims and Jakobsen 2006, p. 23).

In ecological economics, competition is reduced to a far more subordinate function, and cooperation is promoted as the fundamental principle for the coordination of activities. "The competitive autonomous economic man has to be replaced by a co-operative social ecological man" (Ingebrigtsen and Jakobsen 2009). The systems view of life provides a better and more accurate description of the interplay between the actors in the market than an atomized description which refers to autonomous actors in competitive markets. Market behaviour based exclusively on competition will often, as we know, lead to disintegration and egocentric behaviour. We must replace greed, competition and growth with solidarity, cooperation and compassion.

The Earth is understood as a system composed of closely interacting and interdependent subsystems based upon dissipative structures. Since every system is connected to and dependent on others, everything evolves together over time. Co-evolution is characterized by path-dependency, and change is the rule rather than the exception. We have to admit that the Earth itself and all its living and non-living components is a community and that humans are members of this integrated community and find their proper role in advancing the well-being of this whole community. Berry concludes in the following way: "There can be no sustained well-being of any part of the community that does not relate effectively to the well-being of the total community" (Fabel and St. John 2007, p. 63).

One important consequence of accepting the fundamental interrelatedness of reality is that the market is not reducible to atomistic competition between autonomous actors. The market is more like a cooperative web of interrelated economic actors. From this perspective, ecological economics describes the market as consisting of flexible and changing patterns. When the system-perspective is applied, it is important to describe the elements, and especially the relationships between the elements. Based on the fact that both social and environmental structures change through succession, it is of great importance that the economic system is also sufficiently flexible to adjust to this process.

So we can see that our environmental and social challenges should be addressed through building integrated local and regional networks where creative thinking is combined with practical experimentation. Dialogues in cooperative networks make it possible to be open to pluralistic values that far exceed the economy's traditional one-dimensional monetary scale. In economics, as in the management of business organizations, everything depends on an open-minded consideration of life as a whole. We must gain a clear vision of the wholeness of life.

An economy based on local networks linked together globally provides the best basis for developing co-responsible human beings. In such an economy, local and national interests will not seem divisive in our shared responsibility as global citizens, while we can also avoid global uniformity. Internationalizing is based upon a cooperative network of small societies, while globalization represents membership in an abstract global community. Globalization is not about patterns for diverse interactions; it is about the constitution of a single global economy. Diversity is a sure way to keep relations dynamic and to make sure they do not harden into a fixed pattern which could, in the long run, lead to conflict and disunity.

According to the systems view of life, living organisms interact with their environment through "structural coupling", i.e., through recurrent interactions, each of which triggers structural changes in the system (see Capra and Luisi

2014, p. 135). Over time, different environments will trigger different structural changes, and as a consequence, no organism is exactly the same as any other organism of the same species: individuality is a basic property of life.

For a sustainable economy, this means that economic processes directly or indirectly affect and are affected by individuals, businesses, communities and the environment, depending on local and regional circumstances. Economic practice always has to be ready to adapt to changing regional conditions. If economic theory and practice ignore this essential dynamism, then serious negative and unintended consequences may arise as we clearly see in today's environmental, social and financial crises.

Local networks, linked together nationally and globally, provide the best basis for the development of co-responsible human beings. The main thing to emphasize here is that individual citizens, even in the global network, should maintain their individuality and dignity. In addition to local, bottom-up initiatives, the development of global democratic institutions (top-down) with the authority to regulate the world economy are of great importance. A combination of bottom-up (personal responsibility) and top-down principles (international treaties) is necessary to ensure that the total consumption of natural resources is kept within critical levels, though we accept that all economic activity in some shape or form depends on access to natural resources.

In a society based on organic interdependence, economies are characterized by cooperation instead of ruthless competition. Whereas mechanical systems and bureaucracy stifle creativity, decentralized structures, based on local ownership and local decision-making, stimulate creativity. Globalized corporations tend to do business with an abstract competitive market, while small enterprises, nested in networks, cooperate with living actors. In such a real-life context, technological development expands from merely improving eco-efficiency to emphasizing ecological and social resilience.

Concluding remarks

Ecological economics, as a transdisciplinary science, seeks to describe, understand and suggest solutions to some of the most pressing challenges in today's societies at all levels – local, national and global. Ecological economists reject mainstream economy's hard-core values of competition, growth and strategic behaviour. The scientific bases of ecological economics are, first of all, thermodynamics and evolutionary theory, and that means accepting that the economy exists within the principles of eco-systems and cannot be anchored in physical growth.

Within these limits, the goal is to develop sustainable societies based on fairness and focused on satisfying the basic needs of all human beings. The context of interpretation is organic thinking, characterized by the web of life, networks, open systems and cognitive systems. From this theoretical platform, it is possible to draw different practical conclusions. Society could be described as nested networks of smaller communities based on dialogic communication. Human well-being depends on more than material consumption, and a central demand is the opportunity to develop its potential, both individually and collectively. Meaningful activities in a social and natural context are also necessary preconditions for quality of life. Workplaces must offer work that has inherent value and gives opportunities to develop the individual's potential and, even more importantly, it gets people working together to counteract tendencies to egocentrism.

We can draw from this that the economy cannot be based on exponential growth and cannot move into the cultural and natural sectors without transforming inherent values into instrumental values. Commercialization transforms nature and culture into economic resources. Ecological economics challenges the failure of the competitive market economy to capture the complexity of nature and society and argues that the economy should be organized as cooperative decentralized networks.

10 Anarchism as a political platform for ecological economics

Introduction

In the preceding chapters, it became clear that well-known contributors to anarchism and ecological economics address many of the categories of Sustainable Development Goals set out in the UN reports and the Earth Charter: poverty, equity, environmental sustainability, economics, politics, education and cooperation. In addition it became clear that anarchists and ecological economists agree that fair distribution of wealth cannot be achieved within a liberalist economy because the competitive market leads to concentration of money, wealth and power. Environmental sustainability is also virtually impossible given that in order to survive, the liberalist economy has to grow and create more and more profits. Because everything is reduced to economic resources, liberalist economy is both anti-social (it dehumanizes workers) and anti-ecological (it devalues nature to an economic resource). In accordance with the social liberal tradition, the authorities adopt laws and regulations that are designed to reduce the most urgent negative consequences.

Anarchists and ecological economists attack the dominating economy for being caught in a mechanical paradigm and argue that the most important event, if we are to change, is a shift to an organic paradigm. Even if politics are mostly discussed implicitly in ecological economics, some contributors discuss political issues explicitly. For example, a change in the definition of the economic actor from the economic man to a political economic person (PEP) has been suggested by the Swedish ecological economist Peter Söderbaum (2000). Maybe the most unifying idea amongst anarchists and ecological economists is the demand for a shift from an atomistic competitive market to a market characterized by cooperative networks.

Conversion through capitalism

If we are to eradicate the causes of the challenges set out in the UN's Sustainable Development Goals (SDGs), we have to do far more than make changes in the protective belt of (social) liberalist market economy; radical change in the hard core is also required. Ecological economics represents an interesting alternative which points out the necessity of fundamental change in economic theory and practice. However, experience has indicated how hard it is to implement the principles of ecological economics within the current economic and political system, based as it is on diametrically opposed ideas. Referring to Figure 2.1, ecological economics is actually possible and could be implemented in practice, but it is ideologically impossible within the existing system. In other words, ecological economics is an example of a "possible impossibility" – possible in practice but impossible within the dominating capitalist system. Empirical experience shows that when solutions based on ecological economics are put forward, the capitalist system reacts by seeing them as "green" measures, and the deeper problems remain concealed behind changes in the protective belt while the fundamental principles in the hard core stay, conveniently, entirely unchallenged. Circular economy met exactly this fate and stands as a fine example of how the capitalist machinery will commercialize and emasculate all such good intentions.

As long as the political system stays chained to a (social) liberalist ideology, ecological economics, when implemented, will also be transformed and manipulated into a version of green economics (Figure 10.1). Attempts to solve the environmental and social challenges discussed in the UN's MDGs and SDGs and the Earth Charter end up as mere measures that reduce the negative symptoms instead of "putting pain to work" by confronting the real, actual and fundamental problems. In practice this means that all and any solutions based on changes in the protective belt will leave the hard core of the existing system untouched and dominant. To be more precise, the liberalist political context represents a self-protecting frame of reference that makes it extremely difficult to implement the radical changes necessary if we are to achieve the UN's 17 SDGs. Rees argues that green economics has scarcely made any progress whatever towards solving the major environmental challenges faced by today's global societies; rather, "green economy has contributed to concealing the real problems behind a veil of green words and concepts" (Jakobsen 2017, p. 163).

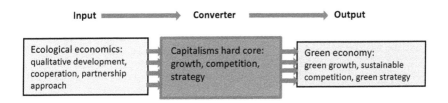

Figure 10.1 Conversion through capitalism

Conversion through anarchism

In the following paragraphs I will set out how a shift towards anarchism as a political platform is relevant in the implementation of ecological economics. Referring to Bjørneboe, it is not a question of anarchism or not, but on degrees of anarchism. So the real question is, which elements of anarchism are most important when it comes to the successful implementation of ecological economics?

In the first chapter I raised the following question: To what extent is philosophical anarchism relevant as a political platform for ecological economics? Because anarchism and ecological economics can both be defined in many different ways, it is helpful to pinpoint the exact definitions used in this book. Anarchism is interpreted as communitarian anarchism, which means freedom in solidarity; ecological economics as the economic system within the eco-systems, and, rather than exploiting nature, we take it as something from which we can learn. From the previous discussion, it is clear that there are many similarities between the ideological foundations of anarchism and ecological economics, but it is also important to identify and assess the discrepancies between them. In Figure 10.2, ecological economics is transformed through an anarchist converter and the result is cooperative economy integrated in nature and society.

The hard core of anarchism can be expressed through concepts such as freedom in solidarity, self-government and mutualism. Basically, people develop responsibility through freedom, and that freedom, in turn, depends on responsibility. One dramatic consequence of this understanding is that external leadership, either by the State or by powerful economic and political leaders, is dispensed with, and in its place we have a decentralized self-organizing social and economic system. Living societies are characterized by individual self-realization within collaborative networks of ecologically balanced small communes.

If ecological economics is realized through a political platform derived from the hard core of anarchism, then the potential for individual, social and environmental responsibility is actualized and amplified.

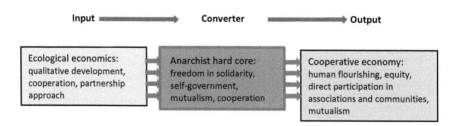

Figure 10.2 Conversion through anarchism

A new collaborative economy based on mutualism is better equipped to handle the challenges described in the SDGs and the Earth Charter and systematized through the six categories of Sustainable Development Goals. The idea is that ecological economics, renewed and reinvigorated by anarchist political philosophy, represents a far deeper solution and one that truly offers the new and radical measures necessary to reach the defined Sustainable Development Goals.

However, it is far from easy to envisage a change towards a society characterized by a high degree of anarchist principles in a world where everything is going the other way, with an increasing focus on market economic solutions working alongside more and more top-down regulations than ever. Maybe, by accelerating the crises, the opportunities to implement fundamental changes both in the individual mindset and at the systemic level will increase. This reasoning is in accordance with Kuhn and Lakatos, who argue that only when the anomalies become serious enough will the paradigm and the hard core be replaced. This indicates that a revolutionary paradigm shift is imminent.

The following evaluation is structured in accordance with the categorization of the SDGs: poverty, environmental sustainability, politics, economy, education and cooperation. Table 10.1 illustrates and compares the UN's SDGs with anarchist philosophy and ecological economics, respectively.

Every model of the good society has shortcomings, and anarchy has its share as well. I will point out several criteria that could serve as standards in the evaluation of anarchy as a political platform for ecological economics. The different criteria are put into perspective by comparing them to the shift in worldview.

Comparing principles

Anarchism is based on an organic worldview which maintains that man is rooted in nature and society and that society is part of nature. Anarchism concludes that since we cannot revolt against nature, we have to act in harmony with ecological principles. Kropotkin argued that anarchism included a lively interaction between nature, society, economics and politics. This is a precondition for understanding the problems we are facing today, locally, nationally and globally. The methodology for understanding this basic interconnectedness was pointed out by Feyerabend, who argued that scientists must be free to ask questions and choose methods that are in total conflict with the scientific establishment. Ecological economics agrees with Kropotkin and emphasizes that the economy is a subsystem of nature and that we should learn from nature instead of degrading it to no more than an economic resource. The integrated perspective on science is expressed in ecological economics as transdisciplinarity, i.e. associate different sciences, link theory and practice and express knowledge through artistic expressions.

Table 10.1 Sustainable Development Goals, anarchism and ecological economics

	UN's Sustainability Development Goals	Anarchist philosophy	Ecological economics
Poverty	End poverty in all its forms everywhere (SDG 1)	The aim of the economy is to produce the greatest amount of goods necessary to the well-being of all (Kropotkin)	The task of the economy is to ensure that human needs are satisfied without disturbing the eco-systems (Georgescu-Roegen)
Environmental sustainability	Initiate action against climate change and protect eco-systems	Eco-communitarian anarchism is the project of creating a way of life consonant with a world of free and just ecologically responsible communities (Clark)	A society based on ecological economics differs from the current society by being ecologically sustainable, fair, efficient and secure (Costanza et al.)
Politics	Protect the rights to freedom of opinion, expression, peaceful assembly, association and dissent	Associative organization is a guarantee of equality and fairness, diversity and dialogue (Proudhon)	Ecological economics presupposes the existence of forums for free exchange of ideas, knowledge, and information (Costanza et al.)
Economy	Strengthen small companies Ensure sustainable consumption and production patterns	Decentralization is important to ensure use of appropriate technology with which people can identify, and that they can understand and control (Ritter)	An economy in harmony with nature and culture has a structure that copes with a multiplicity of small-scale units (Schumacher)

Education	Empower all people to participate in the development of their societies	The primary goal of education is to inspire the individual to develop in harmony with their own nature. The learning methods should combine intellectual and practical activities (Reclus)	Education about civic responsibilities and roles is heavily stressed and is characterized as an interactive balance between online tools and content acquisition, and on-the-ground problem solving (Costanza et al.)
Cooperation	International cooperation to reach the goals	Establish a large number of diverse, fully cooperative communities based on the land, and which would federate with one another to create a new organic whole (Clark)	Global challenges could be addressed through integrated local and regional networks where creative thinking is combined with practical thinking (Holbæk-Hanssen)

Communitarian anarchism's chief principle is freedom in solidarity. The freedom principle fits in perfectly with ecological economics, which calls for freedom in small autonomous units combined with global unity and coordination. There is, though, a discrepancy between anarchism and ecological economics in terms of global coordination: anarchists would say that the norms and values are a result of bottom-up processes in nested networks, while ecological economists acknowledge top-down regulations.

Both anarchism and ecological economics are inspired by process philosophy and argue that relations are more essential than objects. In anarchism, freedom is process and is closely connected to self-realization. In ecological economics, the same insight is expressed through arguments indicating that society is changeable, unfinished, dynamic, and in a constant state of flux.

Maybe the most controversial principle in (classical) anarchism is the declaration of a stateless society, without a ruler. Anarchist philosophy defines society as a self-organizing, living organism defined by its political decentralization. It is regarded as integrated networks of small villages, created bottom-up. Every village is a center in and of itself, and every city has its own unique individuality. The commune is the local decision-making unit consisting of autonomous institutions. In practice, this means voluntary agreements between different groups and associations, which ensure that the economy and the society work in harmonious interaction. Ecological economics parts company with the anarchists on the elimination of the State; on the contrary, ecological economists often refer to the necessity of national and global laws and regulations if a sustainable economy is to be achieved.

In order to understand how a society can live without government, we only need to take a closer look at the current society and notice how a significant part of life in society carries on, even today, in the absence of all government intervention. The liberty we seek for others and ourselves is not

> that absolute, abstract, metaphysical liberty which, in practice, inevitably translates into oppression of the weak, but rather, real liberty, the achievable liberty represented by conscious community of interests and willing solidarity.
>
> (Guérin 2005, p. 363)

However, since ecological economics is embedded in social and ecological systems, the economy must harmonize with the evolutionary principles, cooperation and symbiosis, which refers to a tendency of different organisms to live in close association with one another. Boulding argued that one-way power and one-way communication lines represent a major evil. We are now beginning to see that there is a mutual connection between all forms of life and that all human beings are co-responsible. By inviting community members to participate in making decisions about the things that affect their lives, you allow them to develop their co-responsibility. The social organism is changing through human participation.

Anarchists argue that a fair and equal society should be organized through free and temporary associations. In an association, individuals are free and have the best opportunities to develop their own potential in company with other free individuals. However, Guérin argued that associations imply a sacrifice of individual freedom to secure the common good. In ecological economics we find contributors, such as Holbæk-Hanssen, who argued that associations make it possible to facilitate pluralistic values that exceed the economy's traditional one-dimensional monetary scale. The associations are independent, self-governing parts of a cooperative economy. In common with anarchists, ecological economists point to mutual trust as a prerequisite for a well-functioning associative economy.

In anarchist political philosophy, the main purpose of the economy is to ensure production is in accordance with consumer demands and that individuals have the freedom to make decisions concerning both production and consumption. To reach such a goal, anarchist philosophy maintains that the economy should be made up of decentralized networks of small self-managed enterprises owned by the workers. Anarchists are not against modern technology, far from it, and they argue that appropriate technology is positive. Cooperation and mutual aid are the basic principles. The value of a product should be equivalent to the amount of labour necessary to produce a similar article. Instead of property, anarchists talk about possessions, or, put another way, the right to use. They argue that property is the source of injustice and exploitation. In principle, all people should have free access to all kinds of commodities. The goal is to make the necessities of life free, which is a strong version of the basic-income concept.

Ecological economists argue that the economy depends on its natural base and its legal regulations. The aim of the economy is to enrich life-processes in both nature and society. Anarchists describe the economy by referring to decentralized collaborative networks. In common with anarchists, ecological economists prefer customized technology. According to Boulding, an integrative system based on rational argument, trust and love is essential in a well-functioning economy. Daly maintained that wealth should be distributed based on fairness and that nature cannot be privately owned.

Kropotkin and Tolstoy explicitly expressed pacifist values in anarchist philosophy. They argued that anarchism has to be built on pacifism because violence is based on an authoritarian philosophy. The anarchist pacifist philosophy, as mentioned earlier, is one of the main sources of inspiration in Gandhi's peace project. In ecological economics, peace between humans and nature is every bit as essential as peace between humans.

Education, seen as the key to freedom, is of the greatest importance in anarchist philosophy. The aim of education is the individualization of the self, combined with the development of social consciousness. The pedagogy stresses the importance of combining mental and manual work in education programmes. Reclus argued that there is a link between the problems we are facing in society and the dominating authoritarian systems in schools and universities. He argued that the primary aim of education is to inspire the individual to develop in freedom and in harmony with their nature.

Education is a life-long project in ecological economics. Everyday life and nature are the laboratories of learning. The focus is on cultivating knowledge and wisdom as bases for responsible decision-making. So, even if education does not have an explicit part, it is fair to say that education plays an implicit role in ecological economics. In Table 10.2, I synthesize and compare several dimensions in anarchism and ecological economics.

Anarchy raises deep objections to many of the most generally accepted parts of hard-core liberalist capitalism. Modern society is seriously defective in the way it controls behaviour by means of law, whose generality, permanence and physical coercion makes it problematic for any community to develop their individual potential fully. Criticism of the existing system is important, for sure, it is more important to find a way to solve the problems. The guidance that anarchy gives on social reconstruction is to accept that criticism, in the absence of better alternatives being put forward, is damaging.

Godwin argued that it was not necessary to wait for a majority to agree before the reconstruction of society could start. He recommended "a gradual, voluntary decentralization of power and equalization of ranks, designed to inspire belief in anarchy to spread further" (Ritter 2010, p. 95). The majority could be won over through small-scale practical examples. History indicates that ordinary people, far from being ignorant, are a great source of progress. According to Ritter, the change process depends on the social traits that must abound, such as "honesty and sympathy, and (...) trust and co-operation" (Ritter 2010, p. 110), which need a stable, peaceful climate. Instead of replacing the whole system instantly, many modern-day anarchists argue that the new system should be introduced step by step.

Ritter expresses the view that, contrary to what most people think, anarchists actually give public authority a place and a role in the good society, even if it is, admittedly, extraordinarily limited. Thus, the worth of anarchy as a model for the best system must be deemed outstanding, "judged from a practical, as well as from a theoretical point of view" (Ritter 2010, p. 163). As a concrete standard and guide, anarchy points the way to a realization that combines safety, immediate advantage, and the potential of systemic change.

Central to Kropotkin's interpretation of anarchism is his concern over size and the interconnectedness between production and consumption. Small, integrated units would have a positive impact on the quality of life. Opposition to centralization is common in anarchist philosophy, and this is translated into economic practice. Kropotkin was critical of capitalism's

Table 10.2 Anarchism as political platform for ecological economics

	Anarchism	Ecological economics
Worldview	Organic A holistic vision of humanity in nature and society in nature	Organic Economic system that is consistent with basic principles in ecology
Principles	Associations, decentralized communes and mutualism Freedom in solidarity	Freedom in small autonomous units combined with global unity and coordination
Process	A plural movement of constantly shifting and trans-forming as it is prefigured, performed, pursued and practiced	Everything is changeable, unfinished, dynamic and always in a state of flux
Society	Networks of small, cooperative local societies are the precondition for freedom and responsibility. Freedom is inevitably connected to responsibility, and responsibility is connected to freedom	One-way power and one-way communication lines represent a major evil Self-sufficient local societies The social organism is changing through human participation
Human nature	Twofold: both an essentially egoistic potential and a sociable and altruistic potential. The social context is essential to make individuality flourish	The ecological man is integrated in ecosystems and social systems. The relationship between ecological man and nature is beyond economic self-interest and biological survival.

(*Continued*)

Table 10.2 (Continued)

	Anarchism	Ecological economics
Economy	Decentralized small entities Self-managed enterprises owned by the workers Based on cooperation and mutual aid Free access to all kinds of commodities Property is a source of injustice and exploitation	Enrich life-processes in nature and society Economy depends on the natural base and legal regulations Decentralized collaborative networks Distribution of wealth Nature cannot be privately owned
Associations	In associations, each individual is free A place for free-thinking actors to emerge	Associative cooperation between people with different experiences Mutual trust between people of an association
Peace	Anarchism implies pacifism Violence is authoritarian	Peace between humans and nature, between humans and within the individual human being
Education	Key to freedom, individualization of the self	The only factor that can be changed is human beings
Science	Anything goes	Scientific pluralism, transdisciplinarity
Technology	Appropriate technology	Customized technology

tendency to cluster workers in ever-larger factories, turning them, basically, into little more than machinery. His thinking pointed in another direction, "to a localized consumption and production, realized in the factory amidst the fields" (Adams 2015, p. 151). The anarchist organic ontology understands societies as self-righting and self-ruling and is illuminated and captured by the use of an organismic conceptual vocabulary.

Concluding remarks

Even if the fundamental philosophies of anarchism and ecological economics are for the most part in harmony, there are some challenging discrepancies. Anarchism rejects states, hierarchies and leaders, whereas ecological economists refer to the necessity of both national and global top-down regulations. However, ecological economists argue that leaders should be social and environmentally responsible (change in protective belt). Anarchism also states that the workers should be the owners of firms and companies and that capitalists have no place in anarchism. Few voices in ecological economics argue that the workers should take over all companies, but, close to anarchism, many argue that networks of small firms are better than mammoth-sized globalized companies. Anarchism is also explicit in arguing that it is an ethical right of all people to have free access to fundamental goods and services. Ecological economists argue that the economic system should give priority to the satisfaction of basic needs instead of fulfilling rich people's demand for luxury. Proudhon argued that there will be chaos as long as there is economic inequality in the society, and an harmonious society equalizes the gap between rich and poor.

11 Concluding reflections

According to anarchism, the roots of the environmental crises we face today are not to be found in technology, overpopulation or industrial growth alone, but rather in the hierarchical structure of society itself, and to solve these problems we have to create a society based on freedom. Kropotkin maintained that the economy must become the physiology of society. "It should aim at studying the needs of society and the various means, both hitherto used and available under the present state of scientific knowledge, for their satisfaction" (Kropotkin 1908, p. 72).

We have seen in the preceding chapters that the objective of all human activity is not to be found merely on the material level but also in the development of individual personality and social order. I hope to have provided both the urgency of the challenges we face and a sense that solutions are possible through a rational evaluation of the problem and collective action to bring in meaningful change. The goal is to foster deep change in order to realize the UN's Sustainable Development Goals by creating a new anarchist-inspired political platform for ecological economics, thereby making major changes in business, local communities and governments. Behaviour, in contrast to mainstream economics, is more important than technology. The speed of the change process depends on, and is stimulated by, the level of anarchist principles existing in the society. Ecological economics has little chance of success in a society characterized by top-down regulations and the dominating all-embracing control systems.

The change process has to be conducted from below and not from above. Proudhon wrote, "All revolutions have been carried through by the spontaneous action of the people; if occasionally governments have responded to the initiative of the people it was only because they were forced or constrained to do so" (Guérin 1970, p. 34). According to Bakunin, the masses have spontaneously developed within themselves the most essential elements of the material and moral order of real human unity. He maintained that

> Each individual, each association, commune, or province, each region and nation, has the absolute right to determine its own fate, to associate with others or not, to ally itself with whomever it will, or break any alliance,

without regard to so-called historical claims or the convenience of its neighbors.

(Bakunin in Guérin 1970, p. 67)

Bakunin argued that without the political right to freely unite or separate, centralization will be the consequence. Every organization that exceeds its true limits by expanding into other organizations will lose in strength what they gain in size. When we look at the future through the lens of the current economic paradigm, which focuses solely on growth and short-term profit maximization, the time horizon is far too short and the perspective far too narrow to cover the multifaceted phenomena which include the interactions between ecological sustainability, social welfare and individual quality of life.

Evolution, both biological and cultural, has been characterized by slow development over long periods of time, followed by sudden revolutionary leaps of profound change. Scientific development is, according to Kuhn (1962), characterized by revolutionary paradigm shifts. Kuhn argued that fundamental changes occur only when the established explanations do not make the cut for solving society's challenges. Problems that cannot be solved within the established paradigm are called anomalies. When the anomalies increase in number and severity, science goes into a phase of crisis, and that is the force which brings about a paradigm shift. This presupposes that an alternative paradigm, able to deal with the anomalies, can be developed.

If we accept that the current environmental and social challenges cannot be solved within the present economic and political paradigm, then the way is clear for new and creative ground-breaking solutions. Since problem-solving goes on at the meeting point between past and future, it is necessary to address the challenges with a thorough understanding of the social and economic developments up to the present day. It is also essential to have realistic long-term visions for the future. If we are to identify and address the major challenges, it is important that new ideas are rooted in individual and collective experience. It is neither desirable nor possible to force solutions that have no basis in human intuition, feelings and thoughts. Overwhelmed by "the sheer quantity, complexity and brilliance of scientific knowledge, the interaction between our whole culture and the natural world, has become increasingly ignorant and insensitive" (Naydler 2009, p. 16). Here, then, is an aspect of the relationship between science and the contemporary ecological crisis which, despite being critical, is often overlooked.

Improved technology alone has not significantly reduced CO_2 emissions. Additional measures are required to address the climate crisis, but these are difficult, if not impossible, to implement without the radical switch from a growth to a de-growth economy. This same reasoning applies to the problems arising from the global financial and debt crises. According to Benedikter (2011), it is impossible to restore the established system through legal and ethical adjustments alone. We need to develop new solutions based on a change from a competitive to a cooperative economy, based on an ongoing dialogue between all concerned stakeholders. A new balance between the real and financial economies is our goal. Following this line of reasoning, the disproportionate relationship between the real economy and the financial economy explains some of the necessary conditions behind the financial crisis.

To stimulate the change process, the following actions, described by non-violent anarchism, are of great importance. Movements, withdrawal, cooperatives and associations, communes, local currency and free shops could stimulate changes. All kinds of changes depend on support from the people in the society. Therefore, movements that inform and inspire people into action are necessary for radical change. A revitalization of the discussion concerning the contrast between ideological and utopian thinking is necessary in order to motivate change and achievement. As long as the political discussions focus upon isolated topics with no connection to overall ideas and values, it will be almost impossible to generate the necessary energy amongst people.

Action in non-violent anarchism has to be creative and constructive instead of destructive (as is often, incorrectly and perhaps malevolently, linked to anarchism). Withdrawal means that people perform activities that weaken the dominating capitalist economy by developing an alternative economy based on recycling and re-using all kinds of commodities and by growing increasing amounts of their own food. War tax resistance is another example of withdrawal from the dominating economic paradigm's systems and structures. Withdrawal opens the way, in combination with other practices, to the initiation of a more complete form of anarchist ecological economics.

Developing cooperatives and associations, owned by and managed by their workers, is a significant next step in the development of a living economy in viable societies. Associations include production, distribution, consumption and re-distribution. In a wider perspective, they turn the whole local society into a cooperative force in the economy, nature and culture (the triple helix). Associations also serve to build solidarity and mutual support in a society based on voluntary participation. Westoby and Dowling (2013, p. 24) say building these associations within a community leads to

Connection – building relationships of care
Communication that is oriented towards learning
Commitment – acknowledging the need for people to work together for change

Communes are a kind of self-organized village based on values such as equality, fairness, freedom and respect for all forms of life. Anarchism has a long history of integrating art, such as painting, photography, music, magazines, and theatre, into the process of developing a life-enhancing culture in local societies. This is a kind of non-professional activity where everybody is encouraged to participate. The aim of artistic expression is to disturb, or even shatter, the existing dominating paradigm and to develop alternative ideas which apply to all walks of life, including production of healthy food and creating new, exciting recipes. Hundertwasser was "a radical and fascinating example of an artist using scientific knowledge about nature as the basis for his artistic expressions" (Jakobsen and Storsletten 2018, p. 40).

In recent decades, self-managed cooperatives and associations, through which the actors exchange commodities without focusing on profits, have developed a local currency valid in different societies and regions. Local currency stimulates the exchange of local products and services and stops big multi-national companies from taking the wealth away. Reclus concludes, "anarchists must devote as much attention to such principles as federation, mutual aid, and solidarity as they do to the goals of freedom, justice and decentralization of power, if efforts to transform the larger society are to succeed" (Clark and Martin 2013, p. 63).

Ward (2004) argues that if we begin to look at society from an anarchist point of view, we will be aware of alternatives already present in the interstices of the dominant power structure. In other words, all the necessary parts are at hand and ready if we want to build a free society. "In the final reckoning, darkness can be understood both relationally, as something lacking the basic quality of light, and dialectally, as something whose presence is dependent on the absence of light" (White, Springer and De Souza 2016, p. 10). Reclus maintained that although the members of a society may physically leave the old society behind, they carry with them traces of the institutions that formed their character.

According to anarchism, an ecologically sustainable society is incompatible with the demand for continually growing markets, achieved through the invention of wants and built in obsolescence of consumer goods in capitalism. The utopian anarchist society is described in terms of a "stateless, classless, decentralized society" (Bookchin 2004, p. x) characterized by complex human relationships. Tolstoy looked forward to the day when society would say to its leaders: "Go from us (...) all that matters to us is that we should enjoy, undisturbed the fruits of our toil, and all peace loving people should be permitted to develop their lives in mutual harmony and understanding" (Kumarappa 1952, p. 76).

According to Bookchin, it is impossible "to achieve a harmonization of man and nature without creating a human community that lives in a lasting balance with its natural environment" (Bookchin 2004, p. 21). An anarchist society is a stateless society and also a harmonized society which exposes its people to the stimuli provided by both the agrarian and urban life, by physical and mental activity, and by sensuality and spirituality. It has solidarity and regional uniqueness as well as being part of a worldwide brotherhood given to "spontaneity and self-discipline, to the elimination of toil and the promotion of craftsmanship" (Bookchin 2004, p. 37). Many critics of anarchism have focused on these points (Suissa 2010, p. 15):

1. Are the different values promoted by anarchist theory mutually compatible?
2. Is the anarchist vision of the ideal human society feasible given the structure of human nature (inner consistency and external validity)?

3. Can anarchism be implemented on a large scale in the modern indus-
    trialized world?

As long as the radical imagination exists, according to Clark, "the anarchistic utopia, with its values of freedom, mutuality, joyfulness, and creativity,
will continue to exist, and human beings will seek to realize it with diverse
degrees of passion, imagination, and rationality" and he concludes that,
even if "we do not know whether or not the future will be more a dream or
more a nightmare, (but) we do know that it is quite likely that it will have a
utopian dimension" (Clark 2013, p. 148).

In India and China, for example, there is a high rate of suicide amongst
subsistence farmers who lose their livelihoods due to ongoing "modernization" that replaces unpaid subsistence work and familial exchange with
wage labour in factories and industrial agriculture. "Meaningful lives are
made, quite literally, meaningless" (Spash 2017, p. 11). It is likely that the
list of capabilities considered essential for life will expand, and capabilities
relating to an individual's right to self-identity may also be added.

Kropotkin's fusion of agriculture and industry was essential in anarchism's potential for cultural renewal. Aesthetic sensibility will be stimulated as art and creativity become a part of daily life. "Freed from the
strictures of market logic on the one hand and the demands of the autocratic state on the other, society would finally fully recognise the existential
importance of art" (Adams 2015, p. 181). Thus, its art would be anarchism's true measure of success. Art does not change society, but art can
and does change the consciousness of the people who can change society.
While the move towards lower consumption is necessary and inevitable,
"the only question is whether this is unequally enforced through scarcity
and impoverishment of most while the rich continue to take all, or whether
a more fundamental change in global social and economic organization can
be imagined achieved" (Levitas 2012, p. 335).

> The Communists, the Socialists, the unions – everybody is concentrating
> on trying to get more, to get more money and more of what money can
> buy. What would happen if people instead of asking for more and more
> would ask for less and less? They would be happier, would be healthier,
> wouldn't eat rich food, they'd give up their cars for bicycles, grow
> vegetables in the garden, everyone would need less money – I think that
> would be an interesting experiment.
>
> (Hundertwasser in Rand 2004, p. 32)

Anarchism rejects that living beyond the present is delusional, rejects the
current value structure and its judgement of what is good in the current
society, and rejects all claims that there is no alternative. Even if small-scale
cooperative networks characterize society in the future, we will still need
"hospitals, factories and schools, transport, energy and water infrastructure,

and skilled people to operate these" (Levitas 2017, p. 11). When it becomes necessary, we will also have to organize a system in which there is room for large-scale industries.

The State remains necessary but occupies a role far different from the one it has today and will no longer be a mainstay of the competitive capitalist system. According to Levitas, the advantage of utopian thinking is that it "enables us to think about where we want to get to, and how to get there from here" (Levitas 2007, p. 300). "There is a pressing need to move towards an ecologically and socially sustainable economy and to give up our addiction to economic growth as measured by rises in GDP" (Levitas 2012, p. 335).

Literature

Adams, Matthew S. (2015): *Kropotkin, Read, and the Intellectual History of British Anarchism*, New York, Palgrave Macmillan.

Albritton, Robert (2012): A Practical Utopia for the Twenty-First Century, in *Existential Utopia – New Perspectives on Utopian Thought*, (Vieira, Patricia and Marder, Michael eds.), London, Continuum.

Bakunin, Michael (1970): *God and the State*, New York, Dover Publications.

Balachadaran, P. K. (2006): Gandhi Proclaimed himself a Buddhist, Hindustan Times, June 14.

Beard, T. Randolf and Lozada, Gabriel A. (1999): *Economics, Entropy and the Environment: The Extraordinary Economics of Nicholas Georgescu-Roegen*, Northampton, Edward Elgar Publishing Ltd.

Benedikter, Roland (2011): *Social Banking and Social Finance*, Oxford, Springer.

Bjørneboe, Jens (1972): *Politi Og Anarki*, Oslo, Pax.

Bookchin, Murray (2004): *Post-Scarcity Anarchism*, Oakland, AK Press.

Bouckaert, Luk, Ims, Knut J. and Rona, Peter (2018): *Art, Spirituality and Economics – Liber Amicorum for Laszlo Zsolnai*, Oxford, Springer.

Boulding, Kenneth (1966): The Economics of the Comming Spaceship Earth, Presented at at the Sixth Resources for the Future Forum on Environmental Quality in a Growing Economy in Washington, D.C. on March 8, 1966.

Boulding, Kenneth (1968): *Beyond Economics: Essays on Society, Religion and Ethics*, Ann Arbor, University of Michigan Press.

Boulding, Kenneth (1970): *Economics as a Science, Morality, Ecology, Evolution, Sociology, Mathematics*, New York, McGraw Hill Book Company.

Boulding, Kenneth (1981): *Evolutionary Economics*, London, Sage Publications.

Bregman, Rutger (2017): *Utopia for Realists, and How We Get There*, London, Bloomsbury.

Bryson, Kathleen and Msindai, Nadezda J. (2017): *Charles Darwin's on the Origin of the Species*, London, Routledge, The Macat Library.

Buber, Martin (1996): *Paths in Utopia*, New York, Syracuse University Press.

Capra, Fritjof (1997): *The Web of Life – A New Synthesis of Mind and Matter*, London, Flamingo.

Capra, Fritjof (2012): Ecoliteracy. *Resurgence & Ecologist Magazine* 272, May/June.

Capra, Fritjof and Luisi, Pier L (2014): *The Systems View of Life – A Unifying Vision*, Cambridge University Press.

Capra, Fritjof and Henderson, Hazel (2009): *Outside Insights – Qualitative Growth, Sustainable Business Initiative.* (pp. 1–12). http://beahrselp.berkeley.edu/wp-con tent/uploads/2010/06/Qualitative-Growth2.pdf

Capra, Fritjof and Jakobsen, Ove D (2017): A Conceptual Framework for Ecological Economics Based on Systemic Principles of Life. *International Journal of Social Economics* 44 (6): 831–844.

Chomsky, Noam (2013): *On Anarchism*, New York, Penguin Books.

Clark, John P. (2013): *The Impossible Community – Realizing Communitarian Anarchism*, London, Bloomsbury.

Clark, John and Martin, Camille (2013): *Anarchy, Geography and Modernity, Selected Writings of Elisée Reclus*, Oakland, OK Press.

Costanza, Robert (1989): What Is Ecological Economics? *Ecological Economics* 1 (1): 1–7.

Costanza, Robert, Cumberland, John H., Daly, Herman, Goodland, Robert and Norgaard, Richard (1997): *An Introduction to Ecological Economics*, Boca Raton, St. Lucie Press.

Costanza, Robert (2008): Stewardship for a "Full" World. *Current History*, January 107: 30–35.

Costanza, Robert, Alperovitz, Gar, Daly, Herman, Farley, Joshua, Franco, Carol, Jackson, Tim, Kubiszewski, Ida, Schor, Juliet and Victor, Peter (2012): Building a Sustainable and Desirable Economy-in-Society-in Nature, Report to the United Nations for the 2012 Rio+20 Conference.

Daly, Herman and Cobb, Jr., John.B. (1994): *For the Common Good – Redirecting the Economy toward Community, the Environment, and a Sustainable Future*, Boston, Beacon Press.

Daly, Herman (1996): *Beyond Growth – The Economics of Sustainable Development*, Boston, Beacon Press.

Daly, Herman (1999): *Ecological Economics and the Ecology of Economics – Essays in Criticism*, Northampton, Edward Elgar.

Daly, Herman (2007): *Ecological Economics and Sustainable Development – Selected Essays of Herman Daly*, Northampton, Edward Elgar.

Daly, Herman and Farley, Joshua (2011): *Ecological Economics – Principles and Applications*, Washington, Island Press.

Darwin, John (2010): Kuhn vs. Popper vs. Lakatos vs. Feyerabend: Contested Terrain or Fruitful Collaboration? *Philosophy of Management* 9 (1): 39–57.

Davis, Laurence (2012): History, Politics, and Utopia: Toward a Synthesis of Social Theory and Practise, in *Existential Utopia – New Perspectives on Utopian Thought*, (Vieira, Patricia and Marder, Michael eds.), London, Continuum.

Dunbar, Gary S. (1978): *Elisée Reclus- Historian of Nature*, Hamden, Archon Books.

Eisenstein, Charles (2011): *Sacred Economics – Money, Gift and Society in the Age of Transition*, Berkley, CA, Evolver Editions.

Fabel, Arthur and St. John, Donald (2007): *Teilhard in the 21st Century – The Emerging Spirit of Earth*, New York, Orbis Books.

Fatal, Josh (2006): Was Gandhi an Anarchist? *PeacePower* 2 (1): Winter.

Felber, Christian (2012): *Change Everything – Creating an Economy for the Common Good*, London, Zed books.

Feyerabend, Paul (1975): *Against Method*, London, Verso.

Freire, Paulo (2001): *Pedagogy of Freedom – Ethics, Democracy and Civic Courage*, Oxford, Rowman & Littlefield Publishers.

Fromm, Eric (2013): *To Have or to Be?* New York, Bloomsbury Academic.

Georgescu-Roegen, Nicholas (1975): Energy and Economic Myths. *Southern Economic Journal* 41 (3): January.

Gerasimova, Ksenia (2017): *The Brundtland Report – Our Common Future*, London, Routledge – MaCat.

Giddens, Anthony (1990): *The Consequences of Modernity*, Stanford, Stanford University Press.

Goldman, Emma (2017): *Anarchism and Other Essays*, Los Angeles, Enhanced Media.

Graham, Robert (ed.) (2017): *Anarchism – A Documentary History of Libertarian Ideas*, London, Black Rose Books.

Guérin, Daniel (1970): *Anarchism – From Theory to Practice*, London, Monthly Review Press.

Guérin, Daniel (2005): *No Gods, No Masters – An Anthology of Anarchism*, Edinburgh, AK Press.

Holbæk-Hanssen, Leif (2009): *Økonomi Og Samfunn – Når Mennesket Blir Viktigst*, Oslo, Antropos.

Illich, Ivan (2015): *Beyond Economics and Ecology*, London, Marion Boyars.

Ims, Knut J., and Jakobsen, Ove (2006): Cooperation and Competitionin the Context of Organic and Mechanic Worldviews, *Journal of Business Ethics*, 66: 19–32.

Ims, Knut J., Jakobsen, Ove and Zsolnai, Laszlo (2015): Product as Process – Commodities in Mechanic and Organic Ontology. *Ecological Economics* 110: 11–14.

Ingebrigtsen, Stig and Jakobsen, Ove (2007): *Circulation Economics – Theory and Practice*, Oxford, Peter Lang.

Ingebrigtsen, Stig and Jakobsen, Ove (2009): Moral Development of the Economic Actor. *Ecological Economics* 68: 2777–2784.

Jakobsen, Ove and Storsletten, Vivi. (2017): A Better World Is Possible. *Tvergastein* (9): 70–82.

Jakobsen, Ove and Storsletten, Vivi. (2018): Friedensreich Hundertwasser –The Five Skins of the Ecological Man, in *Art, Spirituality and Economics – Liber Amicorum for Laszlo Zsolnai*, (Bouckaert, Luk, Ims, Knut J. and Rona, Peter eds.), Oxford, Springer.

Jakobsen, Ove (2017): *Transformative Ecological Economics – Process Philosophy, Ideology and Utopia*, London, Routledge.

Jaeger, Hans (1906/2013): *Anarkiets Bibel*, Oslo, Vidarforlaget.

Jones, W.T. (1975): *A History of Western Philosophy – The Twentieth Century to Wittgenstein and Sartre*, London, Harcourt Brace Jovanocich Publishers.

Kelly, Marjorie (2012): *Owning Our Future*, San Francisco, Berrett-Koehler.

Kerman, Cynthia Earl (1974): *Creative Tension: Life and Thought of Kenneth Boulding*, Ann Arbor, University of Michigan Press.

Korten, David C (2015): *Change the Story; Change the Future – A Living Economy for A Living Earth*, San Francisco, Berrett-Koeler Publishers.

Kropotkin, Peter (1908): *Modern Science and Anarchism*, New York, Mother Earth Publishing.

Kropotkin, Peter (1909): *Mutual Aid: A Factor in Evolution*, Hampshire.

Kropotkin, Peter (1912): *Fields, Factories and Workshops*, Brighton, The Perfect Library.

Kropotkin, Peter (1970): *Anarchism – A Collection of Revolutionary Writings*, (ed. Baldwin, R.N.), New York, Dover Publications.

Kropotkin, Peter (2002): *Anarchism – A Collection of Revolutionary Writings*, New York, Dover Publications.

Kropotkin, Peter (2014): *The Conquest of Bread*, Amazon.

Kuhn, Thomas (1962): *The Structure of Scientific Revolutions*, The University of Chicago Press.

Kumarappa, J.C. (1952): *Gandhian Economic Thought*, Sarva Seva Publishing.

Lakatos, Imre and Musgrave, Alan (1982): *Criticism and the Growth of Knowledge*, Cambridge University Press.

Levitas, Ruth (2007): Looking for the Blue: The Necessity of Utopia. *Journal of Political Ideologies* 12 (3): 289–306.

Levitas, Ruth (2011): *The Concept of Utopia*, Peter Lang.

Levitas, Ruth (2012): The Just's Umbrella: Austerity and the Big Society in Coalition Policy and Beyond. *Critical Social Policy* 32 (3): 320–342.

Levitas, Ruth (2013): *Utopia as Method – The Imaginary Reconstruction of Society*, Palgrave Macmillan.

Levitas, Ruth (2017): Where There Is No Vision, the People Perish: A Utopian Ethic for a Transformed Future, www.cusp.ac.uk/essay/m1-5

Lindner, Evelyn (2012): *A Dignity Economy – Creating an Economy that Serves Human Dignity and Preserves Our Planet*, Lake Oswego, Dignity Press.

Lovelock, James (1988): *The ages of Gaia: A Biography of our Living Earth*, Oxford University Press.

Mac Laughlin, Jim (2016): *Kropotkin and the Anarchist Intellectual Tradition*, London, Pluto Press.

Mannheim, Karl (1936): *Ideology and Utopia*, New York, Harvest Books.

Marazzi, Luca (2017): *An Analysis of Mathis Wackernagel and William Rees's Our Ecological Footprint*, London, Routledge.

Marshall, Peter (2008): *Demanding the Impossible – A History of Anarchism*, London, Harper Perennial.

Max-Neef, Manfred (2005): Foundation of Transdisciplinarity. *Ecological Economics* 53: 5–16.

Max-Neef, Manfred (2010): The World on a Collision Course and the Need for a New Economy. *Journal of the Human Environment* 39 (3): 200–210.

May, Todd (1994): *The Political Philosophy of Poststructuralist Anarchism*, University Park, The Pennsylvania State University Press.

McDonough, William and Braungart, Michael. (2002): *Cradle to Cradle: Remaking the Way We Make Things*, New York, North Point Press.

Miletzki, Janna and Broten, Nick (2017): *Amartya Sen's Development on Freedom*, London, Routledge.

More, Thomas (1516/2015): *Utopia*, Amazon.

Morris, Brian (1999): Tolstoy and Anarchism, https://theanarchistlibrary.org/library/brian-morris-tolstoy-and-anarchism

Naydler, Jeremy (2009): *Goethe on Science – An Anthology of Goethe's Scientific Writings*, New York, Floris Books.

Parekh, Bhikhu (2001): *Gandhi – A Very Short Introduction*, Oxford University Press.

Patnaik, S.C. (1991): Gandhian Economic Framework, in *Gandhi and Economic Development*, (Pandey, ed.), London, Sangam Books.

Pearce, Joseph (2001): *Small Is Still Beautiful*, London, Harper Collins Publishers.

Planck, Max (1968): *Scientific Autobiography and Other Papers*, New York, Philosophical Library.

Rand, Harry (2004): *Hundertwasser*, Köln, Midpoint Press.

Rees, William (2008): Human Nature, Eco-Footprints and Environmental Injustice. *Local Environment* 13 (8): 685–701.

Ritter, Alan (2010): *Anarchism – A Theoretical Analysis*, Cambridge University Press.

Schumacher, Ernst Fritz. (1973/1993): *Small Is Beautiful – A Study of Economy as if People Mattered*, London, Vintage.

Schumacher, Ernst Fritz. (1978): *A Guide for the Perplexed*, London, Perennial Library, http://www.smallisbeautiful.org/ (Hjemmeside til Schumacher society).

Sivaraska, Sulak (2009): *The Wisdom of Sustainability – Buddhist Economics for the 21st Century*, London, Souvenir Press.

Smith, Adam (1776/2007): *An Inquiry into the Nature and Causes of the Wealth of Nations*, New York, Metalibri.

Snyder, Gary (1961): Buddhist Anarchism, http://www.bopsecrets.org/CF/garysnyder.htm

Söderbaum, Peter (2000): *Ecological Economics – A Political Economics Approach to Environment and Development*, London, Earthscan.

Spash, Clive L (2013): The Shallow or the Deep Ecological Economics Movement? *Ecological Economics* 93 (September): 351–362.

Spash, Clive (ed.) (2017): *Routledge Handbook of Ecological Economics – Nature and Society*, London, Routledge.

Steiner, Rudolf (1972): *World Economy*, London, Rudolf Steiner Press.

Steiner, Rudolf (1977): *Towards Social Renewal – Basic Issues of the Social Question*, London, Rudolf Steiner Press.

Steiner, Rudolf (1894/1964/1995): *The Philosophy of Freedom*, London, Rudolf Steiner Press.

Stiglitz, Joseph (2012): *The Price of Inequality*, New York, Norton.

Suissa, Judith (2010): *Anarchism and Education – A Philosophical Perspective*, Oakland, CA, PM Press.

The World Commission on Environment and Development (1987): *Our Common Future*, Oxford University Press.

Tudge, Colin (2016): *Six Steps Back to the Land – Why We Need Small Mixed Farms and Millions More Farmers*, Cambridge, Green Books.

Van Parijs, Philippe and Vanderborght, Yannick (2017): *Basic Income – A Radical Proposal for a Free Society and a Sane Economy*, Cambridge, MA, Harvard University Press.

Wackernagel, Mathis and Rees, Williams (1996): *Our Ecological Footprint – Reducing Human Impact on Earth*, Gabriola Island, New Society Publishers.

Ward, Colin (2004): *Anarchism – A Very Short Introduction*, Oxford University Press.

Webster, Ken (2015): *The Circular Economy: A Wealth of Flows*, 2nd Edition, Coves, Ellen McArthur Foundation.

Welford, Richard and Gouldson, Andrew (1995): *Environmental Management and Business Strategy*, London, Pitman Publishing.

Westoby, Peter and Dowling, Gerard (2013): *Theory and Practice of Dialogical Community Development – International Perspectives*, London, Routledge.

White, Richard J., Springer, Simon and De Souza, Marcelo Lopes (2016): *The Practice of Freedom – Anarchism, Geography, and the Spirit of Revolt*, New York, Rowman & Littlefield.

Whitehead, Alfred North (1966): *Modes of Thought*, New York, The Free Press.

Whitehead, Alfred North (1977): *Nature and Life*, New York, Greenwood Press.

Whitehead, Alfred North (1978): *Process and Reality. Corrected Edition*, eds. Griffin, D.R. and Sherburne, D. New York, The Free Press.

Web addresses:

BBC news 2018: *http://news.bbc.co.uk/2/hi/uk_news/6158855.stm*

The Earth Charter: http://earthcharter.org/discover/the-earth-charter/

UN reports: The Millennium Development Goals, Report 2015: http://www.undp.org/content/undp/en/home/librarypage/mdg/the-millennium-development-goals-report-2015.html

The Sustainable Development Goals Report, 2016: https://unstats.un.org/sdgs/report/2016/

Index

For Product Safety Concerns and Information please contact our EU
representative GPSR@taylorandfrancis.com
Taylor & Francis Verlag GmbH, Kaufingerstraße 24, 80331 München, Germany